Coleridge

The Ancient Mariner and Other Poems

A CASEBOOK

EDITED BY

ALUN R. JONES

and

WILLIAM TYDEMAN

MACMILLAN

First published 1973 by
THE MACMILLAN PRESS LTD
Houndmills, Basingstoke, Hampshire RG21 2XS
and London
Companies and representatives
throughout the world

ISBN 0–333–12837–0

A catalogue record for this book is available
from the British Library.

Printed in Hong Kong

Ninth reprint 1994

CONTENTS

6   CONTENTS

ACKNOWLEDGEMENTS

Extract from *The Visionary Company* by Harold Bloom copyright
© 1961 by Harold Bloom, reprinted by permission of Faber &
Faber, Ltd and Doubleday & Co., Inc., New York; extract
adapted from *Coleridge the Poet* by George Watson, Routledge
& Kegan Paul Ltd and Barnes & Noble Publishers, New
York; 'Christabel' by Charles Tomlinson from *Interpretations*
by J. Wain, by permission of Routledge & Kegan Paul Ltd and
Humanities Press, Inc., New York; the extract from *Coleridge*
by Humphry House by permission of Rupert Hart-Davis
Ltd; 'The Nightmare World of "The Ancient Mariner," ' by
E. E. Bostetter, *Studies in Romanticism*, Vol. I (Summer, 1962);
'Wordsworth and Coleridge: The Growth of a Theme' by
A. M. Buchan, *University of Toronto Quarterly*, XXXII (1963),
reprinted by permission of the publisher, University of Toronto
Press; 'Wordsworth, Coleridge and the "Plan" of the *Lyrical
Ballads*' by Mark L. Reed, *University of Toronto Quarterly*,
XXXIV (1965), reprinted (with minor authorial changes) by
permission of the author and of the publisher, University of
Toronto Press; 'The Mariner and the Albatross' by George
Whalley, *University of Toronto Quarterly*, XVI (1946–7), reprinted
(with minor authorial changes) by permission of the author
and of the publisher, University of Toronto Press.

GENERAL EDITOR'S PREFACE

Each of this series of Casebooks concerns either one well-known and influential work of literature or two or three closely linked works. The main section consists of critical readings, mostly modern, brought together from journals and books. A selection of reviews and comments by the author's contemporaries is also included, and sometimes comments from the author himself. The Editor's Introduction charts the reputation of the work from its first appearance until the present time.

The critical forum is a place of vigorous conflict and disagreement, but there is nothing in this to cause dismay. What is attested is the complexity of human experience and the richness of literature, not any chaos or relativity of taste. A critic is better seen, no doubt, as an explorer than as an 'authority', but explorers ought to be, and usually are, well equipped. The effect of good criticism is to convince us of what C. S. Lewis called 'the enormous extension of our being which we owe to authors'. A Casebook will be justified only if it helps to promote the same end.

A single volume can represent no more than a small selection of critical opinions. Some critics have been excluded for reasons of space, and it is hoped that readers will follow up the further suggestions in the Select Bibliography. Other contributions have been severed from their original context, to which some readers may wish to return. Indeed, if they take a hint from the critics represented here, they certainly will.

A. E. DYSON

INTRODUCTION

There is little doubt that Wordsworth and Coleridge planned *Lyrical Ballads* as a joint venture and that the plan fully recognised their basic agreement concerning the nature of poetry and the differences in their creative attitudes. Coleridge believed these differences were complementary and would lead to a clear division of responsibility between them without disturbing the essential unity of the volume as a whole, which would exemplify the centrality of their shared beliefs. In retrospect, Coleridge recalled the original idea behind the 1798 volume;

The thought suggested itself (to which of us I do not recollect) that a series of poems might be composed of two sorts. In the one, the incidents and agents were to be, in part at least, supernatural; and the excellence aimed at was to consist in the interesting of the affections by the dramatic truth of such emotions, as would naturally accompany such situations, supposing them real. . . . For the second class, subjects were to be chosen from ordinary life; the characters and incidents were to be such as will be found in every village and its vicinity, when there is a meditative and feeling mind to seek after them, or to notice them, when they present themselves. (*Biographia Literaria* II 5.)

This was a realistic plan, fully acknowledging what we know to be the different powers of both poets. Coleridge was to concentrate on poems concerning 'persons and characters supernatural, or at least romantic' and endow them with 'a semblance of truth sufficient to procure . . . that willing suspension of disbelief for the moment, which constitutes poetic faith.' Wordsworth for his part was also to concentrate on the kind of poetry he could write best and 'to give the charm of novelty to things of everyday, and to excite a feeling analogous to the supernatural, by awakening the mind's attention to the lethargy of custom, and directing it to the loveliness and the wonders of the world before us'.

Although this division of labour recognised the differences of their poetic powers, they were nonetheless agreed on fundamental objectives, and shared the belief in the 'two cardinal points of poetry'; 'the power of exciting the sympathy of the reader by a faithful adherence to the truth of nature, and the power of giving the interest of novelty by the modifying colours of imagination.' (*Biographia Literaria* II 5–6). Of course, during the period when they lived as neighbours in the Quantocks when the poets were daily in each other's company, they shared a great deal more than these 'two cardinal points of poetry', but the significant point to notice in Coleridge's recollection of their original plan is that from the outset they also recognised the poetic differences that existed between them, for these differences soon became more important than their shared beliefs.

Wordsworth's aim, to endow the objects and experiences of everyday life with feelings analogous to the extraordinary and supernatural, is clear from the poems published in the 1798 volume but, apart from 'The Ancient Mariner', Coleridge's contributions to that volume, 'The Foster-Mother's Tale', 'The Dungeon', and 'The Nightingale' (or 'Lewti')[1] provide little evidence that his objectives were originally significantly different. Without Coleridge's description of the original idea behind the volume, there is little to indicate the original intention in the poems as published, although the fact that this volume was published anonymously may be taken to support the contention that the two poets, however different their poetic gifts, did feel their work to be complementary. Obviously, as is so often the case with Coleridge, the conception outran the execution, and he quite simply failed to produce the poems that would have given him an equal share in the volume. Nevertheless the 1798 *Lyrical Ballads* does achieve a kind of balance, however accidentally, in so far as it opens with 'The Ancient Mariner' and ends with 'Tintern Abbey', two poems that brilliantly embody the antithetical approaches of the two poets described by Coleridge as the original basis of their agreement.

However, whatever the agreement may have been concerning the 1798 volume, it was certainly lost sight of entirely in the preparation of the 1800 *Lyrical Ballads*. Wordsworth abandoned any idea of collaboration with Coleridge, and had in any case already concluded that 'The Ancient Mariner' had damaged the 1798 volume in the eyes of the public. Writing to Joseph Cottle, he says

From what I can gather it seems that 'The Ancyent Mariner' has upon the whole been an injury to the volume, I mean that the old words and the strangeness of it have deterred readers from going on. If the volume should come to a second Edition I would put in its place some little things which would be more likely to suit the common taste. (Letter, 24 June 1799.)

The 'old words and strangeness' of the 1798 version (which in fact is entitled 'The Rime of the Ancyent Marinere') were explained in the *Advertisement* as the poem was 'professedly written in imitation of the *style*, as well as the spirit of the elder poets' and 'the language adopted in it has been equally intelligible for these three last centuries' particularly, we might add, to a public familiar with Percy's *Reliques*. In fact the poem was not excluded from the 1800 edition, but at Wordsworth's suggestion the archaisms were removed, some of the iterations deleted, the title changed to 'The Ancient Mariner, A Poet's Reverie' and the introductory Argument significantly altered. Certainly the language of the poem is not consistent with the concept of poetic diction expounded by Wordsworth in the 1800 Preface, although in purging the poem of its archaisms, something was undoubtedly lost, including a number of fine homely images. Also, the poem was not only moved from its original position at the beginning of the first volume to the end, between 'The Mad Mother' and 'Tintern Abbey', but Wordsworth wrote a most ambiguous note to the poem in which he apologises for the poem's defects, criticising the mariner for having no regular profession and the metre as being unfit for long poems, and praising the poem for its 'delicate touches of passion' that are everywhere true to nature. In the note he insists that Coleridge wished to suppress the poem entirely but was dissuaded from doing so even though there was no hiding its 'defects' or the fact that 'many persons had been much displeased with it.' This note is gratuitous, although it was left to Coleridge's faithful friend Lamb to draw Wordsworth's attention to the fact. By 1800 Coleridge, always self-effacing, was completely overwhelmed by Wordsworth and by his admiration for poetic genius in full flood. As Wordsworth grew in confidence, Coleridge's faith in his own poetic powers ebbed away. He struggled unsuccessfully to complete 'Christabel'[2] for inclusion in the edition about to be published, although Wordsworth had decided in any case not to allow it to be printed with his own poems because, he explains, he 'found that the Style of this Poem was so discordant from my own that it could not be printed along with my poems with any propriety'.[3] There was no question of the 1800 *Lyrical Ballads* being anything other than 'by W. Wordsworth', as the title-pages announce, and Coleridge's contributions are noted in a brief paragraph in the Preface as being included for the sake of variety and for friendship. There is no question of a joint venture or any overall plan. Although the 1800 edition contained all Coleridge's original contributions together with an additional poem of his, 'Love', what was thought to be complementary in 1798 was merely 'discordant' and incompatible in 1800. Nonetheless however much Wordsworth may have changed his attitude towards *Lyrical Ballads*, the fact is that, so far as writing 'supernatural' poems was concerned, 'The Ancient Mariner' remained the only completed example.

Dorothy Wordsworth records the occasions in 1799 when Coleridge read 'Christabel' to her and William and she testifies to the delight and pleasure with which they heard it, but it remains incomplete. Coleridge was haunted by his failure to complete 'Christabel' and, like the mariner repeating his history, he recited what he had done to others whom it also haunted. Sir Walter Scott was directly influenced by its rhythms and phrases in writing 'The Lay of the Last Minstrel' (1805) and as Coleridge himself pointed out, it became as well known among literary men as if it had been published. He gave at different times a number of reasons for his failure to complete the poem, though his inability to complete 'Christabel' is not really very different from his inability to complete so much that he planned and began. He recounted to James Gillman (see page 42 below) a summary of the way he would have completed the poem had he been able to do so. He regarded 'Kubla Khan' also as a fragment, a vision broken off by the interruption of the man from Porlock. The part played by opium-taking in the composition of

this poem – and its influence on his life and character generally –
has been the subject of much speculation,[4] but generally critics
have been happy to accept the poem as complete in itself. 'If
Coleridge had never published his Preface, who would have
thought of "Kubla Khan" as a fragment? Who would have
guessed at a dream?' as Humphry House enquired.[5] The
curious thing about 'Kubla Khan' is the uncertainty of its date
of composition and Coleridge's silence regarding its composition.
Coleridge says it was written in 'the summer of the year 1797',
although the summer of 1798 and the autumn of 1797 have both
been suggested as the correct date of composition. Certainly the
date given by Coleridge is unacceptable. Moreover Wordsworth
does not seem to have been aware of the poem's existence at a
time when the two poets constantly read their poems to each
other. Leigh Hunt reports hearing Coleridge recite the poem to
Byron who was 'highly struck' with it (see page 34 below).
Otherwise there is little reference to the poem at all, either by
Coleridge or by others, and such silence on Coleridge's part con-
trasts strongly with the way in which he returned time and time
again to discussion of 'Christabel'.

The publication of 'Christabel' and 'Kubla Khan' was under-
taken eventually at the instigation of Byron, a strange turn of
events in the history of these strange poems. Byron praised
'Christabel' in a note to his poem 'The Siege of Corinth' where
he acknowledged a debt to the unpublished poem that he
describes as 'wild and singularly original and beautiful poem'
(see page 32 below). There is no doubt that Byron drew the
attention of his publisher to these poems that were published,
finally, in 1816 together with 'The Pains of Sleep'.

The texts of 'Kubla Khan' and 'Christabel' remained largely
unchanged when reprinted in 1828, 1829 and 1834, as compared with the text of 'The Ancient Mariner' which underwent
extensive revisions between 1798 and its publication in 1817 in
Sibylline Leaves where it appeared under Coleridge's name for
the first time and the prose gloss in the margins was first added.
These revisions are, on the whole, improvements, though by
modernising the spelling and language and by introducing
further complexities in the narrative the poem became altogether
a more sophisticated performance than the direct simplicity so

powerfully conveyed in the original 1798 version, yet, to quote
Humphry House, 'when all these changes had been made, it is
still remarkable how many features of ballad idiom and method
the poem still retains and completely assimilates . . . the poem
manages to escape history and yet retains tradition'.[6]

★

'The Ancient Mariner', 'Kubla Khan', and 'Christabel' were composed during Coleridge's most creative period, even though
sections of 'Christabel' seem to anticipate the despair, impotence
and suffering he was to undergo. They were not published together in one volume until 1828, some thirty years after their
composition, though his contemporaries seemed to accept them
for their outlandish beauty, the originality of their effects, the
hypnotic quality of their metrical structures, and the supernatural strangeness of the worlds they disclosed. Modern critics,
however, following J. Livingston Lowes'[7] study of 'Kubla Khan',
Maud Bodkin's[8] study of 'The Ancient Mariner', and I. A.
Richards' analysis of Coleridge's theory of Imagination, have
regarded them as centrally important in the study of the
English Romantic movement. What to Coleridge's contemporaries seemed remote, magical and unique has been seen by modern
critics as embodying in symbolic form the whole mythological
structure of romanticism in individual and general terms. These
have become the three poems of Coleridge that are known and
admired and that invariably attract the attention of critics and
readers. Within 'a narrow range', asserts G. W. Knight without
undue hyperbole, 'these (three poems) show an intensity comparable with that of Dante and Shakespeare'.[10] However that may
be, no one can now deny the serious moral nature of these poems
or their implications for the life of the spirit and of the creative
imagination.

★

Not only did Wordsworth damn 'The Ancient Mariner' with faint
praise by defending it against its author's consciousness of its
deficiencies, while insisting that it 'has indeed great defects', but
also 'Christabel' was severely criticised by the reviewers, and

Coleridge's own estimate of 'Kubla Khan' as a 'psychological curiosity' went unchallenged. Curiously it was left to T. S. Eliot to summarise most effectively the general nineteenth-century view of Coleridge as one who 'for a few years . . . had been visited by the Muse . . . and henceforth was a haunted man'.[11] Some nineteenth-century critics had stood out firmly against the prevailing dismissive treatment of Coleridge, and thus appear more impressive for so doing,[12] but even before the patronising judgement of T. S. Eliot was published, J. Livingston Lowes' *The Road to Xanadu* (1927 : rev. ed. 1930) had decisively initiated an entire reassessment of Coleridge's achievement. *The Road to Xanadu* is essentially a detailed study of Coleridge's source materials but its main effect was to establish beyond argument that, far from being the poet's one isolated achievement, 'The Ancient Mariner' could not be discussed without taking into account the main body of his thought and work.

An impressive body of critical writing has since grown up around his work, and the work itself, including his letters and notebooks, is more substantial and original than even his admirers realised. Much of the critical writing on Coleridge's work has placed his poetry at the centre of a continuing discussion as to the nature of poetry itself. Thus Maud Bodkin's *Archetypal Patterns in Poetry* (1934) treats 'The Ancient Mariner' in terms of the Jungian collective unconsciousness and traces the design of the poem in patterns of death and rebirth similar to those recurring in anthropological studies of comparative religion. G. Wilson Knight in *The Starlit Dome* (1941) lays stress on the sexual symbolism of Coleridge's poetry (specifically in 'The Ancient Mariner', 'Christabel' and 'Kubla Khan') leading from 'general love to man and beast' towards 'a total acceptance of God and his universe'. Kenneth Burke in his book *The Philosophy of Literary Forms* (1941) interprets 'The Ancient Mariner' in terms of sexual guilt and the subconscious stresses, particularly those aroused by his unsatisfactory marriage, which find expression and resolution in the poem itself. It was left to Robert Penn Warren in his article 'A Poem of Pure Imagination'[13] to argue that the subject of Coleridge's 'supernatural' poems was poetic Imagination itself. Humphry House in his Clark lectures of 1951-2 accepts many of Robert Penn Warren's assumptions but sees the poems

as a whole as based on experiences that led Coleridge towards
the foundation of his concept of the workings of the Imagination
rather than a symbolic statement embodying the concept. Yet all
these particular studies are seminal and far from definitive. The
fact remains, however, that since *The Road to Xanadu*, Coleridge's
thought and work have been treated seriously, provocatively, and
as the focal point of a continuing discussion concerning the
nature of poetry, the poetic faculty and the relations between
poetry and a variety of human thought and activity. His poetry
has even given rise to speculation concerning the degenerative
or regenerative effect of drugs on thinking, vision and feeling.
Thus, in one sense at least, Coleridge has defined the terms in
which the discussion of so many central and modern problems
have been conducted. William Empson[14] has interpreted 'The
Ancient Mariner' as 'a very good poem about the European mari-
time expansion' written by a poet pursued by a free-floating sense
of neurotic guilt. Whatever the context of the discussion the
assumption is at least the relevance of Coleridge to the modern
situation.

Certainly scholarly editions of the letters, the notebooks, and
his collected works have somewhat curbed more fanciful speculations. E. M. W. Tillyard's discussion of 'The Ancient Mariner'
in his book *Five Poems 1470–1870* (1948) is a sober account of
the poem's political, social and biographical context, and the prevailing attitude towards Coleridge's poetry is at present, on the
whole, one of more scholarly sobriety.[15] Nonetheless it is no longer
possible to treat his work dismissively or other than with serious
respect. Apart from his friendship with Wordsworth and their
co-operation in the production of *Lyrical Ballads*, Coleridge as
poet and thinker is now firmly established as a significant and
even crucial figure in the history of English Poetry. It is now no
longer possible to maintain the old argument that having written
'The Ancient Mariner' he succumbed to a kind of posthumous
existence sustained only by opium and metaphysics.

★

This Casebook was prepared as a complementary volume to our
Casebook on *Lyrical Ballads*. In selecting modern essays on these
poems we are as aware of those we have omitted, as of those we

have included, but have tried to present as many aspects of these poems as possible within these limits. Because of unusually high copyright fees, Robert Penn Warren's study, 'A Poem of Pure Imagination', has been excluded; it is available in his *Selected Essays* (New York, 1958; London, 1964).

The essays in Part Three by Mark L. Reed, George Watson, and George Whalley have been revised by the respective authors in regard to certain points of detail.

ALUN R. JONES   WILLIAM TYDEMAN

NOTES

1. 'The Nightingale' took the place of 'Lewti' in most copies.

2. He completed Parts I and II of the poem conceived in five parts, and may have composed something of Part III though nothing of this survives.

3. Letter to Messrs. Longman & Rees, 18 December 1800.

4. See E. Schneider, *Coleridge, Opium, and 'Kubla Khan'* (Chicago, 1953) and A. Hayter, *Opium and the Romantic Imagination* (London, 1968).

5. Humphry House, *Coleridge. The Clark Lectures 1951–2* (London, 1953) p. 114. See p. 200 below.

6. Ibid., p. 86.

7. J. Livingston Lowes, *The Road to Xanadu: A Study in the Ways of the Imagination* (Boston, 1927).

8. Maud Bodkin, *Archetypal Patterns in Poetry: Psychological Studies of Imagination* (Oxford, 1934) sect. II.

9. I. A. Richards, *Coleridge on Imagination* (London, 1934).

10. G. W. Knight, *The Starlit Dome* (London, 1941) p. 83.

11. *The Use of Poetry and the Use of Criticism* (London, 1933).

12. See below, pp. 76–114.

13. *Kenyon Review*, XIII (1946) 391–427.

14. 'The Ancient Mariner', *Critical Quarterly*, vol. 6, no. 4 (Winter 1964) pp. 298–319.

15. Cf. *S. T. Coleridge*, ed. R. L. Brett (G. Bell & Son Ltd, 1971).

PART ONE

The History of the Poems

CORRESPONDENCE AND COMMENT: THE WORDSWORTHS, COLERIDGE AND BYRON

WORDSWORTH AND COLERIDGE ABANDON 'THE WANDERINGS OF CAIN' (1797)

The work was to have been written in concert with another [Wordsworth] . . . who was then residing at a small distance from Nether Stowey. The title and subject were suggested by myself, who likewise drew out the scheme and the contents for each of the three books or cantos . . . which, the reader is to be informed, was to have been finished in one night! My partner was to undertake the first Canto, I the second: and whichever had *done first*, was to set about the third. Almost thirty years have passed by, yet at this moment I cannot without something more than a smile moot the question which of the two things was the more impracticable, for a mind so eminently original to compose another man's thoughts and fancies, or for a taste so austerely pure and simple to imitate the Death of Abel? Methinks I see his grand and noble countenance as at the moment when having despatched my own portion of the task at full finger-speed, I hastened to him with my manuscript, – that look of humorous despondency fixed on his almost blank sheet of paper, and then its silent mock-piteous admission of failure struggling with the sense of the exceeding ridiculousness of the whole scheme – which broke up in a laugh: and the 'Ancient Mariner' was written instead.

SOURCE: Coleridge, Prefatory Note to 'The Wanderings of Cain' (1828) – extract.

WORDSWORTH ON 'THE ANCIENT MARINER'

I

In reference to this poem, I will here mention one of the most noticeable facts in my own poetic history, and that of Mr Coleridge. In the autumn of 1797 [Another version reads, 'the spring of the year 1798'.] . . . he, my sister, and myself, started from Alfoxden pretty late in the afternoon, with a view to visit Linton, and the Valley of Stones near to it; and as our united funds were very small, we agreed to defray the expense of the tour by writing a poem, to be sent to the 'New Monthly Magazine,' set up by Phillips, the bookseller, and edited by Dr Aikin. Accordingly we set off, and proceeded, along the Quantock Hills, towards Watchet; and in the course of this walk was planned the poem of the 'Ancient Mariner', founded on a dream, as Mr Coleridge said, of his friend Mr Cruikshank. Much the greatest part of the story was Mr Coleridge's invention; but certain parts I suggested; for example, some crime was to be committed which should bring upon the Old Navigator, as Coleridge afterwards delighted to call him, the spectral persecution, as a consequence of that crime and his own wanderings. I had been reading in Shelvocke's Voyages, a day or two before, that, while doubling Cape Horn, they frequently saw albatrosses in that latitude, the largest sort of seafowl, some extending their wings twelve or thirteen feet. 'Suppose,' said I, 'you represent him as having killed one of these birds on entering the South Sea, and that the tutelary spirits of these regions take upon them to avenge the crime.' The incident was thought fit for the purpose, and adopted accordingly. I also suggested the navigation of the ship by the dead men, but do not recollect that I had anything more to do with the scheme of the poem. The gloss with which it was subsequently accompanied was not thought of by either of us at the time, at least not a hint of it was given to me, and I have no doubt it was a gratuitous after-thought. We began the composition together, on that to me memorable evening : I furnished two or three lines at the beginning of the poem, in particular –

And listen'd like a three years' child;
    The Mariner had his will.

These trifling contributions, all but one, which Mr C. has with unnecessary scrupulosity recorded, slipped out of his mind, as they well might. As we endeavoured to proceed conjointly (I speak of the same evening), our respective manners proved so widely different, that it would have been quite presumptuous in me to do anything but separate from an undertaking upon which I could only have been a clog. We returned after a few days from a delightful tour, of which I have many pleasant, and some of them droll enough, recollections. We returned by Dulverton to Alfoxden. The 'Ancient Mariner' grew and grew till it became too important for our first object, which was limited to our expectation of five pounds; and we began to think of a volume which was to consist, as Mr Coleridge has told the world, of poems chiefly on supernatural subjects, taken from common life, but looked at, as much as might be, through an imaginative medium. Accordingly I wrote 'The Idiot Boy', 'Her Eyes Are Wild', &c., and 'We Are Seven', 'The Thorn', and some others.

SOURCE : Notes dictated to Isobella Fenwick in 1843, published in Moxon's edition, 1857 – extract.

II

When my truly-honoured friend Mr Wordsworth was last in London, he . . . made the following statement which I am quite sure, I give you correctly : 'The Ancient Mariner' was founded on a strange dream which a friend of Coleridge [John Cruikshank, Lord Egmont's agent at Stowey] had, who fancied he saw a skeleton ship with figures in it. We had both determined to write some poetry for a monthly magazine, the profits of which were to defray the expenses of a little excursion we were to make together. 'The Ancient Mariner' was intended for this periodical, but was too long. I had very little share in the composition of it, for I soon found that the style of Coleridge and myself would not assimilate. . . .

SOURCE : The Rev. Alexander Dyce, quoted by H. N. Coleridge in his edition of the *Poems*, 1852.

III

You tell me the poems have not sold ill. If it is possible, I should wish to know *what number* have been sold. From what I can gather it seems that 'The Ancyent Mariner' has upon the whole been an injury to the volume, I mean that the old words and the strangeness of it have deterred readers from going on. If the volume should come to a second Edition I would put in its place some little things which would be more likely to suit the common taste.

SOURCE: Letter to Joseph Cottle, 24 June 1799 – extract.

COLERIDGE ON THE SALE OF 'LYRICAL BALLADS'

Longmans offered me the copyright of the *Lyrical Ballads*, at the same time saying that, if I would write a few more, they would publish my contributions. When I expressed a hope that 3,000 might be circulated, Wordsworth spurned at the idea, and said that twenty times that number must be sold. I was told by Longmans that the greater part of the *Lyrical Ballads* had been sold to seafaring men, who having heard of the 'Ancient Mariner' concluded that it was a naval song-book, or, at all events, that it had some relation to nautical matters.

SOURCE: *Table Talk*, January 1821.

COLERIDGE ON THE COMPOSITION OF 'CHRISTABEL'

I

In my last letter I said I would give you my reasons for thinking 'Christabel', *were* it finished & finished as spiritedly as it commences, yet still an improper opening Poem.[1] My reason is – it

cannot be expected to please all / Those who dislike it will deem it
extravagant Ravings, & go on thro' the rest of the Collection
with the feeling of Disgust – and it is not impossible that were it
liked by any, it would still not harmonize with the *real-life* Poems
that follow. – It ought I think to be the last –

SOURCE : Letter to Robert Southey, 10 November 1799 – extract.

NOTE

1. At this time Southey proposed publishing the poem in the
Annual Anthology, of which he was editor.

II

. . . I am afraid that I have scarce poetic Enthusiasm enough to
finish 'Christabel'. . . .

SOURCE : Letter to Robert Southey, 19 December 1799 – extract.

DOROTHY WORDSWORTH ON 'CHRISTABEL'

Sunday 29th August 1800.
Coleridge read us a part of 'Christabel'.

Saturday 4th October 1800.
Exceedingly delighted with the 2nd part of 'Christabel'.

Sunday Morning 5th October 1800.
Coleridge read a 2nd time 'Christabel' – we had increasing
pleasure.

Monday 6th October 1800.
Determined not to print 'Christabel' with the *L.B.*

SOURCE : The Grasmere Journal, *Journals of Dorothy Wordsworth* – extracts.

COLERIDGE ON 'CHRISTABEL' AGAIN

The 'Christabel' was running up to 1300 lines[1] – and was so much admir'd by Wordsworth, that he thought it indelicate to print two Volumes with *his name* in which so much of another man's was included – & which was of more consequence – the poem was in direct opposition to the very purpose for which the *Lyrical Ballads* were published – viz – an experiment to see how far those passions, which alone give any value to extraordinary Incidents, were capable of interesting, in & for themselves, in the incidents of common life – We mean to publish the 'Christabel' therefore with a long Blank Verse Poem of Wordsworth's entitled 'the Pedlar' – I assure you, I think very differently of CHRISTABEL – I would rather have written 'Ruth', and 'Nature's Lady'[2] than a million such poems. . . .

SOURCE: Letter to Humphry Davy, 9 October 1800 – extract.

NOTES

1. In fact, the extant version of the poem contains 677 lines.
2. Coleridge's title for 'Three years she grew'.

COLERIDGE'S FAILURE TO COMPLETE 'CHRISTABEL'

. . . immediately on my arrival in this country I undertook to finish a poem which I had begun, entitled 'Christabel', for a second volume of the *Lyrical Ballads*. I tried to perform my promise; but the deep unutterable Disgust, which I had suffered in the translation of that accursed Wallenstein, seemed to have stricken me with barrenness – for I tried & tried, & nothing would come of it. I desisted with a deeper dejection than I am willing to remember . . .

SOURCE: Letter to Josiah Wedgwood, 1 November 1800 – extract.

WORDSWORTH ON 'CHRISTABEL'

I have this day sent off the last Sheet of the second Volume of the *Lyrical Ballads*. I am exceedingly sorry that bad health should have prevented me from fulfilling my engagements sooner. A Poem of Mr Coleridge's was to have concluded the Volumes; but upon mature deliberation I found that the Style of this Poem was so discordant from my own that it could not be printed along with my poems with any propriety. I had other poems by me of my own which would have been sufficient for our purpose but some of them being connected with political subjects I judged that they would be injurious to the sale of the Work. I therefore, since my last letter, wrote the last poem[1] of the 2nd Volume. I am sure when you see the work you will approve of this delay, as there can be no doubt that the poem alluded to will be highly serviceable to the Sale.

SOURCE : Letter to Messrs. Longman & Rees, 18 December 1800 – extract.

NOTE

1. 'Michael, A Pastoral'.

WORDSWORTH'S 'NOTE TO THE ANCIENT MARINER'

I cannot refuse myself the gratification of informing such Readers as may have been pleased with this Poem, or with any part of it, that they owe their pleasure in some sort to me; as the Author was himself very desirous that it should be suppressed. This wish had arisen from a consciousness of the defects of the Poem, and from a knowledge that many persons had been much displeased with it. The Poem of my Friend has indeed great defects; first that the principal person has no distinct character, either in his profession of Mariner, or as a human being who having been long under the control of supernatural impressions might be supposed himself to partake of something supernatural : secondly, that he does not act, but is continually acted upon : thirdly, that the events having no necessary connection do not produce each other; and lastly, that the imagery is somewhat too laboriously accumulated. Yet the Poem contains many delicate touches of passion, and indeed the passion is every where true to nature; a great number of the stanzas present beautiful images, and are expressed with unusual felicity of language; and the versification, though the metre is itself unfit for long poems, is harmonious and artfully varied, exhibiting the utmost powers of that metre, and every variety of which it is capable. It therefore appeared to me that these several merits (the first of which, namely that of the passion, is of the highest kind,) gave to the Poem a value which is not often possessed by better Poems. On this account I requested of my Friend to permit me to republish it.

SOURCE : *Lyrical Ballads*, 1800 edition.

COLERIDGE ON THE MORAL OF 'THE ANCIENT MARINER'

Mrs Barbauld once told me that she admired 'The Ancient Mariner' very much, but that there were two faults in it – it was improbable, and had no moral. As for the probability, I owned that that might admit some question; but as to the want of a moral, I told her that in my own judgement the poem had too much; and that the only, or chief fault, if I might say so, was the obtrusion of the moral sentiment so openly on the reader as a principle or cause of action in a work of such pure imagination. It ought to have had no more moral than the *Arabian Nights'* tale of the merchant's sitting down to eat dates by the side of a well, and throwing the shells aside, and lo! a genie starts up, and says he *must* kill the aforesaid merchant, *because* one of the date shells had, it seems, put out the eye of the genie's son.[1]

SOURCE : *Table Talk*, 31 May 1830.

NOTE

1. There he found, at the foot of a great walnut-tree, a fountain of a very clear running water, and alighting, tied his horse to a branch of a tree, and sitting down by the fountain, took some biscuits and dates out of his portmanteau, and, as he ate his dates, threw the shells about on both sides of him. When he had done eating, being a good Mussulman, he washed his hands, his face, and his feet, and said his prayers. He had not made an end, but was still on his knees, when he saw a genie appear, all white with rage, and of a monstrous bulk; who, advancing towards him with a cimetar in his hand, spoke to him in a terrible voice thus : – 'Rise up, that I may kill thee with this cimetar as you have killed my son!' and accompanied these words with a frightful cry. The merchant being as much frightened at the hideous shape of the monster as at these threatening words, answered him trembling : 'Alas! my good lord, of what crime can I be guilty towards you that you should take away my life?' – 'I will', replies the genie, 'kill thee, as thou hast killed my son!' – 'O heaven!' says the merchant, 'how should I kill your son? I did not know him, nor ever saw him.' – 'Did not you sit down when you came hither?' replies the genie. 'Did not you take dates out of your portmanteau, and, as you ate them, did not you throw the shells about on both sides – 'I did all that you say,' answers the merchant, 'I cannot deny it.' – 'If it be so,' replied the genie, 'I tell thee that thou hast killed my son; and the way was thus : when you threw the nutshells about, my son was passing by, and you threw one of them into his eye, which killed him, *therefore* I must kill thee.' – 'Ah! my good lord, pardon me!' cried the merchant. – 'No pardon,' answers the genie, 'no mercy! Is it not just to kill him that has killed another?' – 'I agree to it,' says the merchant, 'but certainly I never killed your son, and if I have, it was unknown to me, and I did it innocently; therefore I beg you to pardon me, and suffer me to live.' – 'No, no,' says the genie, persisting in his resolution, 'I must kill thee, since thou hast killed my son;' and then taking the merchant by the arm, threw him with his face upon the ground, and lifted up his cimetar to cut off his head!' – *The Merchant and the Genie,* First night. – (H. N. Coleridge's Note.)

BYRON ON 'CHRISTABEL'

I

Last spring I saw Wr. Scott. He repeated to me a considerable portion of an unpublished poem of yours – the wildest and finest I ever heard in that kind of composition. The title he did not mention, but I think the heroine's name was Geraldine. At all events, the 'toothless mastiff bitch' and the 'witch Lady', the description of the hall, the lamp suspended from the image, and more particularly of the girl herself as she went forth in the evening – all took a hold on my imagination which I never shall wish to shake off. I mention this, not for the sake of boring you with compliments, but as a prelude to the hope that this poem is or is to be in the volumes you are now about to publish. I do not know that even 'Love' or the 'Antient Mariner' are so impressive – and to me there are few things in our tongue beyond these two productions.

SOURCE: Letter to Coleridge, 18 October 1815 – extract.

II

'Sent that soft and tender moan?' I must here acknowledge a close, though unintentional, resemblance in these twelve lines to a passage in an unpublished poem of Mr Coleridge, called 'Christabel.' It was not till after these lines were written that I heard that wild and singularly original and beautiful poem recited; and the MS. of that production I never saw till very recently, by the kindness of Mr Coleridge himself, who, I hope, is convinced that I have not been a wilful plagiarist. The original idea undoubtedly pertains to Mr Coleridge, whose poem has been composed above fourteen years. Let me conclude by a hope that he will not longer delay the publication of a production, of which I can only add my mite of approbation to the applause of far more competent judges.

SOURCE: Byron's notes to *The Siege of Corinth*, 1816.

COLERIDGE ON THE COMPOSITION OF 'CHRISTABEL'

The 'Christabel', which you have mentioned in so obliging a manner, was composed by me in the [year] 1797 – I should say, that the plan of the whole poem was formed and the first Book and half of the second were finished – and it was not till after my return from Germany in the year 1800 that I resumed it – and finished the second and a part of the third Book. – This is all that Mr W Scott can have seen. Before I went to Malta, I heard from Lady Beaumont, I know not whether more gratified or more surprized, that Mr Scott had recited the 'Christabel' and expressed no common admiration.[1] – What occurred after my return from Italy, and what the disgusts were (most certainly not originating in my own opinion or decision) that indisposed me to the completion of the Poem, I will not trouble your Lordship with. – It is not yet a Whole : and as it will be 5 Books, I meant to publish it by itself : or with another Poem entitled, the 'Wanderings of Cain' – of which, however, as far as it was written, I have unfortunately lost the only Copy—and can remember no part distinctly but the first stanza : —

> Encinctur'd with a twine of Leaves,
> That leafy Twine his only Dress !
> A lovely Boy was plucking fruits
> In a moon-light Wilderness.
> The Moon was bright, the Air was free,
> And Fruits and Flowers together grew
> On many a Shrub and many a Tree :
> And all put on a gentle Hue
> Hanging in the shadowy Air
> Like a Picture rich and rare.
> It was a Climate where, they say,
> The Night is more belov'd than Day.
> But who that beauteous Boy beguil'd,
> That beauteous Boy to linger here?
> Alone, by night, a little child,
> In place so silent and so wild –
> Has he no *Friend*, no loving Mother near?[2]

Sir G. Beaumont, I remember, thought it the most impressive of my compositions – & I shall probably compose it over again. – A Lady is now transcribing the 'Christabel', in the form and as

far as it existed before my voyage to the Mediterranean – I hope
to inclose it for your Lordship's gracious acceptance tomorrow
or next day.[3] I have not learnt with what motive Wordsworth
omitted the original a[d]vertisement prefixed to his 'White Doe',
that the peculiar metre and mode of narration he had imitated
from the 'Christabel'.[4] For this is indeed the same metre, as far
as the *Law* extends – the metre of the 'Christabel' not being
irregular, as Southey's 'Thalaba' or 'Kehama', or Scott's Poems,
but uniformly measured by four Beats in each Line. In other
words, I count by Beats or accents instead of syllables – in the
belief that metre might be thus produced sufficiently uniform &
far more malleable to the Passion & Meaning.[5]

I was much gratified, I confess, by what your Lordship has
said of this Poem, the 'Love', and the 'Ancient Mariner'. , , ,

Source: Letter to Lord Byron, 22 October 1815 – extract.

NOTES

1. Scott would seem to have become first acquainted with the
poem in 1802.

2. These lines first appeared in *Aids to Reflection* (1825).

3. Byron acknowledged receipt of the transcript of the poem on
27 October 1815. (*Letters and Journals,* III 228–9.)

4. Wordsworth acknowledged the debt in a short preface of 1808,
now lost.

5. It has been suggested that Coleridge partly based his 'Preface'
to 'Christabel' on this letter. (See pp. 36–7.)

COLERIDGE READS 'KUBLA KHAN' TO BYRON, 1816

He [Coleridge] recited his 'Kubla Khan' one morning to Lord
Byron, in his lordship's house in Picadilly, when I happened to
be in another room. I remember the other's coming away from
him, highly struck with his poem, and saying how wonderfully
he talked. . . .

Source: *The Autobiography of Leigh Hunt* (1859) – extract.

COLERIDGE'S INTRODUCTION TO THE FRAGMENT OF 'KUBLA KHAN': OR, 'A VISION IN A DREAM' (1816)

The following fragment is here published at the request of a poet of great and deserved celebrity [Lord Byron], and, as far as the Author's own opinions are concerned, rather as a psychological curiosity, than on the ground of any supposed *poetic* merits.

In the summer of the year 1797,[1] the Author, then in ill health, had retired to a lonely farm-house between Porlock and Linton, on the Exmoor confines of Somerset and Devonshire. In consequence of a slight indisposition, an anodyne had been prescribed, from the effects of which he fell asleep in his chair at the moment that he was reading the following sentence, or words of the same substance, in 'Purchas's Pilgrimage': 'Here the Khan Kubla commanded a palace to be built, and a stately garden thereunto. And thus ten miles of fertile ground were inclosed with a wall.'[2] The Author continued for about three hours in a profound sleep, at least of the external senses, during which time he has the most vivid confidence, that he could not have composed less than from two to three hundred lines; if that indeed can be called composition in which all the images rose up before him as *things*, with a parallel production of the correspondent expressions, without any sensation or consciousness of effort. On awaking he appeared to himself to have a distinct recollection of the whole, and taking his pen, ink, and paper, instantly and eagerly wrote down the lines that are here preserved. At this moment he was unfortunately called out by a person on business from Porlock, and detained by him above an hour, and on his return to his room, found, to his no small surprise and mortification, that though he still retained some vague and dim recollection of the general purport of the vision, yet, with the exception of some eight or ten scattered lines and images, all the rest had passed away like the images on the surface of a stream into which a stone has been cast, but, alas! Without the after restoration of the latter!

> Then all the charm
> Is broken – all that phantom-world so fair
> Vanishes, and a thousand circlets spread,

And each mis-shape['s] the other. Stay awhile,
Poor youth ! who scarcely dar'st lift up thine eyes –
The stream will soon renew its smoothness, soon
The visions will return ! And lo, he stays,
And soon the fragments dim of lovely forms
Come trembling back, unite, and now once more
The pool becomes a mirror.

[From 'The Picture, or the Lover's Resolution', ll. 91–100.]

Yet from the still surviving recollections in his mind, the Author has frequently purposed to finish for himself what had been originally, as it were, given to him. 'Αΰριον ἅδιον ἀσῶ³ : but the tomorrow is yet to come.

As a contrast to this vision, I have annexed a fragment of a very different character, describing with equal fidelity the dream of pain and disease.[4]

SOURCE : First Edition of 'Kubla Khan', 1816.

NOTES

1. The incident is, in fact, dated wrongly by Coleridge, but the true date is matter of conjecture.

2. 'In Xamdu did Cublai Can build a stately Palace encompassing sixteene miles of plaine ground with a wall, wherein are fertile Meddowes, pleasant Springs, delightfull Streames, and all sorts of beasts of chase and game, and in the middest thereof a sumptuous house of pleasure.' – *Purchas his Pilgrimage*, London, 1626, bk. IV, chap. xiii, p. 418.

3. Based on Theocritus, *Idylls*, I 145, 'Afterwards I shall sing more sweetly.' Coleridge misquoted the initial word as 'tomorrow'.

4. 'The Pains of Sleep'.

COLERIDGE'S PREFACE TO 'CHRISTABEL' (1816)

The first part of the following poem was written in the year one thousand seven hundred and ninety-seven, at Stowey, in the county of Somerset. The second part, after my return from Germany, in the year one thousand eight hundred, at Keswick.

Cumberland. Since the latter date, my poetic powers have been till very lately, in a state of suspended animation. But as, in my very first conception of the tale I had the whole present to my mind, with the wholeness, no less than the liveliness of a vision; I trust that I shall be able to embody in verse the three parts yet to come, in the course of the present year. It is probable that if the poem had been finished at either of the former periods, or if even the first and second part had been published in the year 1800, the impression of its originality would have been much greater than I dare at present expect. But for this I have only my own indolence to blame. The dates are mentioned for the exclusive purpose of precluding charges of plagiarism or servile imitation from myself. For there is amongst us a set of critics, who seem to hold, that every possible thought and image is traditional; who have no notion that there are such things as fountains in the world, small as well as great; and who would therefore charitably derive every rill they behold flowing, from a perforation made in some other man's tank. I am confident, however, that as far as the present poem is concerned the celebrated poets[1] whose writings I might be suspected of having imitated either in particular passages, or in the tone and the spirit of the whole, would be among the first to vindicate me from the charge, and who, on any striking coincidence, would permit me to address them in this doggrel version of two monkish Latin hexameters.

'Tis mine and it is likewise yours;
But an if this will not do;
Let it be mine, good friend! for I
Am the poorer of the two.

I have only to add that the metre of 'Christabel' is not, properly speaking, irregular, though it may seem so from its being founded on a new principle: namely, that of counting in each line the accents, not the syllables. Though the latter may vary from seven to twelve, yet in each line the accents will be found to be only four. Nevertheless, this occasional variation in number of syllables is not introduced wantonly, or for the mere ends of convenience, but in correspondence with some transition in the nature of the imagery or passion.

SOURCE: First Edition of 'Christabel', 1816.

NOTE

1. Sir Walter Scott and Lord Byron.

COLERIDGE ON THE RECEPTION OF 'CHRISTABEL'

During the many years which intervened between the composition and the publication of the 'Christabel', it became almost as well known among literary men as if it had been on common sale, the same references were made to it, and the same liberties taken with it, even to the very names of the imaginary persons in the poem. From almost all of our most celebrated Poets, and from some with whom I had no personal acquaintance, I either received or heard of expressions of admiration that (I can truly say) appeared to myself utterly disproportionate to a work, that pretended to be nothing more than a common Faery Tale. Many, who had allowed no merit to my other poems, whether printed or manuscript, and who have frankly told me as much, uniformly made an exception in favour of the 'Christabel' and the Poem entitled 'Love'. Year after year, and in societies of the most different kinds, I had been entreated to recite it : and the result was still the same in all, and altogether different in this respect from the effect produced by the occasional recitation of any other poems I had composed. – This before the publication. And since then with very few exceptions, I have heard nothing but abuse, and this too in a spirit of bitterness at least as disproportionate to the pretensions of the poem, had it been the most pitiably below mediocrity, as the previous eulogies, and far more inexplicable. In the *Edinburgh Review* it was assailed with a malignity and a spirit of personal hatred that ought to have injured only the work in which such a tirade appeared : and this review was generally attributed (whether rightly or no I know not) to a man, who both in my presence and in my absence has repeatedly pronounced it the finest poem in the language.[1] – This may serve as a warning to authors, that in their calculations on the probable reception of a poem, they must subtract to a large amount from the panegyric,

which may have encouraged them to publish it, however unsuspicious and however various the sources of this panegyric
may have been. And, first, allowances must be made for private
enmity, of the very existence of which they had perhaps entertained no suspicion – for personal enmity behind the mask of
anonymous criticism : secondly for the necessity of a certain proportion of abuse and ridicule in a Review, in order to make it
saleable, in consequence of which, if they have no friends behind
the scenes, the chances must needs be against them; but lastly
and chiefly, for the excitement and temporary sympathy of feeling, which the recitation of the poem by an admirer, especially
if he be at once a warm admirer, and a man of acknowledged
celebrity, calls forth in the audience. For this is really a species
of Animal Magnetism, in which the enkindling reciter, by perpetual comment of looks and tones, lends his own will and appre-
hensive faculty to his auditors. They *live* for the time within the
dilated sphere of his intellectual being. It is equally possible,
though not equally common, that a reader left to himself should
sink below the poem, as that the poem left to itself should flag
beneath the feelings of the reader.

SOURCE : *Biographia Literaria* (1817), ch. XXIV – extract.

NOTE

1. Coleridge is alluding to William Hazlitt, but the *Edinburgh
Review's* critique was, in fact, the work of Thomas Moore. (See pp.
66–76 below.)

COLERIDGE ON THE WORDSWORTHS

. . . I have loved with enthusiastic self-oblivion those who have
been so well pleased that I should, year after year, flow with a
hundred nameless Rills into *their* Main Stream, that they could
find nothing but cold praise and effective discouragement of every
attempt of mine to roll onward in a distinct current of my own
– who *admiited* that the 'Ancient Mariner', the 'Christabel', the
Remorse, and *some* pages of the 'Friend' were not without merit,
but were abundantly anxious to acquit their judgements of any
blindness to the very numerous defects. Yet they *knew* that to

Praise, as mere Praise, I was characteristically, almost constitutionally indifferent. In Sympathy alone I found at once Nourishment and Stimulus: and for Sympathy alone did my heart crave. . . .

SOURCE : Letter to Thomas Allsop, 2 December 1818 – extract.

COLERIDGE ON CRASHAW

Crashaw seems in his poems to have given the first ebullience of his imagination, unshapen into form, or much of, what we now term, sweetness. In the poem, 'Hope', by way of question and answer, his superiority to Cowley is self-evident. In that on the name of Jesus equally so; but his lines on St Theresa are the finest.

Where he does combine richness of thought and diction nothing can excel, as in the lines you so much admire—

> Since 'tis not to be had at home,
> She'l travel to a martyrdome.
> No home for her confesses she,
> But where she may a martyr be.
> She'l to the Moores, and trade with them
> For this invalued diadem,
> She offers them her dearest breath
> With Christ's name in't, in change for death.
> She'l bargain with them, and will give
> Them God, and teach them how to live
> In Him, or if they this deny,
> For Him she'l teach them how to die,
> So shall she leave amongst them sown,
> The Lord's blood, or, at least, her own.
> Farewell then, all the world – adieu,
> Teresa is no more for you :
> Farewell all pleasures, sports and joys,
> Never till now esteemed toys –
> Farewell whatever dear'st may be,
> Mother's arms or father's knee;
> Farewell house, and farewell home,
> She's for the Moores and martyrdom.

These verses were ever present to my mind whilst writing the second part of 'Christabel'; if, indeed, by some subtle process of the mind they did not suggest the first thought of the whole poem.

SOURCE: *Table Talk*, January 1821 – extract.

COLERIDGE ON CONCLUDING 'CHRISTABEL'

I

If I should finish 'Christabel', I shall certainly extend it and give new characters, and a greater number of incidents. This the 'reading public' require, and this is the reason that Sir Walter Scott's Poems, though so loosely written, are pleasing, and interest us by their picturesqueness.

If a genial recurrence of the ray divine should occur for a few weeks, I shall certainly attempt it. I had the whole of the two cantos in my mind before I began it; certainly the first canto is more perfect, has more of the true wild weird spirit than the last. I laughed heartily at the continuation in Blackwood, which I I have been told is by Maginn: it is in appearance, and in appearance *only*, a good imitation; I do not doubt but that it gave more pleasure, and to a greater number, than a continuation by myself in the *spirit* of the two first cantos.

The 'Ancient Mariner' cannot be imitated, nor the poem, 'Love'. *They may be excelled; they are not imitable.*

SOURCE: *Table Talk*, p. 425.

II

The reason of my not finishing 'Christabel' is not, that I don't know how to do it – for I have, as I always had, the whole plan entire from beginning to end in my mind; but I fear I could not carry on with equal success the execution of the idea, an extremely subtle and difficult one. Besides, after this continuation of *Faust*, which they tell me is very poor, who can have courage to attempt a reversal of the judgement of all criticism against continuations?

SOURCE : *Table Talk*, 6 July 1833 – extract.

THE CONTINUATION OF 'CHRISTABEL'

The following relation was to have occupied a third and fourth Canto, and to have closed the tale.

Over the mountains, the Bard, as directed by Sir Leoline, 'hastes' with his disciple; but in consequence of one of those inundations supposed to be common to this country, the spot only where the Castle once stood is discovered – the edifice itself being washed away. He determines to return. Geraldine being acquainted with all that is passing, like the Weird Sisters in *Macbeth*, vanishes. Reappearing, however, she waits the return of the Bard, exerting in the meantime, by her wily arts, all the anger she could rouse in the Baron's breast, as well as that jealousy of which he is described to have been susceptible. The old Bard and the youth at length arrive, and therefore she can no longer personate the character of Geraldine, the daughter of Lord Roland de Vaux, but changes her appearance to that of the accepted though absent lover of Christabel. Next ensues a courtship most distressing to Christabel, who feels – she knows not why – great disgust for her once favoured knight. This coldness is very painful to the Baron, who has no more conception than herself of the supernatural transformation. She at last yields to her father's entreaties, and consents to approach the altar with this hated suitor. The real lover, returning, enters at this moment, and produces the ring which she had once given him in sign of her betrothment. Thus defeated, the supernatural being Geraldine disappears. As predicted, the Castle bell tolls, the mother's voice is heard, and to the exceeding great joy of the parties, the rightful marriage takes place, after which follows a reconciliation and explanation between the father and daughter.

SOURCE : James Gillman, *The Life of Samuel Taylor Coleridge*, 1838 – extract.

PART TWO

Nineteenth-Century Opinions

Anonymous Reviews

I

There is something sensible in these remarks,[1] and they certainly serve as a very pertinent introduction to the studied simplicity which pervades many of the poems. 'The Rime of the Ancyent Marinere', a ballad in seven parts, is written professedly in imitation of the style as well as of the spirit of the ancient poets. We are not pleased with it. . . .

SOURCE: *Analytical Review*, XXVIII (December 1798) – extract.

NOTE

1. *Advertisement.*

II

'The Poem of the Ancyent Marinere' with which the collection opens, has many excellencies, and many faults; the beginning and the end are striking and well-conducted; but the intermediate part is too long, and has, in some places, a kind of confusion of images, which loses all effect, from not being quite intelligible. The author, who is confidently said to be Mr Coleridge, is not correctly versed in the old language, which he undertakes to employ. 'Noises of a swound' and 'broad as a weft,' are both nonsensical; but the ancient style is well imitated, while the antiquated words are so very few, that the latter might with advantage be entirely removed without any detriment to the effect of the Poem. . . .

Whether the remaining poems of the volume are by Mr Coleridge, we have not been informed; but they seem to proceed from the same mind; and in the *Advertisement*, the Writer speaks of himself as a single person accountable for the whole. They all have merit, and many among them a very high rank of merit, which our feelings respecting some parts of the supposed author's character do not authorize or incline us to deny. 'The Poem on the Nightingale', which is there styled *a conversational Poem*, is very good, but we do not perceive it to be more conversational than Cowper's *Task*, which is the best poem in that style that our language possesses. . . .

SOURCE : *British Critic*, xiv (October 1799) – extract.

III

In our Review for October, 1799, we noticed, with considerable satisfaction, the first edition of this work, then comprised in one anonymous volume. It is now extended by the addition of another volume; and the author has given his name to it, with the exception of the 'Ancient Mariner', the 'Foster Mother's Tale', the 'Nightingale', the 'Dungeon', and the poem entitled 'Love'; all of which, as he informs us, are furnished by a friend, whose opinions on the subject of poetry agree most entirely with his own. From this similarity of mind, and from some expressions in the *Advertisement* prefixed to the first edition, we were led to attribute the whole to Mr Coleridge, the supposed author of the 'Ancient Marinere'; we now, therefore, add to the list of our Poets another name, no less likely to do it honour. Mr Wordsworth has, indeed, appeared before the public some years ago, as author of 'Descriptive Sketches in Verse', and of 'An Evening Walk'; compositions in which were discoverable the fire and fancy of a true poet, though obscured by diction, often and intentionally inflated. His style is now wholly changed, and he has adopted a purity of expression, which, to the fastidious ear, may sometimes perhaps sound poor and low, but which is infinitely more correspondent with true feeling than what, by the courtesy of the day, is usually called poetical language. . . .

SOURCE : *British Critic,* xvii (February 1801), reviewing *Lyrical Ballads* – extract.

Charles Lamb

I. TO WORDSWORTH

Thanks for your Letter and Present. I had already borrowed your second volume. What most please me are, the 'Song of Lucy'. . . . *Simon's sickly daughter* in the 'Sexton' made me *cry*. Next to these are the description of the continuous Echoes in the story of Joanna's laugh where the mountains and all the scenery absolutely seem alive – and that fine Shakesperian character of the Happy Man, in the 'Brothers',

> ———that creeps about the fields,
> Following his fancies by the hour, to bring
> Tears down his cheek, or solitary smiles
> Into his face, *until the Setting Sun*
> *Write Fool upon his forehead.*

I will mention one more : the delicate and curious feeling in the wish for the Cumberland Beggar, that he may have about him the melody of Birds, altho' he hears them not. Here the mind knowingly passes a fiction upon herself, first substituting her own feelings for the Beggar's, and, in the same breath detecting the fallacy, will not part with the wish. – 'The Poet's Epitaph' is disfigured, to my taste by the vulgar satire upon parsons and lawyers in the beginning, and the coarse epithet of pin point in the 6th stanza. All the rest is eminently good, and your own. I will just add that it appears to me a fault in the 'Beggar', that the instructions conveyed in it are too direct and like a lecture : they don't slide into the mind of the reader, while he is imagining no such matter. An intelligent reader finds a sort of insult in being told, I will teach you how to think upon this subject. This fault, if I am right, is in a ten-thousandth worse degree to be found in Sterne and many many novelists & modern poets, who continually put a sign post up to shew where you are to feel. They set out with assuming their readers to be stupid. Very different from *Robinson Crusoe*, the *Vicar of Wakefield*, *Roderick Random*, and other beautiful bare narratives. There is implied an unwritten compact between Author and reader; I will tell you a story, and I suppose you will understand it. Modern novels

St Leons[1] and the like are full of such flowers as these 'Let not
my reader suppose,' 'Imagine, *if you can*' – modest! – &c. – I
will here have done with praise and blame. I have written so
much, only that you may not think I have passed over your
book without observation. – I am sorry that Coleridge has
christened his 'Ancient Marinere' 'a poet's Reverie' – it is as
bad as Bottom the Weaver's declaration that he is not a Lion but
only the scenical representation of a Lion. What new idea is
gained by this Title, but one subversive of all credit, which the
tale should force upon us, of its truth? For me, I was never so
affected with any human Tale. After first reading it, I was
totally possessed with it for many days – I dislike all the miraculous part of it, but the feelings of the man under the operation
of such scenery dragged me along like Tom Piper's magic whistle.
I totally differ from your idea that the Marinere should have had
a character and profession. This is a Beauty in *Gulliver's Travels*,
where the mind is kept in a placid state of little wonderments;
but the 'Ancient Marinere' undergoes such Trials, as overwhelm
and bury all individuality or memory of what he was, like the
state of a man in a Bad dream, one terrible peculiarity of which
is : that all consciousness of personality is gone. Your other observation is I think as well a little unfounded : the Marinere from
being conversant in supernatural events *has* acquired a supernatural and strange cast of *phrase*, eye, appearance, &c. which
frighten the wedding guest. You will excuse my remarks, because
I am hurt and vexed that you should think it necessary, with a
prose apology, to open the eyes of dead men that cannot see.
To sum up a general opinion of the second vol. – I do not feel
any one poem in it so forcibly as the 'Ancient Marinere', the 'Mad
Mother,' and the 'Lines at Tintern Abbey' in the first. – I could,
too, have wished the Critical preface had appeared in a separate
treatise. All its dogmas are true and just, and most of them new,
as criticism. But they associate a *diminishing* idea with the Poems
which follow, as having been written for *Experiment* on the
public taste, more than having sprung (as they must have done)
from living and daily circumstances. . . .

SOURCE : Letter to Wordsworth, 30 January 1801 – extract.

NOTE

1. Written by William Godwin.

II. TO THOMAS MANNING

I had need be cautious henceforward what opinion I give of the *Lyrical Ballads*. All the North of England are in a turmoil. Cumberland and Westmoreland have already declared a state of war. I lately received from Wordsworth a copy of the second volume, accompanied by an acknowledgement of having received from me many months since a copy of a certain Tragedy, with excuses for not having made any acknowledgement sooner, it being owing to an 'almost insurmountable aversion from Letter-writing.' This letter I answered in due form and time, and enumerated several of the passages which had most affected me, adding, unfortunately, that no single piece had moved me so forcibly as the 'Ancient Mariner', 'The Mad Mother', or the 'Lines at Tintern Abbey'. The Post did not sleep a moment. I received almost instantaneously a long letter of four sweating pages from my Reluctant Letter-Writer, the purport of which was, that he was sorry his 2d vol. had not given me more pleasure (Devil a hint did I give that it had *not pleased me*), and 'was compelled to wish that my range of sensibility was more extended, being obliged to believe that I should receive large influxes of happiness and happy Thoughts' (I suppose from the *L. B.*) – With a deal of stuff about a certain Union of Tenderness and Imagination, which in the sense he used Imagination was not the characteristic of Shakespeare, but which Milton possessed in a degree far exceeding other Poets : which Union, as the highest species of Poetry, and chiefly deserving that name, 'He was most proud to aspire to'; then illustrating the said Union by two quotations from his own 2d vol. (which I had been so unfortunate as to miss). 1st Specimen – a father addresses his son :

When thou

First camest into the World, as it befalls
To new-born Infants, thou didst sleep away
Two days : and *Blessings from Thy father's Tongue
Then fell upon thee.*

The lines were thus undermarked, and then followed 'This Passage, as combining in an extraordinary degree that Union of Imagination and Tenderness which I am speaking of, I consider as one of the Best I ever wrote!'

2d Specimen. – A youth, after years of absence, revisits his native place, and thinks (as most people do) that there has been strange alteration in his absence : –

> And that the rocks
> And everlasting Hills themselves were changed.

You see both these are good Poetry : but after one has been reading Shakspeare twenty of the best years of one's life, to have a fellow start up, and prate about some unknown quality, which Shakspeare possessed in a degree inferior to Milton and *somebody else!!* This was not to be *all* my castigation. Coleridge, who had not written to me some months before, starts up from his bed of sickness to reprove me for my hardy presumption : four long pages, equally sweaty and more tedious, came from him; assuring me that, when the works of a man of true genius such as W. undoubtedly was, do not please me at first sight, I should suspect the fault to lie 'in me and not in them,' etc. etc. etc. etc. etc. What am I to do with such people? I certainly shall write them a very merry Letter. Writing to *you*, I may say that the 2d vol. has no such pieces as the three I enumerated. It is full of original thinking and an observing mind, but it does not often make you laugh or cry. – It too artfully aims at simplicity of expression. And you sometimes doubt if Simplicity be not a cover for Poverty. . . .

SOURCE : Letter to Thomas Manning, 15 February 1801 – extract.

William Hazlitt

RECOLLECTIONS OF WORDSWORTH AND COLERIDGE IN THE QUANTOCKS (1797–8)

I arrived, and was well received. The country about Nether Stowey is beautiful, green and hilly, and near the sea-shore. I saw it but the other day, after an interval of twenty years, from a hill near Taunton. How was the map of my life spread out before me, as the map of the country lay at my feet! In the afternoon, Coleridge took me over to All-Foxden, a romantic old family-mansion of the St Aubins, where Wordsworth lived. It was then in the possession of a friend of the poet's who gave him the free use of it. Somehow that period (the time just after the French Revolution) was not a time when *nothing was given for nothing*. The mind opened, and a softness might be perceived coming over the heart of individuals, beneath 'the scales that fence' our self-interest. Wordsworth himself was from home, but his sister kept house, and set before us a frugal repast; and we had free access to her brother's poems, the *Lyrical Ballads*, which were still in manuscript, or in the form of *Sybilline Leaves*. I dipped into a few of these with great satisfaction, and with the faith of a novice. I slept that night in an old room with blue hangings, and covered with the round-faced family-portraits of the age of George I and II, and from the wooded declivity of the adjoining park that overlooked my window, at the dawn of day, could

———hear the loud stag speak.

In the outset of life (and particularly at this time I felt it so) our imagination has a body to it. We are in a state between sleeping and waking, and have indistinct but glorious glimpses of strange shapes, and there is always something to come better than what we see. As in our dreams the fulness of the blood gives warmth and reality to the coinage of the brain, so in youth our ideas are clothed, and fed, and pampered with our good spirits; we breathe thick with thoughtless happiness, the weight of future years presses on the strong pulses of the heart, and we repose with undisturbed faith in truth and good. As we advance, we exhaust our fund of enjoyment and of hope. We are no longer

wrapped in *lamb's-wool*, lulled in Elysium. As we taste the
pleasures of life, their spirit evaporates, the sense palls; and nothing is left but the phantoms, the lifeless shadows of what *has
been*!

That morning, as soon as breakfast was over, we strolled out
into the park, and seating ourselves on the trunk of an old ash-
tree that stretched along the ground, Coleridge read aloud with
a sonorous and musical voice, the ballad of 'Betty Foy'. I was not
critically or sceptically inclined. I saw touches of truth and nature,
and took the rest for granted. But in the 'Thor', the 'Mad
Mother', and the 'Complaint of a Poor Indian Woman', I felt
that deeper power and pathos which have been since acknowledged,

> In spite of pride, in erring reason's spite,

as the characteristics of this author; and the sense of a new style
and a new spirit in poetry came over me. It had to me something of the effect that arises from the turning up of the fresh
soil, or of the first welcome breath of Spring,

> While yet the trembling year is unconfirmed.

Coleridge and myself walked back to Stowey that evening, and his
voice sounded high

> Of Providence, foreknowledge, will, and fate,
> Fix'd fate, free-will, foreknowledge absolute,

as we passed through echoing grove, by fairy stream or waterfall,
gleaming in the summer moonlight! He lamented that Wordsworth was not prone enough to believe in the traditional superstitions of the place, and that there was a something corporeal,
a *matter-of-fact-ness*, a clinging to the palpable, or often to the
petty, in his poetry, in consequence. His genius was not a spirit
that descended to him through the air; it sprung out of the
ground like a flower, or unfolded itself from a green spray, on
which the gold-finch sang. He said, however (if I remember
right), that this objection must be confined to his descriptive
pieces, that his philosophic poetry had a grand and comprehensive spirit in it, so that his soul seemed to inhabit the universe like
a palace, and to discover truth by intuition, rather than by
deduction. The next day Wordsworth arrived from Bristol at

Coleridge's cottage. I think I see him now. He answered in some degree to his friend's description of him, but was more gaunt and Don Quixote-like. He was quaintly dressed (according to the *costume* of that unconstrained period) in a brown fustian jacket and striped pantaloons. There was something of a roll, a lounge in his gait, not unlike his own Peter Bell. There was a severe, worn pressure of thought about his temples, a fire in his eye (as if he saw something in objects more than the outward appearance), an intense high narrow forehead, a Roman nose, cheeks furrowed by strong purpose and feeling, and a convulsive inclination to laughter about the mouth, a good deal at variance with the solemn, stately expression of the rest of his face. Chantry's bust wants the marking traits; but he was teazed into making it regular and heavy : Haydon's head of him, introduced into the *Entrance of Christ into Jerusalem*, is the most like his drooping weight of thought and expression. He sat down and talked very naturally and freely, with a mixture of clear gushing accents in his voice, a deep guttural intonation, and a strong tincture of the northern *burr*, like the crust on wine. He instantly began to make havoc of the half of a Cheshire cheese on the table, and said triumphantly that 'his marriage with experience had not been so unproductive as Mr Southey's in teaching him a knowledge of the good things of this life.' He had been to see the *Castle Spectre* by Monk Lewis, while at Bristol, and described it very well. He said 'it fitted the taste of the audience like a glove.' This *ad captandum* merit was however by no means a recommendation of it, according to the severe principles of the new school, which reject rather than court popular effect. Wordsworth, looking out of the low, latticed window, said, 'How beautifully the sun sets on that yellow bank !' I thought within myself, 'With what eyes these poets see nature !' and ever after, when I saw the sun-set stream upon the objects facing it, conceived I had made a discovery, or thanked Mr. Wordsworth for having made one for me ! We went over to All-Foxden again the day following, and Wordsworth read us the story of Peter Bell in the open air; and the comment made upon it by his face and voice was very different from that of some later critics ! Whatever might be thought of the poem, 'his face was as a book where men might read strange matters,' and he announced the fate of his

hero in prophetic tones. There is a *chaunt* in the recitation both
of Coleridge and Wordsworth, which acts as a spell upon the
hearer, and disarms the judgment. Perhaps they have deceived
themselves by making habitual use of this ambiguous accompani-
ment. Coleridge's manner is more full, animated, and varied;
Wordsworth's more equable, sustained, and internal. The one
might be termed more *dramatic*, the other more *lyrical.* Coleridge
had told me that he himself liked to compose in walking over un-
even ground, or breaking through the straggling branches of a
copse-wood; whereas Wordsworth always wrote (if he could)
walking up and down a straight gravel-walk, or in some spot
where the continuity of his verse met with no collateral interruption. Returning that same evening, I got into a metaphysical
argument with Wordsworth, while Coleridge was explaining the
different notes of the nightingale to his sister, in which we neither
of us succeeded in making ourselves perfectly clear and intelligible.
Thus I passed three weeks at Nether Stowey and in the neighbourhood, generally devoting the afternoons to a delightful chat
in an arbour made of bark by the poet's friend Tom Poole,
sitting under two fine elm-trees, and listening to the bees humming
round us, while we quaffed our *flip*. It was agreed, among other
things, that we should make a jaunt down the Bristol-Channel,
as far as Linton. We set off together on foot, Coleridge, John
Chester,[1] and I. . . . We walked for miles and miles on dark brown
heaths overlooking the Channel, with the Welsh hills beyond, and
at times descended into little sheltered valleys close by the sea-
side, with a smuggler's face scowling by us, and then had to
ascend conical hills with a path winding up through a coppice to
a barren top, like a monk's shaven crown, from one of which I
pointed out to Coleridge's notice the bare masts of a vessel on the
very edge of the horizon and within the red-orbed disk of the
setting sun, like his own spectre-ship in the 'Ancient Mariner'.
At Linton the character of the sea-coast becomes more marked
and rugged. There is a place called the *Valley of Rocks* (I suspect
this was only the poetical name for it) bedded among precipices
overhanging the sea, with rocky caverns beneath, into which the
waves dash, and where the sea-gull for ever wheels its screaming
flight. On the tops of these are huge stones thrown transverse, as
if an earthquake had tossed them there, and behind these is a

fretwork of perpendicular rocks, something like the *Giant's Cause-way*. A thunder-storm came on while we were at the inn, and Coleridge was running out bare-headed to enjoy the commotion of the elements in the *Valley of Rocks,* but as if in spite, the clouds only muttered a few angry sounds, and let fall a few refreshing drops. Coleridge told me that he and Wordsworth were to have made this place the scene of a prose-tale, which was to have been in the manner of, but far superior to, the 'Death of Abel', but they had relinquished the design. In the morning of the second day, we breakfasted luxuriously in an old-fashioned parlour, on tea, toast, eggs, and honey, in the very sight of the bee-hives from which it had been taken, and a garden full of thyme and wild flowers that had produced it. On this occasion Coleridge spoke of Virgil's Georgics, but not well. I do not think he had much feeling for the classical or elegant. It was in this room that we found a little worn-out copy of the *Seasons*, lying in a window-seat, on which Coleridge exclaimed, '*That* is true fame!' He said Thomson was a great poet, rather than a good one; his style was as meretricious as his thoughts were natural. He spoke of Cowper as the best modern poet. He said the *Lyrical Ballads* were an experiment about to be tried by him and Wordsworth, to see how far the public taste would endure poetry written in a more natural and simple style than had hitherto been attempted; totally discarding the artifices of poetical diction, and making use only of such words as had probably been common in the most ordinary language since the days of Henry II. Some comparison was introduced between Shakespear and Milton. He said 'he hardly knew which to prefer. Shakespear appeared to him a mere stripling in the art; he was as tall and as strong, with infinitely more activity than Milton, but he never appeared to have come to man's estate; or if he had, he would not have been a man, but a monster.' He spoke with contempt of Gray, and with intolerance of Pope. He did not like the versification of the latter. He observed that 'the ears of these couplet-writers might be charged with having short memories, that could not retain the harmony of whole passages.' He thought little of Junius as a writer; he had a dislike of Dr Johnson; and a much higher opinion of Burke as an orator and politician, than of Fox or Pitt. He however thought him very inferior in richness of style and imagery to some of our elder prose-writers, particularly Jeremy Taylor. He liked Richardson, but not Fielding; nor could I get him to enter into the merits of *Caleb Williams*. In short, he was profound and discriminating with respect to those authors whom he liked, and where he gave his judgment fair play; capricious, perverse, and prejudiced in his antipathies and distastes. We loitered on the 'ribbed sea-sands,' in such talk as this, a whole morning, and I recollect met with a curious sea-weed, of which John Chester told us the country name! A fisherman gave Coleridge an account of a boy that had been drowned the day before, and that they had tried to save him at the risk of their own lives. He said 'he did not know how it was that they ventured, but, Sir, we have a *nature* towards one another.' This expression, Coleridge remarked to me, was a fine illustration of that theory of disinterestedness which I (in common with Butler) had adopted. I broached to him an argument of mine to prove that *likeness* was not mere association of ideas. I said that the mark in the sand put one in mind of a man's foot, not because it was part of a former impression of a man's foot (for it was quite new) but because it was like the shape of a man's foot. He assented to the justness of this distinction (which I have explained at length elsewhere, for the benefit of the curious) and John Chester listened; not from any interest in the subject, but because he was astonished that I should be able to suggest any thing to Coleridge that he did not already know. We returned on the third morning, and Coleridge remarked the silent cottage-smoke curling up the valleys where, a few evenings before, we had seen the lights gleaming through the dark.

SOURCE : 'On My First Acquaintance with Poets', – extract.

NOTE

1. John Chester was a friend of Coleridge, who later followed him into Germany.

Thomas De Quincey

It was, I think, in the month of August, but certainly in the summer season, and certainly in the year 1807, that I first saw this illustrious man. My knowledge of him as a man of most original genius began about the year 1799. A little before that time Wordsworth had published the first edition (in a single volume) of the *Lyrical Ballads,* and into this had been introduced Mr Coleridge's poem of the 'Ancient Mariner', as the contribution of an anonymous friend. It would be directing the reader's attention too much to myself if I were to linger upon this, the greatest event in the unfolding of my own mind. Let me say, in one word, that, at a period when neither the one nor the other writer was valued by the public – both having a long warfare to accomplish of contumely and ridicule before they could rise into their present estimation – I found in these poems 'the ray of a new morning,' and an absolute revelation of untrodden worlds teeming with power and beauty as yet unsuspected amongst men. I may here mention that, precisely at the same time, Professor Wilson,[1] entirely unconnected with myself, and not even known to me until ten years later, received the same startling and profound impressions from the same volume. With feelings of reverential interest, so early and so deep, pointing towards two contemporaries, it may be supposed that I inquired eagerly after their names. But these inquiries were self-baffled; the same deep feelings which prompted my curiosity causing me to recoil from all casual opportunities of pushing the inquiry, as too generally lying amongst those who gave no sign of participating in my feelings; and, extravagant as this may seem, I revolted with as much hatred from coupling my question with any occasion of insult to the persons whom it respected as a primitive Christian from throwing frankincense upon the altars of Cæsar, or a lover from giving up the name of his beloved to the coarse license of a Bacchanalian party. It is laughable to record for how long a period my curiosity in this particular was thus self-defeated. Two years passed before I ascertained the two names. Mr Wordsworth published *his* in the second and enlarged edition of the poems; and for Mr Coleridge's I was 'indebted' to a private source; but I discharged that debt ill, for I quarrelled with my informant for what I considered his profane way of dealing with a subject so hallowed in my own thoughts. After this I searched, east and west, north and south, for all known works or fragments of the same authors. . . .

SOURCE: *Confessions of an English Opium Eater* – extract.

NOTE

1. John Wilson, 'Christopher North' (1785–1854).

Thomas Noon Talfourd

Little as Mr Coleridge has written, he has manifested not only a depth but a variety of genius, from which the most brilliant results might be expected . . . In spell poetry he is far more potent than any writer of the present age, – his enchantments are more marvellous and deeper woven, – his fictions wilder, – and his mysteries more heart-touching and appalling. In his 'Ancient Mariner', the solemn helplessness of the narrator, condemned to live amidst supernatural horrors, is awfully expressed by the lines, – 'a thousand thousand slimy things liv'd on and so did I.' How the image of strange loneliness strikes upon the heart, when he with the fatal ship and her ghastly crew burst into the sea, 'where God himself' scarcely seemed to be present! And with how pure a thrill of delight are we refreshed, in the midst of this terrible witchery, when the poor creature, whom superior power has enchanted, sees the water-snakes sporting in the sun, which at happier seasons would have filled him with disgust, bursts into a blessing of these 'happy living things,' and a 'gush of love' comes from a spirit haunted with unutterable terrors. . . .

SOURCE: 'An Attempt to Estimate the Poetical Talent of the Present Age', *The Pamphleteer*, v (1815) – extract.

Critical Review 1816

'Christabel' is a romantic fragment; the first part, as the author
informs us, having been written in 1797, and the second in 1800,
during which interval Mr Coleridge visited Germany, still retaining the fabric of the complete story in his mind 'with the
wholeness no less than with the liveliness of a vision', and as the
vivid impression continues to the present day, he undertakes 'to
embody in verse the three parts yet to come, in the course of the
present year'. We sincerely hope that this promise will be realized,
but we fear that the task will be at least wearisome to a man of the
listless habits of Mr Coleridge. For ourselves we confess, that
when we read the story in MS. two or three years ago, it appeared
to be one of those dreamlike productions whose charm partly
consisted in the undefined obscurity of the conclusion – what that
conclusion may be, no person who reads the commencement will
be at all able to anticipate. The reader, before he opens the
poem, must be prepared to allow for the superstitions of necro-
mancy and sorcery, and to expect something of the glorious and
unbounded range which the belief in those mysteries permits;
the absurd trammels of mere physical possibility are here thrown
aside, like the absurd swaddling clothes of infants, which
formerly obstructed the growth of the fair symmetry of nature.

The lady Christabel, in consequence of ill-boding dreams, re-
pairs at midnight in April to the forest, a furlong from the castle
of Sir Leoline, her father, and while in the fearlessness of innocence she is engaged in prayer 'for the weal of her lover that's far
away', she hears behind the old oak, at the foot of which she is
kneeling, a low moan ...

Christabel stealing to the other side of the tree, beholds a lovely
lady in distress, who informs her that her name is Geraldine, that
she had been conveyed to the forest by five warriors, and that she
had lain there devoid of sense, till awakened by the distant sound
of a castle bell. Christabel . . . takes compassion on the unhappy
lady ...

What a beautiful picture is here afforded of these two delicate and lovely females passing the iron'd gate, contrasted with an army in battle array, that had shortly before marched through it. Geraldine faints at the gate, but is revived by her companion, who afterwards requires her to join in praise to the Virgin who had rescued her in the forest

> Alas, alas ! said Geraldine,
> I cannot pray for weariness.

The truth is that she is one of those evil ministers, who are fancifully supposed for a time to obtain power over the innocent. The manner in which the reader is prepared for this disclosure is gradual and beautiful, though it fails at first to alarm the unsuspicious Christabel. The first indication we have above given – the next is an involuntary and angry moan made by an old faithful mastiff that lay asleep in one of the baillies of the castle : a third is thus conveyed :

> They pass'd the hall, that echoes still,
> Pass as lightly as you will,
> The brands were flat, the brands were dying,
> Amid their own white ashes lying;
> But when the lady pass'd there came
> A tongue of light a fit of flame;
> And Christabel saw the lady's eyes,
> But nothing else she saw thereby.

The distinguishing of Geraldine's bright eye reflecting back the flame, is a most effective finish. When they reach the chamber of Christabel, the weary Geraldine again sinks to the floor, and is again recovered. Her evil designs are soon afterwards fully disclosed when she appears to be contending for masterdom with the unseen spirit of the dead mother of Christabel.

Geraldine requested Christabel to unrobe, while she pretended to employ herself in prayer; the daughter of Sir Leoline complied, 'and lay down in her loveliness' . . .

By a poetical and most judicious abruption the poet leaves it to the imagination of the reader to figure what terrible and disgusting sight presented itself to Christabel. Geraldine then pressed Christabel to her bosom, where worked a spell that restrained the utterance of what she had just beheld. After a night of fearful visions, Christabel awakes, and finding the lady Geraldine sleeping in renovated beauty at her side, she imagines she had but dreamt what had given her such alarm. She introduces Geraldine to her father, Sir Leoline, who learns that she was the daughter of Sir Roland de Vaux of Tryermaine . . .

Pity for Geraldine supersedes all other considerations, and Sir Leoline swears to revenge her wrongs : he summons his Bard, Bracy, whom he commands to repair to the castle of Lord Roland, to inform him of the safety of his daughter, but Bracy alleges as a reason for postponement, a dream he had had, that he had seen the gentle dove of Christabel struggling with a green serpent round its neck in the forest, and as he fancied that some 'thing unblest' lingered there, he had vowed to expel it by music. While the bard was relating his dream, Geraldine turned towards her victim . . .

When (Christabel) awoke from this trance, she entreated her father to send Geraldine away, but the powerful spell prevented her from assigning any reason, and Sir Leoline who had marked this 'look of dull and treacherous hate', which was the mere reflection of Geraldine's countenance on the pure mirror of his daughter's face, is instantly struck with the conviction that Christabel is the serpent of whom Bracy had dreamt, and Geraldine the innocent and trembling dove; for to Sir Leoline she appeared all beauty and simplicity . . .

We lament that our limits will not allow us to give more of this very graceful and fanciful poem, which we may say, without fear of contradiction, is enriched with more beautiful passages than have ever been before included in so small a compass. Nothing can be better contrasted than Christabel and Geraldine – both exquisite, but both different – the first all innocence, mildness, and grace; the last all dignity, grandeur, and majesty : the one with all those innate virtues, that working internally, mould the external shape to corresponding perfectness – the other possessing merely the charm of superficial excellence : the one the gentle soul-delighting Una – the other the seeming fair, but infamous Duessa.

Of the rich and luxuriant imagery with which this poem abounds, our imperfect sketch will afford but a faint idea, and we have been compelled to omit many descriptive passages of the first order. For these we must refer to the original, assured that, after reading our extracts, none will throw it aside because they meet with a passage or two in the threshold not exactly according with their pre-conceived notions of excellence.

'Kubla Khan, a Vision', is one of those pieces that can only speak for itself . . .

SOURCE : ·*Critical Review*, III (May 1816) – extract.

William Hazlitt (1816)

ON 'CHRISTABEL' AND 'KUBLA KHAN'

The fault of Mr Coleridge is, that he comes to no conclusion. He is a man of that universality of genius, that his mind hangs suspended between poetry and prose, truth and falsehood, and an infinity of other things, and from an excess of capacity, he does little or nothing. Here are two unfinished poems, and a fragment. 'Christabel', which has been much read and admired in manuscript, is now for the first time confided to the public. 'The Vision of Kubla Khan' still remains a profound secret; for only a few lines of it ever were written.

The poem of 'Christabel' sets out in the following manner.

> 'Tis the middle of night by the castle clock,
> And the owls have awaken'd the crowing cock;
> Tu—whit! Tu——whoo!
> And hark, again! the crowing cock,
> How drowsily it crew.
> Sir Leoline, the Baron rich,
> Hath a toothless mastiff bitch;
> From her kennel beneath the rock
> She makes answer to the clock,
> Four for the quarters and twelve for the hour;
> Ever and aye, moonshine or shower,
> Sixteen short howls, not over loud;
> Some say, she sees my lady's shroud.

We wonder that Mr Murray,[1] who has an eye for things, should suffer this 'mastiff bitch' to come into his shop. Is she a sort of Cerberus to fright away the critics? But – gentlemen, she is toothless.

There is a dishonesty as well as affectation in all this. The secret of this pretended contempt for the opinion of the public, is that it is a sorry subterfuge for our self-love. The poet, uncertain of the approbation of his readers, thinks he shews his superiority to it by shocking their feelings at the outset, as a clown, who is at a loss how to behave himself, begins by affronting the company. This is what is called *throwing a crust to the critics.* If the beauties of 'Christabel' should not be sufficiently admired, Mr Coleridge may lay it all to two lines which he had too much manliness to omit in complaisance to the bad taste of his contemporaries.

We the rather wonder at this bold proceeding in the author, as his courage has cooled in the course of the publication, and he has omitted, from mere delicacy, a line which is absolutely necessary to the understanding the whole story. The Lady Christabel, wandering in the forest by moonlight, meets a lady in apparently great distress, to whom she offers her assistance and protection, and takes her home with her to her own chamber. This woman,

> beautiful to see,
> Like a lady of a far countree,

is a witch. Who she is else, what her business is with Christabel, upon what motives, to what end her sorceries are to work, does not appear at present; but this much we know : that she is a witch, and that Christabel's dread of her arises from her discovering this circumstance, which is told in a single line, which line, from an exquisite refinement in efficiency, is here omitted. When the unknown lady gets to Christabel's chamber, and is going to undress, it is said :

> Then drawing in her breath aloud
> Like one that shuddered, she unbound
> The cincture from beneath her breast :
> Her silken robe and inner vest
> Dropt to her feet, and full in view
> *Behold! her bosom and half her side* –
> A sight to dream of, not to tell !
> And she is to sleep by Christabel !

The manuscript runs thus, or nearly thus :

Behold her bosom and half her side –
Hideous, deformed, and pale of hue.

This line is necessary to make common sense of the first and second part. 'It is the keystone that makes up the arch'. For that reason Mr Coleridge left it out. Now this is a greater physiological curiosity than even the fragment of 'Kubla Khan'.

In parts of 'Christabel' there is a great deal of beauty, both of thought, imagery, and versification; but the effect of the general story is dim, obscure, and visionary. It is more like a dream than a reality. The mind, in reading it, is spell-bound. The sorceress seems to act without power – Christabel to yield without resistance. The faculties are thrown into a state of metaphysical suspense and theoretical imbecility. The poet, like the witch in Spenser, is evidently

Busied about some wicked gin.

But we do not foresee what he will make of it. There is something disgusting at the bottom of his subject, which is but ill glossed over by a veil of Della Cruscan sentiment and fine writing – like moonbeams playing on a charnel-house, or flowers strewed on a dead body. Mr Coleridge's style is essentially superficial, pretty, ornamental, and he has forced it into the service of a story which is petrific. In the midst of moon-light, and fluttering ringlets, and flitting clouds, and enchanted echoes, and airy abstractions of all sorts, there is one genuine burst of humanity, worthy of the author, when no dream oppresses him, no spell binds him. We give the passage entire :

But when he heard the lady's tale,
And when she told her father's name,
Why waxed Sir Leoline so pale,
Murmuring o'er the name again,
Lord Roland de Vaux of Tryermaine?
Alas ! they had been friends in youth;
But whispering tongues can poison truth;
And constancy lives in realms above;
And life is thorny, and youth is vain;
And to be wroth with one we love,

Doth work like madness in the brain.
And thus it chanced, as I divine,
With Roland and Sir Leoline.
Each spake words of high disdain,
And insult to his heart's best brother :
They parted – ne'er to meet again !
But never either found another
To free the hollow heart from paining –
They stood aloof, the scars remaining
Like cliffs which had been rent asunder;
A dreary sea now flows between,
But neither heat nor frost nor thunder,
Shall wholly do away, I ween,
The marks of that which once hath been.
Sir Leoline a moment's space
Stood gazing in the damsel's face;
And the youthful Lord of Tryermaine
Came back upon his heart again.

Why does not Mr Coleridge always write in this manner, that we might always read him? The description of the Dream of Bracy the bard, is also very beautiful and full of power.

The conclusion of the second part of 'Christabel', about 'the little limber elf', is to us absolutely incomprehensible. 'Kubla Khan', we think, only shews that Mr Coleridge can write better *nonsense* verses than any man in England. It is not a poem, but a musical composition.

A damsel with a dulcimer
In a vision once I saw :
It was an Abyssinian maid,
And on her dulcimer she play'd,
Singing of Mount Abora.

We could repeat these lines to ourselves not the less often for not knowing the meaning of them.

SOURCE : *Examiner* (2 June 1816) – extract.

NOTE

1. John Murray (1778–1843), the publisher.

Thomas Moore

The advertisement by which this work was announced to the publick, carried in its front a recommendation from Lord Byron, who, it seems, has somewhere praised 'Christabel', as 'a wild and singularly original and beautiful poem'. Great as the noble bard's merits undoubtedly are in poetry, some of his latest *publications* dispose us to distrust his authority, where the question is what ought to meet the public eye; and the works before us afford an additional proof, that his judgment on such matters is not absolutely to be relied on. Moreover, we are a little inclined to doubt the value of the praise which one poet lends another. It seems now-a-days to be the practice of that once irritable race to laud each other without bounds; and one can hardly avoid suspecting, that what is thus lavishly advanced may be laid out with a view to being repaid with interest. Mr Coleridge, however, must be judged by his own merits.

It is remarked, by the writers upon the Bathos, that the true *profound* is surely known by one quality – its being wholly bottomless; insomuch, that when you think you have attained its utmost depth in the work of some of its great masters, another, or peradventure the same, astonishes you, immediately after, by a plunge so much more vigorous, as to outdo all his former outdoings. So it seems to be with the new school, or, as they may be termed, the wild or lawless poets. After we had been admiring their extravagance for many years, and marvelling at the ease and rapidity with which one exceeded another in the unmeaning or infantine, until not an idea was left in the rhyme – or in the insane, until we had reached something that seemed the untamed effusion of an author whose thoughts were rather more free than his actions – forth steps Mr Coleridge, like a giant refreshed with sleep, and as if to redeem his character after so long a silence (his poetic powers having been, he says, from 1808 till very lately, in a state of suspended animation) and breaks out in these precise words :

'Tis the middle of night by the castle clock,
And the owls have awaken'd the crowing cock ;

Tu—whit!——Tu—whoo!
And hark, again! the crowing cock,
How drowsily it crew.

Sir Leoline, the Baron rich,
Hath a toothless mastiff bitch;
From her kennel beneath the rock
She makes answer to the clock,
Four for the quarters, and twelve for the hour;
Ever and aye, moonshine or shower,
Sixteen short howls, not over loud;
Some say she sees my lady's shroud.
Is the night chilly and dark?
The night is chilly, but not dark.

It is probable that Lord Byron may have had this passage in his eye, when he called the poem 'wild' and 'original'; but how he discovered it to be 'beautiful', is not quite so easy for us to imagine.

Much of the art of the wild writers consists in sudden transitions – opening eagerly upon some topic, and then flying from it immediately. This indeed is known to the medical men, who not unfrequently have the care of them, as an unerring symptom. Accordingly, here we take leave of the Mastiff Bitch, and lose sight of her entirely, upon the entrance of another personage of a higher degree,

The lovely Lady Christabel,
Whom her father loves so well –

And who, it seems, has been rambling about all night, having, the night before, had dreams about her lover, which 'made her moan and *leap*'. While kneeling, in the course of her rambles, at an old oak, she hears a noise on the other side of the stump, and going round, finds, to her great surprize, another fair damsel in white silk, but with her dress and hair in some disorder; at the mention of whom, the poet takes fright, not as might be imagined, because of her disorder, but on account of her beauty and her fair attire:

I guess, 'twas frightful there to see
A lady so richly clad as she –
Beautiful exceedingly!

Christabel naturally asks who she is, and is answered, at some length, that her name is Geraldine; that she was, on the morning before, seized by five warriors, who tied her on a white horse, and drove her on, they themselves following, also on white horses; and that they had rode all night. Her narrative now gets to be a little contradictory, which gives rise to unpleasant suspicions. She protests vehemently, and with oaths, that she has no idea who the men were; only that one of them, the tallest of the five, took her and placed her under the tree, and that they all went away, she knew not whither; but how long she had remained there she cannot tell:

> Nor do I know how long it is,
> For I have lain in fits, I *wis*;

although she had previously kept a pretty exact account of the time. The two ladies then go home together, after this satisfactory explanation, which appears to have conveyed to the intelligent mind of Lady C. every requisite information. They arrive at the castle, and pass the night in the same bed-room; not to disturb Sir Leoline, who, it seems, was poorly at the time, and, of course, must have been called up to speak to the chambermaids, and have the sheets aired, if Lady G. had had a room to herself. They do not get to their bed, however, in the poem, quite so easily as we have carried them. They first cross the moat, and Lady C. 'took the key that fitted well', and opened a little door, 'all in the middle of the gate'. Lady G. then sinks down 'belike through pain'; but it should seem more probably from laziness; for her fair companion having lifted her up, and carried her a little way, she then walks on 'as she were not in pain'. Then they cross the court – but we must give this in the poet's words, for he seems so pleased with them, that he inserts them twice over in the space of ten lines.

> So free from danger, free from fear,
> They crossed the court – right glad they were.

Lady C. is desirous of a little conversation on the way, but Lady G. will not indulge her Ladyship, saying, she is too much tired to speak. We now meet our old friend, the mastiff bitch, who is much too important a person to be slightly passed by:

Outside her kennel, the mastiff old
Lay fast asleep, in moonshine cold.
The mastiff old did not awake,
Yet she an angry moan did make !
And what can ail the mastiff bitch?
Never till now she uttered yell
Beneath the eye of Christabel.
Perhaps it is the owlet's scritch :
For what can ail the mastiff bitch?

Whatever it may be that ails the bitch, the ladies pass forward, and take off their shoes, and tread softly all the way up stairs, as Christabel observes that her father is a bad sleeper. At last, however, they do arrive at the bed-room, and comfort themselves with a dram of some home-made liquor, which proves to be very old; for it was made by Lady C.'s mother; and when her new friend asks if she thinks the old lady will take her part, she answers, that this is out of the question, in as much as she happened to die in childbed of her. The mention of the old lady, however, gives occasion to the following pathetic couplet. Christabel says,

O mother dear, that thou wert here !
I would, said Geraldine, she were !

A very mysterious conversation next takes place between Lady Geraldine and the old gentlewoman's ghost, which proving extremely fatiguing to her, she again has recourse to the bottle – and with excellent effect, as appears by these lines.

Again the wild-flower wine she drank ;
Her fair eyes 'gan glitter bright,
And from the floor whereon she sank,
The lofty Lady stood upright :
    She was most beautiful to see,
Like a Lady of a far countrée.

From which, we may gather among other points, the exceeding great beauty of all women who live in a distant place, no matter where. The effects of the cordial speedily begin to appear; as no one, we imagine, will doubt, that to its influence must be ascribed the following speech :

And thus the lofty lady spake –
All they, who live in the upper sky,
Do love you, holy Christabel!
And you love them – and for their sake
And for the good which me befel,
Even I in my degree will try,
Fair maiden, to requite you well.

Before going to bed, Lady G. kneels to pray, and desires her friend to undress, and lie down; which she does 'in her loveliness'; but being curious, she leans 'on her elbow', and looks towards the fair devotee – where she sees something which the poet does not think fit to tell us very explicitly.

Her silken robe, and inner vest,
Dropt to her feet, and full in view,
Behold! her bosom and half her side –
A sight to dream of, not to tell!
And she is to sleep by Christabel.

She soon rises, however, from her knees; and as it was not a double-bedded room, she turns in to Lady Christabel, taking only 'two paces and a stride'. She then clasps her tight in her arms, and mutters a very dark spell, which we apprehend the poet manufactured by shaking words together at random; for it is impossible to fancy that he can annex any meaning whatever to it. This is the end of it.

But vainly thou warrest,
  For this is alone in
Thy power to declare,
  That in the dim forest
Thou heard'st a low moaning,
And found'st a bright lady, surpassing fair :
And didst bring her home with thee in love and in charity,
To shield her and shelter her from the damp air.

The consequence of this incantation is, that Lady Christabel has a strange dream – and when she awakes, her first exclamation is, 'Sure I have sinn'd' – 'Now heaven be praised if all be well!' Being still perplexed with the remembrance of her 'too lively' dream – she then dresses herself, and modestly prays to be forgiven for 'her sins unknown'. The two companions now go to the

Baron's parlour, and Geraldine tells her story to him. This, however, the poet judiciously leaves out, and only signifies that the Baron recognized in her the daughter of his old friend Sir Roland, with whom he had had a deadly quarrel. Now, however, he despatches his tame poet, or laureate, called Bard Bracy, to invite him and his family over, promising to forgive every thing, and even make an apology for what had passed. To understand what follows, we own, surpasses our comprehension. Mr Bracy, the poet, recounts a strange dream he has just had, of a dove being almost strangled by a snake; whereupon the Lady Geraldine falls a hissing, and her eyes grow small, like a serpent's, – or at least so they seem to her friend; who begs her father to 'send away that woman'. Upon this the Baron falls into a passion, as if he had discovered that his daughter had been seduced; at least, we can understand him in no other sense, though no hint of such a kind is given; but, on the contrary, she is painted to the last moment as full of innocence and purity. Nevertheless,

> His heart was cleft with pain and rage,
> His cheeks they quiver'd, his eyes were wild,
> Dishonour'd thus in his old age;
> Dishonour'd by his only child;
> And all his hospitality
> To th' insulted daughter of his friend
> By more than woman's jealousy,
> Brought thus to a disgraceful end –

Nothing further is said to explain the mystery; but there follows incontinently, what is termed '*The conclusion of Part the Second*'. And as we are pretty confident that Mr Coleridge holds this passage in the highest estimation; that he prizes it more than any other part of 'that wild, and singularly original and beautiful poem Christabel', excepting always the two passages touching the 'toothless mastiff Bitch'; we shall extract it for the amazement of our readers – premising our own frank avowal that we are wholly unable to divine the meaning of any portion of it.

> A little child, a limber elf,
> Singing, dancing to itself,
> A fairy thing with red round cheeks,
> That always finds and never seeks;

Makes such a vision to the sight
As fills a father's eyes with light;
And pleasures flow in so thick and fast
Upon his heart, that he at last
Must needs express his love's excess
With words of unmeant bitterness.
Perhaps 'tis pretty to force together
Thoughts so all unlike each other;
To mutter and mock a broken charm,
To dally with wrong that does no harm.
Perhaps 'tis tender too, and pretty,
At each wild word to feel within
A sweet recoil of love and pity.
And what if in a world of sin
(O sorrow and shame should this be true !)
Such giddiness of heart and brain
Comes seldom save from rage and pain,
So talks as it's most used to do.

Here endeth the Second Part, and, in truth, the 'singular' poem itself; for the author has not yet written, or, as he phrases it, 'embodied in verse', the 'three parts yet to come'; though he trusts he shall be able to do so 'in the course of the present year'.

One word as to the metre of 'Christabel', or, as Mr Coleridge terms it, '*the* Christabel' – happily enough; for indeed we doubt if the peculiar force of the definite article was ever more strongly exemplified. He says, that though the reader may fancy there prevails a great *irregularity* in the metre, some lines being of four, others of twelve syllables, yet in reality it is quite regular; only that it is 'founded on a new principle, namely, that of counting in each line the accents, not the syllables'. We say nothing of the monstrous assurance of any man coming forward coolly at this time of day, and telling the readers of English poetry, whose ear has been tuned to the lays of Spenser, Milton, Dryden, and Pope, that he makes his metre 'on a new principle' ! but we utterly deny the truth of the assertion, and defy him to show us *any* principle upon which his lines can be conceived to tally. We give two or three specimens, to confound at once this miserable piece of coxcombry and shuffling. Let our 'wild, and singularly original and beautiful' author, show us how these lines agree either in number of accents or of feet.

Ah wel-a-day ! –
For this is alone in –
And didst bring her home with thee in love and in charity –
I pray you drink this cordial wine –
Sir Leoline –
And found a bright lady surpassingly fair –
Tu—whit !——Tu—whoo !

'Kubla Khan' is given to the public, it seems, 'at the request of a poet of great and deserved celebrity'; but whether Lord Byron the praiser of 'the Christabel', or the Laureate, the praiser of Princes, we are not informed. As far as Mr Coleridge's 'own opinions are concerned', it is published, 'not upon the ground of any *poetic* merits', but 'as a Psychological Curiosity' ! In these opinions of the candid author, we entirely concur; but for this reason we hardly think it was necessary to give the minute detail which the Preface contains, of the circumstances attending its composition. Had the question regarded *Paradise Lost*, or Dryden's 'Ode', we could not have had a more particular account of the circumstances in which it was composed. It was in the year 1797, and in the summer season. Mr Coleridge was in bad health; the particular disease is not given; but the careful reader will form his own conjectures. He had retired very prudently to a lonely farm-house; and whoever would see the place which gave birth to the 'psychological curiosity', may find his way thither without a guide; for it is situated on the confines of Somerset and Devonshire, and on the Exmoor part of the boundary; and it is, moreover, between Porlock and Linton. In that farmhouse, he had a slight indisposition, and had taken an anodyne, which threw him into a deep sleep in his chair (whether after dinner or not he omits to state)' 'at the moment that he was reading a sentence in Purchas's Pilgrims', relative to a palace of Kubla Khan. The effects of the anodyne, and the sentence together, were prodigious : they produced the 'curiosity' now before us; for, during his three-hours sleep, Mr Coleridge 'has the most vivid confidence that he could not have composed less than from two to three hundred lines'. On awakening, he 'instantly and eagerly' wrote down the verses here published; when he was (he says, '*unfortunately*') called out by a 'person on business from Porlock, and detained by him above an hour'; and when he returned, the vision was gone. The lines here given smell strongly, it must be owned, of the anodyne; and, but that an under dose of a sedative produces contrary effects, we should inevitably have been lulled by them into forgetfulness of all things. Perhaps a dozen more such lines as the following would reduce the most irritable of critics to a state of inaction.

> A damsel with a dulcimer
> In a vision once I saw :
> It was an Abyssinian maid
> And on her dulcimer she play'd,
> Singing of Mount Abora.
> Could I revive within me
> Her symphony and song,
> To such a deep delight 'twould win me
> That with music loud and long,
> I would build that dome in air,
> That sunny dome ! those caves of ice !
> And all who heard should see them there,
> And all should cry, Beware ! Beware !
> His flashing eyes, his floating hair !
> Weave a circle round him thrice,
> And close your eyes with holy dread :
> For he on honey-dew hath fed, &c. &c.

There is a good deal more altogether as exquisite – and in particular a fine description of a wood, 'ancient as the hills'; and 'folding sunny spots of *greenery*' ! But we suppose this specimen will be sufficient.

Persons in this poet's unhappy condition, generally feel the want of sleep as the worst of their evils; but there are instances, too, in the history of the disease, of sleep being attended with new agony, as if the waking thoughts, how wild and turbulent soever, had still been under some slight restraint, which sleep instantly removed. Mr Coleridge appears to have experienced this symptom, if we may judge from the title of his third poem, 'The Pains of Sleep'; and, in truth, from its composition – which is mere raving, without any thing more affecting than a number of incoherent words, expressive of extravagance and incongruity. We need give no specimen of it.

Upon the whole, we look upon this publication as one of the

most notable pieces of impertinence of which the press has lately
been guilty; and one of the boldest experiments that has yet been
made on the patience or understanding of the public. It is impossible, however, to dismiss it, without a remark or two. The other
productions of the Lake School have generally exhibited talents
thrown away upon subjects so mean, that no power of genius
could ennoble them; or perverted and rendered useless by a false
theory of poetical composition. But even in the worst of them,
if we except the 'White Doe' of Mr Wordsworth and some of
the laureate odes, there were always some gleams of feeling or of
fancy. But the thing now before us, is utterly destitute of value.
It exhibits from beginning to end not a ray of genius; and we
defy any man to point out a passage of poetical merit in any of
the three pieces which it contains, except, perhaps, the following
lines, and even these are not very brilliant; nor is the leading
thought original :

> Alas ! they had been friends in youth;
> But whispering tongues can poison truth;
> And constancy lives in realms above;
> And life is thorny; and youth is vain;
> And to be wroth with one we love,
> Doth work like madness in the brain.

With this one exception, there is literally not one couplet in
the publication before us which would be reckoned poetry, or
even sense, were it found in the corner of a newspaper or upon
the window of an inn. Must we then be doomed to hear such a
mixture of raving and driv'ling, extolled as the work of a *'wild and
original'* genius, simply because Mr Coleridge has now and then
written fine verses, and a brother poet chooses, in his milder
mood, to laud him from courtesy or from interest? And are such
panegyrics to be echoed by the mean tools of a political faction,
because they relate to one whose daily prose is understood to be
dedicated to the support of all that courtiers think should be
supported? If it be true that the author has thus earned the
patronage of those liberal dispensers of bounty, we can have no objection that they should give him proper proofs of their gratitude;
but we cannot help wishing, for his sake, as well as our own, that
they would pay in solid pudding instead of empty praise; and

adhere, at least in this instance, to the good old system of rewarding their champions with places and pensions, instead of
puffing their bad poetry, and endeavouring to cram their nonsense down the throats of all the loyal and well affected.

SOURCE: *Edinburgh Review*, XXVII (September 1816).

John G. Lockhart

There is no question many of our readers will think we are doing
a very useless, if not a very absurd thing, in writing, at this time
of day, any thing like a review of the poetry of Mr Coleridge.
Several years have elapsed since any poetical production, entitled
to much attention, has been published by him – and of those
pieces in which the true strength and originality of his genius
have been expressed, by far the greater part were presented to
the world before any of the extensively popular poetry of the
present day existed. In the midst, however, of the many new
claimants which have arisen on every hand to solicit the ear and
the favour of the readers of poetry, we are not sure that any one
has had so much reason to complain of the slowness and inade-
quacy of the attention bestowed upon him as this gentleman, who
is, comparatively speaking, a veteran of no inconsiderable standing...

Our only wish for the present, is to offer a few remarks in
regard to one or two of his individual productions, which may
perhaps excite the attention of such of our readers as have never
yet paid any considerable attention to any of them. ...

The longest poem in the collection of the Sibylline Leaves, is
the 'Rime of the Ancient Mariner' – and to our feeling, it is by
far the most wonderful also – the most original – and the most
touching of all the productions of its author. From it alone, we
are inclined to think an idea of the whole poetical genius of Mr
Coleridge might be gathered, such as could scarcely receive any
very important addition either of extent or of distinctness, from a
perusal of the whole of his other works. To speak of it at all is

extremely difficult; above all the poems with which we are
acquainted in any language – it is a poem to be felt – cherished
– mused upon – not to be talked about – not capable of being
described – analyzed – or criticised. It is the wildest of all the
creations of genius – it is not like a thing of the living, listening, moving world – the very music of its words is like the
melancholy mysterious breath of something sung to the sleeping
ear – its images have the beauty – the grandeur – the incoherence
of some mighty vision. The loveliness and the terror glide before
us in turns – with, at one moment, the awful shadowy dimness
– at another, the yet more awful distinctness of a majestic dream.

. . . We have no difficulty in confessing, that the ideas on which
the intent of this poem hinges, and which to us seem to possess all
beauty and pathos, may, after all, have been selected by the poet
with a too great neglect of the ordinary sympathies. But if any one
will submit himself to the magic that is around him, and suffer
his senses and his imagination to be blended together, and
exalted by the melody of the charmed words, and the splendour
of the unnatural apparitions with which the mysterious scene is
opened, surely he will experience no revulsion towards the centre
and spirit of this lovely dream. There is the very essence of tenderness in the remorseful delight with which the Mariner dwells
upon the image of the 'pious bird of omen good,' as it

> Every day, for food or play,
> Came to the Mariner's hollo !

And the convulsive shudder with which he narrates the treacherous issue, bespeaks to us no pangs more than seem to have followed justly on that inhospitable crime. It seems as if the very
spirit of the universe had been stunned by the wanton cruelty of
the Mariner – as if earth, sea, and sky, had all become dead and
stagnant in the extinction of the moving breath of love and
gentleness.

. . . Had the ballad been more interwoven with sources of prolonged emotion extending throughout – and had the relation of
the imagery to the purport and essence of the piece been a little
more close – it does not seem to us that any thing more could
have been desired in a poem such as this. As it is, the effect of the
wild wandering magnificence of imagination in the details of the

dream-like story is a thing that cannot be forgotten. It is as if we had seen real spectres, and were for ever to be haunted. The unconnected and fantastic variety of the images that have been piled up before us works upon the fancy, as an evening sky made up of half lurid castellated clouds – half of clear unpolluted azure – would upon the eye. It is like the fitful concert of fine sounds which the Mariner himself hears after his spirit has been melted, and the ship has begun to sail homewards. . . .

The conclusion has always appeared to us to be happy and graceful in the utmost degree. The actual surface-life of the world is brought close into contact with the life of sentiment – the soul that is as much alive, and enjoys, and suffers as much in dreams and visions of the night as by daylight. One feels with what a heavy eye the Ancient Mariner must look and listen to the pomps and merry-makings – even to the innocent enjoyments – of those whose experience has only been of things tangible. One feels that to him another world – we do not mean a supernatural, but a more exquisitely and deeply natural world – has been revealed – and that the repose of his spirit can only be in the contemplation of things that are not to pass away. The sad and solemn indifference of his mood is communicated to his hearer – and we feel that even after reading what he had heard, it were better to 'turn from the bridegroom's door'. . . .

Of all the author's productions, the one which seems most akin to the Ancient Mariner, is Christabel, a wonderful piece of poetry, which has been far less understood, and is as yet far less known than the other. This performance does not make its appearance in the Sibylline Leaves – but we hope Mr Coleridge will never omit it in any future collection. The reception it met with was no doubt a very discouraging one, more particularly when contrasted with the vehement admiration which seems to have been expressed by all who saw it while yet in MS. Mr Coleridge, however, should remember that the opinions of the few who saw and admired Christabel then, may very well, without any overweening partiality on his part, be put into competition with the many who have derided it since. Those who know the secret history of the poem, and compare it with the productions of the most popular poets of our time, will have no difficulty in perceiving how deep an impression his remarkable creation had made on the minds of those of his contemporaries, whose approbation was most deserving to be an object of ambition with such a man as Mr Coleridge. . . .

It is impossible to gather from the part which has been published any conception of what is the meditated conclusion of the story of Christabel. Incidents can never be fairly judged of till we know what they lead to. Of those which occur in the first and second cantos of this poem, there is no doubt many appear at present very strange and disagreeable, and the sooner the remainder comes forth to explain them, the better. One thing is evident, that no man need sit down to read Christabel with any prospect of gratification, whose mind has not rejoiced habitually in the luxury of visionary and superstitious reveries. He that is determined to try every thing by the standard of what is called common sense, and who has an aversion to admit, even in poetry, of the existence of things more than are dreamt of in philosophy, had better not open this production, which is only proper for a solitary couch and a midnight taper. Mr Coleridge is the prince of superstitious poets; and he that does not read Christabel with a strange and harrowing feeling of mysterious dread, may be assured that his soul is made of impenetrable stuff. . . .

In these two poems – we might even say in the extracts we have made from them – the poetical faculties of Coleridge are abundantly exhibited in the whole power and charm of their native beauty. That such exercise of these faculties may have been so far injudicious as not calculated to awaken much of the ordinary sympathies of mankind – but rather addressing every thing to feelings of which in their full strength and sway only a few are capable – all this is a reproach easy to be made, and in a great measure perhaps it may be a well-founded reproach. But nothing surely can be more unfair, than to overlook or deny the existence of such beauty and such strength on any grounds of real or pretended misapplication. That the author of these productions is a poet of a most noble class – a poet most original in his conceptions – most masterly in his execution – above all things a most inimitable master of the language of poetry – it is impossible to deny. His powers indeed – to judge from what of them that has been put forth and exhibited – may not be of the widest – or even of the very highest kind. So far as they go, surely, they are the

most exquisite of powers. In his mixture of all the awful and all
the gentle graces of conception – in his sway of wild – solitary –
dreamy phantasies – in his music of words – and magic of numbers – we think he stands absolutely alone among all the poets of
the most poetical age. ...

Source: *Blackwood's Edinburgh Magazine*, vi (October
1819) – extract.

Leigh Hunt

Mr Coleridge speaks very modestly of his poetry – not affectedly
so, but out of a high notion of the art in his predecessors. He
delighted the late Mr Keats, in the course of conversation, with
adding, after he had alluded to it – 'if there is any thing I have
written which may be *called poetry*' : and the writer of the present
article heard him speak of verses, as the common tribute which
a young mind on its entrance into the world of letters pays to the
love of intellectual beauty. His poetry however has an 'image and
superscription' very different from this current coin. We do not,
it is true, think that it evinces the poetical habit of mind – or that
tendency to regard every thing in its connexion with the imaginative world, which in a minor sense was justly attributed to the
author of the *Seasons*, and in its greater belonged to Spenser and
Milton. But it is full of imagination and of a sense of the beautiful,
as suggested by a great acquaintance with books and thoughts,
acting upon a benevolent mind. It is to the scholar of old books
and metaphysics, what Milton's was to the Greek and Italian
scholar. It is the essence of the impression made upon him by that
habit of thinking and reading, which is his second nature. Mr
Coleridge began with metaphysics when at school; and what the
boy begins with, the man will end with, come what will between.
He does not turn metaphysical upon the strength of his poetry,
like Spenser and Tasso; but poet upon the strength of his metaphysics. Thus in the greater part of his minor poems he only
touches upon the popular creeds, or wilful creations of their

own, which would occupy other poets, and then falls musing upon the nature of things, and analysing his feelings. In his voyage to Germany, he sees a solitary wildfowl upon 'the objectless desert of waters', and says how interesting it was. It was most probably from a train of reflection on the value of this link between land and the ship, that he produced his beautiful wild poem of the 'Ancient Mariner', which he precedes with a criticophilosophical extract from Burnet's *Archaeologia*. We do not object to this as belonging to his genius. We only instance it, as shewing the nature of it. In the same spirit, he interrupts his 'Christabel' with an explanation of the wish sometimes felt to give pain to the innocent; and instead of being content to have written finely under the influence of laudanum, recommends 'Kubla-Khan' to his readers, not as a poem, but as 'a psychological curiosity'. All this however is extremely interesting of its kind, and peculiar. It is another striking instance of what we have often remarked, the tendency of all great knowledge and deep delight in it, of whatever kind, to extend itself into poetry, which lies like a heaven in the centre of the intellectual world for those to go to and be refreshed with, more or less, who are not bound to the physical world like slaves to the soil. Every lover of books, scholar or not, who knows what it is to have his quarto open against a loaf at his tea, to carry his duodecimo about in his pocket, to read along country roads or even streets, and to scrawl his favourite authors with notes (as 'S.T.C.' is liberally sanctioned to do those of others by a writer in the *London Magazine*)[1] ought to be in possession of Mr Coleridge's poems, if it is only for 'Christabel', 'Kubla Khan', and the 'Ancient Mariner'. The first comprises all that is ancient and courteous in old rhythm, and will also make any studious gentleman, who is not sufficiently imaginative, turn himself round divers times in his chair, as he ought to do, to see if there is not 'something in the room'. 'Kubla Khan' is a voice and a vision, an everlasting tune in our mouths, a dream fit for Cambuscan and all his poets, a dance of pictures such as Giotto or Cimabue, revived and re-inspired, would have made for a Storie of Old Tartarie, a piece of the invisible world made visible by a sun at midnight and sliding before our eyes.

> Beware, beware,
> His flashing eyes, his floating hair !
> Weave a circle round him thrice,
> And close your lips with holy dread,
> For he on honey dew hath fed,
> And drank of the milk of Paradise.

Justly is it thought that to be able to present such images as these
to the mind, is to realise the world they speak of. We could repeat
such verses as the following down a green glade, a whole summer's morning :

> A damsel with a dulcimer
> In a vision once I saw,
> A lovely Abyssinian maid;
> And on her dulcimer she played,
> Singing of Mount Aborah.

As to the 'Ancient Mariner', we have just this minute read it
again, and all that we have been saying about the origin of the
author's poetry, appears to be nonsense. Perhaps it is, and we
are not sorry that it should be. All that we are certain of is, that
the 'Ancient Mariner' is very fine poetry, and that we are not the
'one of three' to whom the sea-faring old greybeard is fated to
tell his story, for we are aware of the existence of other worlds
beside the one about us, and we would not have shot the solitary
bird of good omen, nor one out of a dozen of them. . . .

The Ancient Mariner was one of a crew, who were driven by a
storm to the south pole. An albatross appeared, who became
familiar with the sailors, and a good wind sprang up. The
Mariner not having the fear of violation of kindness and gentleness before his eyes, killed the albatross, for which the others said
he would be pursued with a misfortune. . . .

This is a lesson to those who see nothing in the world but their
own unfeeling common-places, and are afterwards visited with a
dreary sense of their insufficiency. Not to have sympathy for all,
is not to have the instinct that suffices instead of imagination.
Not to have imagination, to supply the want of the instinct, is to
be left destitute and forlorn when brute pleasure is gone, and
to be *dead-in-life*. This poem would bear out a long marginal
illustration in the style of the old Italian critics, who squeeze a
sonnet of Petrarch's into the middle of the page with a crowd of

fond annotations. Be the source of its inspiration what it may, it is a poem that may serve as a test to any one who wishes to know whether he has a real taste for poetry or not. And be Mr Coleridge what he may, whether an author inspired by authors or from himself, whether a metaphysical poet or a poetical metaphysician, whether a politician baulked and rendered despairing like many others by the French Revolution, or lastly, and totally, a subtle and good-natured casuist fitted for nothing but contemplation, and rewarded by it with a sense of the beautiful and wonderful *above* his casuistry, we can only be grateful for the knowledge and delight he affords us by his genius, and recognise in him an instance of that departure from ordinary talent, which we are far from being bound to condemn, because it does not fall in with our own humours. If it is well for the more active that his prose does not talk quite well or vivaciously enough to turn them from their stream of action, and so unfit them for *their* purposes, they ought to be glad that they have such men to talk to them when they are at rest, and to maintain in them that willingness to be impartial, and that power of 'looking abroad into universality', without which action itself would never be any thing but a mischievous system of reaction and disappointment, fretting and to fret.

They also serve, who only stand and wait.

SOURCE: *Examiner* (21 October 1821) – extract.

NOTE

1. Charles Lamb in 'The Two Races of Men', *London Magazine*, December 1820, II 625.

Henry Nelson Coleridge

... the 'Ancient Mariner' is, and will ever be, one of the most perfect pieces of imaginative poetry, not only in our language, but in the literature of all Europe. We have, certainly, sometimes doubted whether the miraculous destruction of the vessel in the presence of the pilot and hermit, was not an error, in respect of

its bringing the purely preternatural into too close contact with
the actual framework of the poem. The only link between those
scenes of out-of-the-world wonders, and the wedding guest,
should, we rather suspect, have been the blasted, unknown being
himself who described them. There should have been no other
witnesses of the truth of any part of the tale, but the 'Ancient
Mariner' himself. This by the way : but take the work altogether,
there is nothing else like it; it is a poem by itself; between it and
other compositions, in *pari materia*,[1] there is a chasm which you
cannot overpass; the sensitive reader feels himself insulated, and
a sea of wonder and mystery flows round him as round the spell-
stricken ship itself. It was a sad mistake in the able artist – Mr
Scott,[2] we believe – who in his engravings has made the ancient
mariner an old decrepit man. That is not the true image; no! he
should have been a growthless, decayless being, impassive to time
or season, a silent cloud – the wandering Jew. The curse of the
dead men's eyes should not have passed away. But this was, perhaps, too much for any pencil, even if the artist had fully entered
into the poet's idea. Indeed, it is no subject for painting. The
'Ancient Mariner' displays Mr Coleridge's peculiar mastery over
the wild and preternatural in a brilliant manner; but in his next
poem, 'Christabel', the exercise of his power in this line is still
more skilful and singular. The thing attempted in 'Christabel'
is the most difficult of execution in the whole field of romance –
witchery by daylight; and the success is complete. Geraldine, so
far as she goes, is perfect. She is *sui generis*. The reader feels
the same terror and perplexity that Christabel in vain struggles to
express, and the same spell that fascinates her eyes. Who and what
is Geraldine – whence come, whither going, and what designing?
What did the poet mean to make of her? What could he have
made of her? Could he have gone on much farther without having had recourse to some of the ordinary shifts of witch tales?
Was she really the daughter of Roland de Vaux, and would the
friends have met again and embraced? . . .

We are not amongst those who wish to have 'Christabel'
finished. It cannot be finished. The poet has spun all he could
without snapping. The theme is too fine and subtle to bear much
extension. It is better as it is, imperfect as a story, but complete
as an exquisite production of the imagination, differing in form

and colour from the 'Ancient Mariner,' yet differing in effect from it only so as the same powerful faculty is directed to the feudal or the mundane phases of the preternatural. . . .

SOURCE : *Quarterly Review*, LII (August 1834) – extract.

NOTES

1. *Of equal (or equivalent) matter.*
2. David Scott (1806–49).

A. C. Swinburne

The great man of whom I am about to speak seems to me a figure more utterly companionless, more incomparable with others, than any of his kind. Receptive at once and communicative of many influences, he has received from none and to none did he communicate any of those which mark him as a man memorable to all students of men. What he learnt and what he taught are not the precious things in him. He has founded no school of poetry, as Wordsworth has, or Byron, or Tennyson; happy in this, that he has escaped the plague of pupils and parodists. Has he founded a school of philosophy? He has helped men to think; he has touched their thought with passing colours of his own thought; but has he moved and moulded it into new and durable shapes? Others may judge better of this than I, but to me, set beside the deep direct work of those thinkers who have actual power to break down and build up thought, to construct faith or destroy it, his work seems not as theirs is. And yet how very few are even the great names we could not better afford to spare, would not gladlier miss from the roll of 'Famous men and our fathers that were before us'. Of his best verses I venture to affirm that the world has nothing like them, and can never have : that they are of the highest kind, and of their own. They are jewels of the diamond's price, flowers of the rose's rank, but unlike any rose or diamond known. In all times there have been gods that alighted and giants that appeared on earth; the ranks of great men are properly divisible, not into thinkers and workers, but into Titans and Olympians. Sometimes a supreme poet is both at once : such above all men is Æschylus; so also Dante, Michel Angelo, Shakespeare, Milton, Goethe, Hugo, are gods at once and giants; they have the lightning as well as the light of the world, and in hell they have command as in heaven; they can see in the night as by day. As godlike as these, even as the divinest of them, a poet such as Coleridge needs not the thews and organs of any Titan to make him greater. Judged by the justice of other men, he is assailable and condemnable on several sides; his good work is the scantiest in quantity ever done by a man so famous in so long a life; and much of his work is bad. His genius is fluctuant and moonstruck as the sea is, and yet his mind is not, what he described Shakespeare's to be, 'an oceanic mind'. His plea against all accusers must be that of Shakespeare, a plea unanswerable :

> I am that I am; and they that level
> At my abuses reckon up their own.

'I am that I am'; it is the only solid and durable reply to any impertinence of praise or blame. We hear too much and too often of circumstances or accidents which extenuate this thing or qualify that; and such, no doubt, there always may be; but usually – at least it seems so to me – we get out of each man what he has in him to give. Probably at no other time, under no other conditions, would Coleridge for example have done better work or more. His flaws and failures are as much ingrained in him as his powers and achievements.

For from the very first the two sides of his mind are visible and palpable. Among all verses of boys who were to grow up great, I remember none so perfect, so sweet and deep in sense and sound, as those which he is said to have written at school, headed 'Time, Real and Imaginary.' And following hard on these come a score or two of 'poems' each more feeble and more flatulent than the last. Over these and the like I shall pass with all due speed, being undesirous to trouble myself or any possible reader with the question whether 'Religious Musings' be more damnable than 'Lines to a Young Ass', or less damnable. Even when clear of these brambles, his genius walked for some time over much waste ground with irregular and unsure steps. Some poems, touched with exquisite grace, with clear and pure harmony, are tainted with somewhat of feeble and sickly which impairs our relish; 'Lewti' for instance, an early sample of his admirable melody, of tender colour and dim grace as of clouds, but effeminate in build, loose-hung, weak of eye and foot. Yet nothing of more precious and rare sweetness exists in verse than that stanza of the swans disturbed. His style indeed was a plant of strangely slow growth, but perfect and wonderful in its final flower. Even in the famous verses called 'Love' he has not attained to that strength and solidity of beauty which was his special gift at last. For melody rather than for harmony it is perfect; but in this œnomel there is as yet more of honey than of wine.

Coleridge was the reverse of Antæus; the contact of earth took all strength out of him. He could not handle to much purpose any practical creed; his political verse is most often weak of foot and hoarse of accent. There is a graceful Asiatic legend cited by his friend Southey of 'the footless birds of Paradise' who have only wings to sustain them, and live their lives out in a perpetual flight through the clearest air of heaven. Ancient naturalists, Cardan and Aldrovandus, had much dispute and dissertation as to the real or possible existence of these birds, as to whether the female did in effect lay her eggs in a hollow of the male's back, designed by nature to that end; whether they could indeed live on falling dew; and so forth. These questions we may presume to be decided; but it is clear and certain enough that men have been found to live in much this fashion. Such a footless bird of Paradise was Coleridge; and had his wings always held out it had been well for him and us. Unhappily this winged and footless creature would perforce too often furl his wings in mid air and try his footing on earth, where his gait was like a swan's on shore.

Of his flight and his song when in the fit element, it is hard to speak at all, hopeless to speak adequately. It is natural that there should be nothing like them discoverable in any human work; natural that his poetry at its highest should be, as it is, beyond all praise and all words of men. He who can define it could 'unweave a rainbow'; he who could praise it aright would be such another as the poet. The 'Christabel', the Kubla Khan', with one or two more, are outside all law and jurisdiction of ours. When it has been said that such melodies were never heard, such dreams never dreamed, such speech never spoken, the chief thing remains unsaid, and unspeakable. There is a charm upon these poems which can only be felt in silent submission of wonder. Any separate line has its own heavenly beauty, but to cite separate lines is intolerable. They are to be received in a rapture of silence; such a silence as Chapman describes; silence like a god 'peaceful and young,' which

> Left so free mine ears,
> That I might hear the music of the spheres,
> *And all the angels singing out of heaven.*[1]

More amenable to our judgment, and susceptible of a more definite admiration, 'The Ancient Mariner', and the few other poems cast in something of a ballad type which we may rank around or below it, belong to another class. The chief of these is so well known that it needs no fresh comment. Only I will say that to some it may seem as though this great sea-piece might have had more in it of the air and savour of the sea. Perhaps it is none the worse; and indeed any one speaking of so great and famous a poem must feel and know that it cannot but be right, although he or another may think it would be better if this were retrenched or that appended. And this poem is beyond question one of the supreme triumphs of poetry. Witness the men who brought batteries to bear on it right and left. Literally : for one critic said that the 'moral sentiment' had impaired the imaginative excellence; another, that it failed and fell through for want of a moral foothold upon facts. Remembering these things, I am reluctant to proceed – but desirous to praise, as I best may. Though I doubt if it be worth while, seeing how 'The Ancient Mariner' – praised or dispraised – lives and is like to live for the delight equally of young boys and old men; and seeing also that the last critic cited was no less a man than Hazlitt. It is fortunate – among many misfortunes – that for Coleridge no warning word was needed against the shriek of the press-gang from this side or that. He stooped once or twice to spurn them; but he knew that he stooped. His intense and overwrought abstraction from things of the hour or day did him no evil service here.

'The Ancient Mariner' has doubtless more of breadth and space, more of material force and motion, than anything else of the poet's. And the tenderness of sentiment which touches with significant colour the pure white imagination is here no longer morbid or languid, as in the earlier poems of feeling and emotion. It is soft and piteous enough, but womanly rather than effeminate; and thus serves indeed to set off the strange splendours and boundless beauties of the story. For the execution, I presume no human eye is too dull to see how perfect it is, and how high in kind of perfection. Here is not the speckless and elaborate finish which shows everywhere the fresh rasp of file or chisel on its smooth and spruce excellence; this is faultless after the fashion of a flower or a tree. Thus it has grown : not thus has it been carved.

Nevertheless, were we compelled to the choice, I for one would rather preserve 'Kubla Khan' and 'Christabel' than any other of Coleridge's poems. It is more conceivable that another man should be born capable of writing 'The Ancient Mariner' than one capable of writing these. The former is perhaps the most wonderful of all poems. In reading it we seem rapt into that paradise revealed to Swedenborg, where music and colour and perfume were one, where you could hear the hues and see the harmonies of heaven. For absolute melody and splendour it were hardly rash to call it the first poem in the language. An exquisite instinct married to a subtle science of verse has made it the supreme model of music in our language, a model unapproachable except by Shelley. All the elements that compose the perfect form of English metre, as limbs and veins and features a beautiful body of man, were more familiar, more subject as it were, to this great poet than to any other. How, for instance, no less than rhyme, assonance and alliteration are forces, requisite components of high and ample harmony, witness once for all the divine passage[2] which begins : –

Five miles meandering with a mazy motion, etc.

All these least details and delicacies of work are worth notice when the result of them is so transcendent. Every line of the poem might be subjected to the like scrutiny, but the student would be none the nearer to the master's secret. The spirit, the odour

in it, the cloven tongue of fire that rests upon its forehead, is a
thing neither explicable nor communicable.

Of all Coleridge's poems the loveliest is assuredly 'Christabel'.
It is not so vast in scope and reach of imagination as 'The Ancient
Mariner'; it is not so miraculous as 'Kubla Khan'; but for simple
charm of inner and outer sweetness it is unequalled by either.
The very terror and mystery of magical evil is imbued with this
sweetness; the witch has no less of it than the maiden; their contact has in it nothing dissonant or disfiguring, nothing to jar or
to deface the beauty and harmony of the whole imagination.
As for the melody, here again it is incomparable with any other
poet's. Shelley indeed comes nearest; but for purity and volume
of music Shelley is to Coleridge as a lark to a nightingale; his
song heaven-high and clear as heaven, but the other's more rich
and weighty, more passionately various and warmer in effusion
of sound.[3] On the other hand, the nobler nature, the clearer spirit
of Shelley, fills his verse with a divine force of meaning, which
Coleridge, who had it not in him, could not affect to give. That
sensuous fluctuation of soul, that floating fervour of fancy, whence
his poetry rose as from a shifting sea, in faultless completion of
form and charm, had absorbed – if indeed there were any to
absorb – all emotion of love or faith, all heroic beauty of moral
passion, all inner and outer life of the only kind possible to such
other poets as Dante or Shelley, Milton or Hugo. This is
neither blameable nor regrettable; none of these could have done
his work; nor could he have done it had he been in any way
other or better than he was. Neither, for that matter, could we
have had a Hamlet or a Faust from any of these, the poets of
moral faith and passion, any more than a 'Divina Commedia'
from Shakespeare, a 'Prometheus Unbound' from Goethe. Let
us give thanks for each after their kind to nature and the fates.

Alike by his powers and his impotences, by his capacity and his
defect, Coleridge was inapt for dramatic poetry. It were no dis-
credit to have fallen short of Shelley on this side, to be overcome
by him who has written the one great English play of modern
times; but here the very comparison would seem a jest. There
is little worth praise or worth memory in the *Remorse* except such
casual fragments of noble verse as may readily be detached from
the loose and friable stuff in which they lie embedded. In the

scene of the incantation, in the scene of the dungeon, there are two such pure and precious fragments of gold. In the part of Alhadra there are lofty and sonorous interludes of declamation and reflection. The characters are flat and shallow; the plot is at once languid, violent, and heavy. To touch the string of the spirit, thread the weft of evil and good, feel out the way of the soul through dark places of thought and rough places of action, was not given to this the sweetest dreamer of dreams. In *Zapolya* there are no such patches of imperial purple sewn on, but there is more of air and motion; little enough indeed of high dramatic quality, but a native grace and ease which give it something of the charm of life. In this lighter and more rapid work, the song of Glycine flashes out like a visible sunbeam; it is one of the brightest bits of music ever done into words.

The finest of Coleridge's odes is beyond all doubt the 'Ode to France'. Shelley declared it the finest of modern times, and justly, until himself and Keats had written up to it at least. It were profitless now to discuss whether it should take or yield precedence when weighed with the 'Ode to Liberty' or the 'Ode to Naples'. There is in it a noble and loyal love of freedom, though less fiery at once and less firm than Shelley's, as it proved in the end less durable and deep. The prelude is magnificent in music, and in sentiment and emotion far above any other of his poems; nor are the last notes inadequate to this majestic overture. Equal in force and sweetness of style, the 'Ode on Dejection' ranks next in my mind to this one; some may prefer its vaguer harmonies and sunset colours to the statelier movement, the more august and solemn passion of the earlier ode.

It is noticeable that only his supreme gift of lyrical power could sustain Coleridge on political ground. His attempts of the kind in blank verse are poor indeed : –

Untimely breathings, sick and short assays.

Compare the nerveless and hysterical verses headed 'Fears in Solitude' (exquisite as is the overture, faultless in tone and colour, and worthy of a better sequal) with the majestic and masculine sonnet of Wordsworth, written at the same time on the same subject : the lesser poet – for, great as he is, I at least cannot hold Wordsworth, though so much the stronger and more admir-

able man, equal to Coleridge as mere poet – speaks with a calm
force of thought and resolution; Coleridge wails, appeals, depre-
cates, objurgates in a flaccid and querulous fashion without heart
or spirit. This debility of mind and manner is set off in strong
relief by the loveliness of landscape touches in the same poem. The
eclogue of 'Fire, Famine, and Slaughter', being lyrical, is worthier
of a great name; it has force and motion enough to keep it alive
yet and fresh, impeded and trammelled though it usually be by
the somewhat vain and verbose eloquence of a needlessly 'Apolo-
getic Preface'. Blank verse Coleridge could never handle with
the security of conscious skill and a trained strength; it grows in
his hands too facile and feeble to carry the due weight or accomplish the due work. I have not found any of his poems in this
metre retouched and reinvigorated as a few have been among
his others. One such alteration is memorable to all students of his
art; the excision from 'The Ancient Mariner' of a stanza (eleventh
of the Third Part) which described the Death-mate of the
Spectre-Woman, his bones foul with leprous scurf and green cor-
ruption of the grave, in contrast to the red lips and yellow locks
of the fearfuller Nightmare Life-in-Death. Keats in like manner
cut off from the 'Ode on Melancholy' a first stanza preserved for
us by his biographer, who has duly noted the delicate justice of
instinct implied by this rejection of all ghastly and violent images,
however noble and impressive in their violence and ghastliness,
from a poem full only of the subtle sorrow born of beauty. The
same keen and tender sense of right made Coleridge reject from
his work the horrors while retaining the terrors of death. But of
his studies in blank verse he seems to have taken no such care.
They remain mostly in a hybrid or an embryonic state, with birth-
marks on them of debility or malformation. Two of these indeed
have a charm of their own, not shallow or transient: 'The
Nightingale' and 'Frost at Midnight'. In colour they are perfect,
and not (as usual) too effusive and ebullient in style. Others,
especially some of the domestic or religious sort, are offensive
and grievous to the human sense on that score. Coleridge had
doubtless a sincere belief in his own sincerity of belief, a true feeling of his own truth of feeling; but he leaves with us too often
an unpleasant sense of taste – as it were a tepid dilution of sentiment, a rancid unction of piety. A singular book published in

1835 without author's name – the work, as I find, of a Mr Alsop, long after to be advertised for on public placards as an accomplice in the enterprise which clouded the fiery fame and closed the heroic life of Felice Orsini—gives further samples of this in *Letters, Conversations and Recollections*; samples that we might well have spared. A selection from his notes and remains, from his correspondence and the records of his 'Table-Talk,' even from such books as Cottle's and this anonymous disciple's, would be of real interest and value, if well edited, sifted and weeded of tares and chaff. The rare fragments of work done or speech spoken in his latter years are often fragments of gold beyond price. His plastic power and flexible charm of verse, though shown only in short flashes of song, lose nothing of the old freshness and life. To the end he was the same whose 'sovereign sway and master-dom' of music could make sweet and strong even the feeble and tuneless form of metre called hexameters in English; if form of metre that may be called which has neither metre nor form. But the majestic rush and roll of that irregular anapæstic measure used once or twice by this supreme master of them all, no student can follow without an exultation of enjoyment. The 'Hymn to the Earth' has a sonorous and oceanic strength of harmony, a grace and a glory of life, which fill the sense with a vigorous de-light. Of such later work as the divine verses on 'Youth and Age', 'The Garden of Boccaccio', sun-bright and honey-sweet, 'Work without Hope' (what more could be left to hope for when the man could already do such work?) – of these, and of how many more! what can be said but that they are perfect, flawless, priceless? Nor did his most delicate and profound power of criti-cism ever fail him or fall off. To the perfection of that rare faculty there were but two things wanting: self-command and the natural cunning of words which has made many lesser men as strong as he was weak in the matter of verbal emendation. In that line of labour his hand was unsure and infirm. Want of self-command, again, left him often to the mercy of a caprice which swept him through tangled and tortuous ways of thought, through brakes and byways of fancy, where the solid subject in hand was either utterly lost and thrown over, or so transmuted and transfigured that any recognition of it was as hopeless as any profit. In an essay well worth translating out of jargon into some human language, he speaks of 'the holy jungle of transcendental metaphysics.' Out of that holy and pestilential jungle he emerged but too rarely into sunlight and clear air. It is not depth of thought which makes obscure to others the work of a thinker; real and offensive obscurity comes merely of inadequate thought embodied in inadequate language. What is clearly comprehended or conceived, what is duly thought and wrought out, must find for itself and seize upon the clearest and fullest expression. That grave and deep matter should be treated with the fluency and facility proper to light and slight things, no fool is foolish enough to desire: but we may at least demand that whatever of message a speaker may have for us be delivered without impediment of speech. A style that stammers and rambles and stumbles, that stagnates here, and there overflows into waste marsh relieved only by thick patches of powdery bulrush and such bright flowerage of barren blossom as is bred of the fogs and the fens – such a style gives no warrant of depth or soundness in the matter thus arrayed and set forth. What grains of truth or seeds of error were borne this way or that on the perpetual tide of talk concerning 'subject and object', 'reason and understanding', those who can or who care may at their leisure determine with the due precision. If to the man's critical and philosophic faculty there had been added a formative power as perfect as was added to his poetic faculty, the fruit might possibly have been wellnigh as precious after its kind. As it is, we must judge of his poetic faculty by what is accomplished; of the other we must judge, not by what is accomplished, but by what is suggested. And the value of this is sometimes great, though the value of that be generally small: so great indeed that we cannot weigh or measure its influence and its work.

Our study and our estimate of Coleridge cannot now be discoloured or misguided by the attraction or repulsion to which all contemporary students or judges of a great man's work cannot but be more or less liable. Few men, I suppose, ever inspired more of either feeling than he in his time did. To us his moral or social qualities, his opinion on this matter and his action in that, are nothing except in so far as they affect the work done, the inheritance bequeathed us. With all fit admiration and gratitude for the splendid fragments so bequeathed of a critical and philosophic sort, I doubt his being remembered, except by a small body of his elect, as other than a poet. His genius was so great, and in its greatness so many-sided, that for some studious disciples of the rarer kind he will doubtless, seen from any possible point of view, have always something about him of the old magnetism and magic. The ardour, delicacy, energy of his intellect, his resolute desire to get at the root of things and deeper yet, if deeper might be, will always enchant and attract all spirits of like mould and temper. But as a poet his place is indisputable. It is high among the highest of all time. An age that should forget or neglect him might neglect or forget any poet that ever lived. At least, any poet whom it did remember such an age would remember as something other than a poet; it would prize and praise in him, not the absolute and distinctive quality, but something empirical or accidental. That may be said of this one which can hardly be said of any but the greatest among men; that come what may to the world in course of time, it will never see his place filled. Other and stronger men, with fuller control and concentration of genius, may do more service, may bear more fruit; but such as his was they will not have in them to give. The highest lyric work is either passionate or imaginative; of passion Coleridge's has nothing; but for height and perfection of imaginative quality he is the greatest of lyric poets. This was his special power, and this is his special praise.

SOURCE : 'Coleridge', *Essays and Studies* (London, 1875).

NOTES

1. *Euthymiæ Raptus; The Tears of Peace* (1609).

2. Witness also the matchless fragments of metrical criticism in Coleridge's 'Remains', which prove with what care and relish the most sweet and perfect melodist among all our poets would set himself to examine and explain the alternations and sequences of sound in the noblest verse of others.

3. From this general rule I except of course the transcendent antiphonal music which winds up the 'Prometheus' of Shelley, and should perhaps except also the 'Ode to the West Wind', and the close of the 'Ode to Naples'. Against 'Christabel' it would for example be fairer to set 'The Sensitive Plant' for comparison of harmonies.

Walter Pater

Coleridge's prose writings on philosophy, politics, religion, and criticism, were, in truth, but one element in a whole lifetime of endeavours to present the then recent metaphysics of Germany to English readers, as a legitimate expansion of the older, classical and native masters of what has been variously called the *a priori*, or absolute, or spiritual, or Platonic, view of things. His criticism, his challenge for recognition in the concrete, visible, finite work of art, of the dim, unseen, comparatively infinite, soul or power of the artist, may well be remembered as part of the long pleading of German culture for the things 'behind the veil'. To introduce that spiritual philosophy, as represented by the more transcendental parts of Kant, and by Schelling, into all subjects, as a system of reason in them, one and ever identical with itself, however various the matter through which it was diffused, became with him the motive of an unflagging enthusiasm, which seems to have been the one thread of continuity in a life otherwise singularly wanting in unity of purpose, and in which he was certainly far from uniformly at his best. Fragmentary and obscure, but often eloquent, and always at once earnest and ingenious, those writings, supplementing his remarkable gift of conversation, were directly and indirectly influential, even on some the furthest removed from Coleridge's own masters; on John Stuart Mill, for instance, and some of the earlier writers of the 'high-church' school. Like his verse, they display him also in two other characters — as a student of words, and as a psychologist, that is, as a more minute observer or student than other men of the phenomena of mind. To note the recondite associations of words, old or new; to expound the logic, the reasonable soul, of their various uses; to recover the interest of older writers who had had a phraseology of their own – this was a vein of inquiry allied to his undoubted gift of tracking out and analysing curious modes of thought. A quaint fragment of verse on *Human Life* might serve to illustrate his study of the earlier English philosophical poetry. The latter gift, that power of the 'subtle-souled psychologist', as Shelley calls him, seems to have been connected with some tendency to disease in the physical temperament, something of a morbid want of balance in those parts where the physical and intellectual elements mix most closely together, with a kind of languid visionariness, deep-seated in the very constitution of the 'narcotist,' who had quite a gift for 'plucking the poisons of self-harm', and which the actual habit of taking opium, accidentally acquired, did but reinforce. This morbid languor of nature, connected both with his fitfulness of purpose and his rich delicate dreaminess, qualifies Coleridge's poetic composition even more than his prose; his verse, with the exception of his avowedly political poems, being, unlike that of the 'Lake School', to which in some respects he belongs, singularly unaffected by any moral, or professional, or personal effort or ambition, – 'written,' as he says, 'after the more violent emotions of sorrow, to give him pleasure, when perhaps nothing else could;' but coming thus, indeed, very close to his own most intimately personal characteristics, and having a certain languidly soothing grace or cadence, for its most fixed quality, from first to last. After some Platonic soliloquy on a flower opening on a fine day in February, he goes on –

> Dim similitudes
> Weaving in mortal strains, I've stolen one hour
> From anxious self, life's cruel taskmaster!
> And the warm wooings of this sunny day
> Tremble along my frame and harmonize
> The attempered organ, that even saddest thoughts
> Mix with some sweet sensations, like harsh tunes
> Played deftly on a sweet-toned instrument.

The expression of two opposed, yet allied, elements of sensibility in these lines, is very true to Coleridge : – the grievous agitation, the grievous listlessness, almost never entirely relieved, together with a certain physical voluptuousness. He has spoken several times of the scent of the bean-field in the air : – the tropical touches in a chilly climate; his is a nature that will make the most of these, which finds a sort of caress in such things. 'Kubla Khan', the fragment of a poem actually composed in some certainly not quite healthy sleep, is perhaps chiefly of interest as showing, by the mode of its composition, how physical, how much of a diseased or valetudinarian temperament, in its moments of relief, Coleridge's happiest gift really was; and side by side with 'Kubla Khan' should be read, as Coleridge placed it,

the 'Pains of Sleep', to illustrate that retarding physical burden
in his temperament, that 'unimpassioned grief,' the source of
which lay so near the source of those pleasures. Connected also
with this, and again in contrast with Wordsworth, is the limited
quantity of his poetical performance, as he himself regrets so
eloquently in the lines addressed to Wordsworth after his recitation of *The Prelude*. It is like some exotic plant, just managing
to blossom a little in the somewhat un-english air of Coleridge's
own south-western birthplace, but never quite well there.

In 1798 he joined Wordsworth in the composition of a volume
of poems – the *Lyrical Ballads*. What Wordsworth then wrote
already vibrates with that blithe impulse which carried him to
final happiness and self-possession. In Coleridge we feel already
that faintness and obscure dejection which clung like some con-
tagious damp to all his work. Wordsworth was to be distinguished
by a joyful and penetrative conviction of the existence of certain latent affinities between nature and the human mind, which
reciprocally gild the mind and nature with a kind of 'heavenly
alchemy'.

> My voice proclaims
> How exquisitely the individual mind
> (And the progressive powers, perhaps, no less
> Of the whole species) to the external world
> Is fitted; and how exquisitely, too,
> The external world is fitted to the mind;
> And the creation, by no lower name
> Can it be called, which they with blended might
> Accomplish.

In Wordsworth this took the form of an unbroken dreaming
over the aspects and transitions of nature – a reflective, though
altogether unformulated, analysis of them.

There are in Coleridge's poems expressions of this conviction
as deep as Wordsworth's. But Coleridge could never have
abandoned himself to the dream, the vision, as Wordsworth did,
because the first condition of such abandonment must be an
unvexed quietness of heart. No one can read the 'Lines composed above Tintern' without feeling how potent the physical
element was among the conditions of Wordsworth's genius –
'felt in the blood and felt along the heart'.

My whole life I have lived in quiet thought!

The stimulus which most artists require of nature he can renounce. He leaves the ready-made glory of the Swiss mountains that he may reflect glory on a mouldering leaf. He loves best to watch the floating thistledown, because of its hint at an unseen life in the air. Coleridge's temperament, ἀεί ἐν σφοδρᾷ ὀρέξει, with its faintness, its grieved dejection, could never have been like that.

> My genial spirits fail;
> And what can these avail
> To lift the smothering weight from off my breast?
> It were a vain endeavour,
> Though I should gaze for ever
> On that green light that lingers in the west :
> I may not hope from outward forms to win
> The passion and the life whose fountains are within.

Wordsworth's flawless temperament, his fine mountain atmosphere of mind, that calm, sabbatic, mystic, wellbeing which De Quincey, a little cynically, connected with worldly (that is to say, pecuniary) good fortune, kept his conviction of a latent intelligence in nature within the limits of sentiment or instinct, and confined it to those delicate and subdued shades of expression which alone perfect art allows. In Coleridge's sadder, more purely intellectual, cast of genius, what with Wordsworth was sentiment or instinct became a philosophical idea, or philosophical formula, developed, as much as possible, after the abstract and metaphysical fashion of the transcendental schools of Germany.

The period of Coleridge's residence at Nether Stowey, 1797–8, was for him the *annus mirabilis*. Nearly all the chief works by which his poetic fame will live were then composed or planned. What shapes itself for criticism as the main phenomenon of Coleridge's poetic life, is not, as with most true poets, the gradual development of a poetic gift, determined, enriched, retarded, by the actual circumstances of the poet's life, but the sudden blossoming, through one short season, of such a gift already perfect in its kind, which thereafter deteriorates as suddenly, with something like premature old age. Connecting this phenomenon with the leading motive of his prose writings, we might note it as the deterioration of a productive or creative power into one merely metaphysical or discursive. In his unambitious conception of his function as a poet, and in the very limited quantity of his poetical performance, as I have said, he was a contrast to his friend Wordsworth. That friendship with Wordsworth, the chief 'developing' circumstance of his poetic life, comprehended a very close intellectual sympathy; and in such association chiefly, lies whatever truth there may be in the popular classification of Coleridge as a member of what is called the 'Lake School'. Coleridge's philosophical speculations do really turn on the ideas which underlay Wordsworth's poetical practice. His prose works are one long explanation of all that is involved in that famous distinction between the Fancy and the Imagination. Of what is understood by both writers as the imaginative quality in the use of poetic figures, we may take some words of Shakespeare as an example. –

> My cousin Suffolk,
> My soul shall thine keep company to heaven :
> Tarry, sweet soul, for mine, then fly abreast.

The complete infusion here of the figure into the thought, so vividly realised, that, though birds are not actually mentioned, yet the sense of their flight, conveyed to us by the single word 'abreast', comes to be more than half of the thought itself : – this, as the expression of exalted feeling, is an instance of what Coleridge meant by Imagination. And this sort of identification of the poet's thought, of himself, with the image or figure which serves him, is the secret, sometimes, of a singularly entire realisation of that image, such as makes these lines of Coleridge, for instance, 'imaginative' –

> Amid the howl of more than wintry storms,
> The halcyon hears the voice of vernal hours
> Already on the wing.

There are many such figures both in Coleridge's verse and prose. He has, too, his passages of that sort of impassioned contemplation on the permanent and elementary conditions of nature and humanity, which Wordsworth held to be the essence of a poet; as it would be his proper function to awaken such contemplation in other men – those 'moments', as Coleridge says, addressing him –

> Moments awful,
> Now in thy inner life, and now abroad,
> When power streamed from thee, and thy soul received
> The light reflected, as a light bestowed.

The entire poem from which these lines are taken, 'composed on the night after Wordsworth's recitation of a poem on the growth of an individual mind', is, in its high-pitched strain of meditation, and in the combined justice and elevation of its philosophical expression –

> high and passionate thoughts
> To their own music chanted;

wholly sympathetic with *The Prelude* which it celebrates, and of which the subject is, in effect, the generation of the spirit of the 'Lake poetry', The 'Lines to Joseph Cottle' have the same philosophically imaginative character; the 'Ode to Dejection' being Coleridge's most sustained effort of this kind.

It is in a highly sensitive apprehension of the aspects of external nature that Coleridge identifies himself most closely with one of the main tendencies of the 'Lake School'; a tendency instinctive, and no mere matter of theory, in him as in Wordsworth. That record of the

> green light
> Which lingers in the west,

and again, of

> the western sky,
> And its peculiar tint of yellow green,

which Byron found ludicrously untrue, but which surely needs no defence, is a characteristic example of a singular watchfulness for the minute fact and expression of natural scenery pervading all he wrote – a closeness to the exact physiognomy of nature, having something to do with that idealistic philosophy which sees in the external world no mere concurrence of mechanical agencies, but an animated body, informed and made expressive, like the body of man, by an indwelling intelligence. It was a tendency, doubtless, in the air, for Shelley too is affected by it, and

Turner, with the school of landscape which followed him. 'I had found,' Coleridge tells us,

> That outward forms, the loftiest, still receive
> Their finer influence from the world within;
> Fair ciphers of vague import, where the eye
> Traces no spot, in which the heart may read
> History and prophecy : . . .

and this induces in him no indifference to actual colour and form and process, but such minute realism as this –

> The thin gray cloud is spread on high,
> It covers but not hides the sky.
> The moon is behind and at the full;
> And yet she looks both small and dull;

or this, which has a touch of 'romantic' weirdness –

> Nought was green upon the oak
> But moss and rarest misletoe :

or this –

> There is not wind enough to twirl
> The one red leaf, the last of its clan,
> That dances as often as dance it can,
> Hanging so light, and hanging so high,
> On the topmost twig that looks up at the sky :

or this, with a weirdness, again, like that of some wild French etcher –

> Lo ! the new-moon winter-bright !
> And overspread with phantom light
> (With swimming phantom light o'erspread,
> But rimmed and circled with a silver thread)
> I see the old moon in her lap, foretelling
> The coming on of rain and squally blast.

He has a like imaginative apprehension of the silent and unseen processes of nature, its 'ministries' of dew and frost, for instance; as when he writes, in April –

> A balmy night ! and though the stars be dim,
> Yet let us think upon the vernal showers
> That gladden the green earth, and we shall find
> A pleasure in the dimness of the stars.

Of such imaginative treatment of landscape there is no better
instance than the description of 'The Dell', in 'Fears in Solitude' –

> A green and silent spot amid the hills,
> A small and silent dell ! O'er stiller place
> No singing skylark ever poised himself –
>   But the dell,
> Bathed by the mist is fresh and delicate
> As vernal cornfield, or the unripe flax
> When, through its half-transparent stalks, at eve,
> The level sunshine glimmers with green light : –
>   The gust that roared and died away
> To the distant tree –
>   heard and only heard
> In this low dell, bowed not the delicate grass.

This curious insistence of the mind on one particular spot, till
it seems to attain actual expression and a sort of soul in it – a
mood so characteristic of the 'Lake School' – occurs in an earnest
political poem, 'written in April 1798, during the alarm of an
invasion'; and that silent dell is the background against which
the tumultuous fears of the poet are in strong relief, while the
quiet sense of the place, maintained all through them, gives a
true poetic unity to the piece. Good political poetry – political
poetry that shall be permanently moving – can, perhaps, only be
written on motives which, for those they concern, have ceased
to be open questions, and are really beyond argument; while
Coleridge's political poems are for the most part on open questions. For although it was a great part of his intellectual ambition to subject political questions to the action of the fundamental
ideas of his philosophy, he was nevertheless an ardent partisan,
first on one side, then on the other, of the actual politics proper
to the end of the last and the beginning of the present century,
where there is still room for much difference of opinion. Yet 'The
Destiny of Nations', though formless as a whole, and unfinished,
presents many traces of his most elevated manner of speculation,
cast into that sort of imaginative philosophical expression, in
which, in effect, the language itself is inseparable from, or essentially a part of, the thought. 'France, an Ode', begins with a
famous apostrophe to Liberty –

Ye Clouds ! that far above me float and pause,
    Whose pathless march no mortal may control !
  Ye Ocean-waves ! that wheresoe'er ye roll,
Yield homage only to eternal laws !
Ye Woods ! that listen to the night-bird's singing,
    Midway the smooth and perilous slope reclined,
Save when your own imperious branches swinging,
    Have made a solemn music of the wind !
Where like a man beloved of God,
Through glooms which never woodman trod,
    How oft, pursuing fancies holy,
My moonlight way o'er flowering weeds I wound,
Inspired, beyond the guess of folly,
By each rude shape and wild unconquerable sound !
O ye loud Waves ! and O ye Forests high !
    And O ye Clouds that far above me soar'd !
Thou rising Sun ! thou blue rejoicing Sky !
Yea, everything that is and will be free !
Bear witness for me, wheresoe'er ye be,
With what deep worship I have still adored
      The spirit of divinest liberty.

And the whole ode, though, after Coleridge's way, not quite
equal to that *exordium*, is an example of strong national sentiment, partly in indignant reaction against his own earlier sympathy with the French Republic, inspiring a composition which,
in spite of some turgid lines, really justifies itself as poetry, and
has that true unity of effect which the ode requires. Liberty, after
all his hopes of young France, is only to be found in nature : –

    Thou speedest on thy subtle pinions,
The guide of homeless winds, and playmate of the waves !

In his changes of political sentiment, Coleridge was associated
with the 'Lake School'; and there is yet one other very different
sort of sentiment in which he is one with that school, yet all
himself, his sympathy, namely, with the animal world. That was a
sentiment connected at once with the love of outward nature in
himself and in the 'Lake School', and its assertion of the natural
affections in their simplicity; with the homeliness and pity, con-
sequent upon that assertion. The 'Lines to a Young Ass', teth-
ered –

> Where the close-eaten grass is scarcely seen,
> While sweet around her waves the tempting green,

which had seemed merely whimsical in their day, indicate a vein of interest constant in Coleridge's poems, and at its height in his greatest poems – in 'Christabel', where it has its effect, as it were antipathetically, in the vivid realisation of the serpentine element in Geraldine's nature; and in 'The Ancient Mariner', whose fate is interwoven with that of the wonderful bird, at whose blessing of the water-snakes the curse for the death of the albatross passes away, and where the moral of the love of all creatures, as a sort of religious duty, is definitely expressed.

'Christabel', though not printed till 1816, was written mainly in the year 1797 : 'The Rhyme of the Ancient Mariner' was printed as a contribution to the *Lyrical Ballads* in 1798; and these two poems belong to the great year of Coleridge's poetic production, his twenty-fifth year. In poetic quality, above all in that most poetic of all qualities, a keen sense of, and delight in beauty, the infection of which lays hold upon the reader, they are quite out of proportion to all his other compositions. The form in both is that of the ballad, with some of its terminolgy, and some also of its quaint conceits. They connect themselves with that revival of ballad literature, of which Percy's *Relics*, and, in another way, Macpherson's *Ossian* are monuments, and which afterwards so powerfully affected Scott –

> Young-eyed poesy
> All deftly masked as hoar antiquity.

'The Ancient Mariner', as also, in its measure, 'Christabel', is a 'romantic' poem, impressing us by bold invention, and appealing to that taste for the supernatural, that longing for *le frisson*, a shudder, to which the 'romantic' school in Germany, and its derivations in England and France, directly ministered. In Coleridge, personally, this taste had been encouraged by his odd and out-of-the-way reading in the old-fashioned literature of the marvellous – books like Purchas's *Pilgrims*, early voyages like Hakluyt's, old naturalists and visionary moralists, like Thomas Burnet, from whom he quotes the motto of 'The Ancient Mariner', *'Facile credo, plures esse naturas invisibles quam visibles in rerum universitate, etc.'* Fancies of the strange things which may very well happen, even in broad daylight, to men shut up alone in ships far off on the sea, seem to have occurred to the human mind in all ages with a peculiar readiness, and often have about them, from the story of the stealing of Dionysus downwards, the fascination of a certain dreamy grace, which distinguishes them from other kinds of marvellous inventions. This sort of fascination 'The Ancient Mariner' brings to its highest degree: it is the delicacy, the dreamy grace, in his presentation of the marvellous, which makes Coleridge's work so remarkable. The too palpable intruders from a spiritual world in almost all ghost literature, in Scott and Shakespeare even, have a kind of crudity or coarseness. Coleridge's power is in the very fineness with which, as by some really ghostly finger, he brings home to our inmost sense his inventions, daring as they are – the skeleton ship, the polar spirit, the inspiriting of the dead corpses of the ship's crew. 'The Rhyme of the Ancient Mariner' has the plausibility, the perfect adaptation to reason and the general aspect of life, which belongs to the marvellous, when actually presented as part of a credible experience in our dreams. Doubtless, the mere experience of the opium-eater, the habit he must almost necessarily fall into of noting the more elusive phenomena of dreams, had something to do with that: in its essence, however, it is connected with a more purely intellectual circumstance in the development of Coleridge's poetic gift. Some one once asked William Blake, to whom Coleridge has many resemblances, when either is at his best (that whole episode of the re-inspiriting of the ship's crew in 'The Ancient Mariner' being comparable to Blake's well-known design of the 'Morning Stars singing together') whether he had ever seen a ghost, and was surprised when the famous seer, who ought, one might think, to have seen so many, answered frankly, 'Only once!' His 'spirits', at once more delicate, and so much more real, than any ghost – the burden, as they were the privilege, of his *temperament* – like it, were an integral element in his everyday life. And the difference of mood expressed in that question and its answer, is indicative of a change of temper in regard to the supernatural which has passed over the whole modern mind, and of which the true measure is the influence of the writings of Swedenborg. What that change is we may see if we compare the vision by which Swedenborg was 'called', as he thought, to his work, with the ghost which called Hamlet, or the spells of Marlowe's *Faust* with those of Goethe's. The modern mind, so minutely self-scrutinising, if it is to be affected at all by a sense of the supernatural, needs to be more finely touched than was possible in the older, romantic presentment of it. The spectral object, so crude, so impossible, has become plausible, as

> The blot upon the brain,
> That *will* show itself without;

and is understood to be but a condition of one's own mind, for which, according to the scepticism, latent at least, in so much of our modern philosophy, the so-called real things themselves are but *spectra* after all.

It is this finer, more delicately marvellous supernaturalism, fruit of his more delicate psychology, that Coleridge infuses into romantic adventure, itself also then a new or revived thing in English literature; and with a fineness of weird effect in 'The Ancient Mariner', unknown in those older, more simple, romantic legends and ballads. It is a flower of medieval or later German romance, growing up in the peculiarly compounded atmosphere of modern psychological speculation, and putting forth in it wholly new qualities. The quaint prose commentary, which runs side by side with the verse of 'The Ancient Mariner, illustrates this – a composition of quite a different shade of beauty and merit from that of the verse which it accompanies, connecting this, the chief poem of Coleridge, with his philosophy, and emphasising therein that psychological interest of which I have spoken, its curious soul-lore.

Completeness, the perfectly rounded wholeness and unity of the impression it leaves on the mind of a reader who fairly gives himself to it – that, too, is one of the characteristics of a really excellent work, in the poetic as in every other kind of art; and by this completeness, 'The Ancient Mariner' certainly gains upon 'Christabel' – a completeness, entire as that of Wordsworth's 'Leech-gatherer', or Keats's 'Saint Agnes' Eve', each typical in its way of such wholeness or entirety of effect on a careful reader. It is Coleridge's one great complete work, the one really finished thing, in a life of many beginnings. 'Christabel' remained a fragment. In 'The Ancient Mariner' this unity is secured in part by

the skill with which the incidents of the marriage-feast are made
to break in dreamily from time to time upon the main story.
And then, how pleasantly, how reassuringly, the whole nightmare story itself is made to end, among the clear fresh sounds
and lights of the bay, where it began, with

> The moon-light steeped in silentness,
> The steady weather-cock.

So different from 'The Rhyme of the Ancient Mariner' in regard
to this completeness of effect, 'Christabel' illustrates the same
complexion of motives, a like intellectual situation. Here, too,
the work is of a kind peculiar to one who touches the characteristic motives of the old romantic ballad, with a spirit made subtle
and fine by modern reflection; as we feel, I think, in such passages as –

> But though my slumber had gone by,
> This dream it would not pass away –
> It seems to live upon mine eye; –

and –

> For she, belike, hath drunken deep
> Of all the blessedness of sleep;

and again –

> With such perplexity of mind
> As dreams too lively leave behind.

And that gift of handling the finer passages of human feeling,
at once with power and delicacy, which was another result of
his finer psychology, of his exquisitely refined habit of self-reflec-
tion, is illustrated by a passage on Friendship in the *Second Part* –

> Alas ! they had been friends in youth;
> But whispering tongues can poison truth;
> And constancy lives in realms above;
> And life is thorny; and youth is vain;
> And to be wroth with one we love,
> Doth work like madness in the brain.
> And thus it chanced, as I divine,
> With Roland and Sir Leoline.
> Each spake words of high disdain
> And insult to his heart's best brother :

> They parted – ne'er to meet again !
> But never either found another
> To free the hollow heart from paining –
> They stood aloof the scars remaining,
> Like cliffs which had been rent asunder;
> A dreary sea now flows between;
> But neither heat, nor frost, nor thunder,
> Shall wholly do away, I ween,
> The marks of that which once hath been.

I suppose these lines leave almost every reader with a quickened sense of the beauty and compass of human feeling; and it is the sense of such richness and beauty which, in spite of his 'dejection', in spite of that burden of his morbid lassitude, accompanies Coleridge himself through life. A warm poetic joy in everything beautiful, whether it be a moral sentiment, like the friendship of Roland and Leoline, or only the flakes of falling light from the water-snakes – this joy, visiting him, now and again, after sickly dreams, in sleep or waking, as a relief not to be forgotten, and with such a power of felicitous expression that the infection of it passes irresistibly to the reader – such is the predominant element in the matter of his poetry, as cadence is the predominant quality of its form. 'We bless thee for our creation !' he might have said, in his later period of definite religious assent, 'because the world is so beautiful : the world of ideas – living spirits, detached from the divine nature itself, to inform and lift the heavy mass of material things; the world of man, above all in his melodious and intelligible speech; the world of living creatures and natural scenery; the world of dreams.' What he really did say, by way of 'A Tombless Epitaph', is true enough of himself –

> Sickness, 'tis true,
> Whole years of weary days, besieged him close,
> Even to the gates and inlets of his life !
> But it is true, no less, that strenuous, firm,
> And with a natural gladness, he maintained
> The citadel unconquered, and in joy
> Was strong to follow the delightful Muse.
> For not a hidden path, that to the shades
> Of the beloved Parnassian forest leads,
> Lurked undiscovered by him; not a rill

There issues from the fount of Hippocrene,
But he had traced it upward to its source,
Through open glade, dark glen, and secret dell,
Knew the gay wild flowers on its banks, and culled
Its med'cinable herbs. Yea, oft alone,
Piercing the long-neglected holy cave,
The haunt obscure of old Philosophy,
He bade with lifted torch its starry walls
Sparkle, as erst they sparkled to the flame
Of odorous lamps tended by saint and sage.
O framed for calmer times and nobler hearts!
O studious Poet, eloquent for truth!
Philosopher! contemning wealth and death,
Yet docile, childlike, full of Life and Love.

The student of empirical science asks, Are absolute principles attainable? What are the limits of knowledge? The answer he receives from science itself is not ambiguous. What the moralist asks is, Shall we gain or lose by surrendering human life to the relative spirit? Experience answers that the dominant tendency of life is to turn ascertained truth into a dead letter, to make us all the phlegmatic servants of routine. The relative spirit, by its constant dwelling on the more fugitive conditions or circumstances of things, breaking through a thousand rough and brutal classifications, and giving elasticity to inflexible principles, begets an intellectual *finesse* of which the ethical result is a delicate and tender justice in the criticism of human life. Who would gain more than Coleridge by criticism in such a spirit? We know how his life has appeared when judged by absolute standards. We see him trying to 'apprehend the absolute', to stereotype forms of faith and philosophy, to attain, as he says, 'fixed principles' in politics, morals, and religion, to fix one mode of life as the essence of life, refusing to see the parts as parts only; and all the time his own pathetic history pleads for a more elastic moral philosophy than his, and cries out against every formula less living and flexible than life itself.

'From his childhood he hungered for eternity'. There, after all, is the incontestable claim of Coleridge. The perfect flower of any elementary type of life must always be precious to humanity, and Coleridge is a true flower of the *ennuyé*, of the type of René. More than Childe Harold, more than Werther, more than

René himself, Coleridge, by what he did, what he was, and what he failed to do, represents that inexhaustible discontent, languor, and homesickness, that endless regret, the chords of which rang all through our modern literature. It is to the romantic element in literature that those qualities belong. One day, perhaps, we may come to forget the distant horizon, with full knowlege of the situation, to be content with 'what is here and now'; and herein is the essence of classical feeling. But by us of the present moment, certainly – by us for whom the Greek spirit, with its engaging naturalness, simple, chastened, debonair, τρυφῆς, ἀβρότητος, χλιδῆς, χαρίτων, ἱμέρου, πόθου πατήρ, is itself the Sangrail of an endless pilgrimage, Coleridge, with his passion for the absolute, for something fixed where all is moving, his faintness, his broken memory, his intellectual disquiet, may still be ranked among the interpreters of one of the constituent elements of our life.

SOURCE: *Appreciations* (1889) – extract.

William Watson

It is usual to think of Coleridge the metaphysician as directly responsible for the gradual supersession, if not extinction, of Coleridge the bard; and it is clear that he himself, at a comparatively early date, was conscious of – and not unalarmed at – the growing ascendency exercised by his philosophical over his creative powers. It is in 1802, when he has still thirty-two years of life before him, that he acknowledges himself in the singular position of a man unable, so to speak, to get at his own genius or imagination except by a circuitous route, – *viâ* his intellect.

> By abstruse research to steal
> From my own nature all the natural man, –

this, he says, has become his 'sole resource', his 'only plan',

> Till that which suits a part infects the whole,
> And now is almost grown the habit of my soul.

But although his speculative faculty did ultimately dominate and overbear his poetic powers, we are inclined to think there was a time when it co-operated with them not disloyally. One is a little apt to forget that his metaphysical bent was no less innate than his poetical, – even at Christ's Hospital, his spiritual potation was a half-and-half in which the waters of a more or less authentic Castaly, and the 'philosophic draughts' from such fountains as Jamblichus and Plotinus, were equally mingled. Whether or not a born 'maker', he was certainly a born theorist; and we believe not only that under all his most important artistic achievements there was a basis of intellectual theory, but that the theory, so far from being an alien and disturbing presence, did duty as the unifying principle which co-ordinated the whole. We think we can see such a theory underlying. 'The Ancient Mariner', and securing the almost unqualified imaginative success of that poem; and we further think we can see it departed from in one isolated instance, with temporary artistic disaster as the result.

Anyone examining the poem with a critical eye for its machinery and groundwork, will have noticed that Coleridge is careful not to introduce any element of the marvellous or supernatural until he has transported the reader beyond the pale of definite geographical knowledge, and thus left behind him all those conditions of the known and the familiar, all those associations with recorded fact and experience, which would have created an inimical atmosphere. Indeed, there is perhaps something rather inartistic in his undisguised haste to convey us to the aesthetically necessary region. In some half-dozen stanzas, beginning with 'The ship was cheered', we find ourselves crossing the Line and driven far towards the Southern Pole. Beyond a few broad indications thus vouchsafed, Coleridge very astutely takes pains to avoid anything like geography. We reach that silent sea into which we are the first that ever burst, and that is sufficient for imaginative ends. It is enough that the world, as known to actual navigators, is left behind, and a world which the poet is free to colonise with the wildest children of his dreaming brain, has been entered. Forthwith, to all intents and purposes, we may say, in the words of Goethe as rendered by Shelley : –

'The bound of true and false are passed ; –
Lead us on, thou wandering gleam.'

Thenceforth we cease to have any direct relations with the verifiable. Natural law is suspended; standards of probability have ceased to exist. Marvel after marvel is accepted by us, as by the Wedding-Guest, with the unquestioning faith of 'a three years' child'. We become insensibly acclimatised to this dreamland. Nor is it the chaotic, anarchic, incoherent world of arabesque romance, where the real and unreal by turns arbitrarily interrupt and supplant each other, and are never reconciled at heart. On the contrary, here is no inconsistency, for with the constitution of *this* dream-realm nothing except the natural and the probable could be inconsistent. Here is no danger of the intellect or the reason pronouncing an adverse judgment, for the venue has been changed to a court where the jurisdiction of fantasy is supreme. Thus far then, the Logic of the Incredible is perfect, and the result, from the view point of art, magnificent. But at last we quit this consistently, unimpeachably, more satisfactorily impossible world; we are restored to the world of common experience; and when so restoring us, the poet makes his first and only mistake. For the concluding miracle, or rather brace of miracles – the apparition of the angelic forms standing over the corpses of the crew, and the sudden preternatural sinking of the ship – take place just when we have returned to the province of the natural and regular, to the sphere of the actual and the known; just when, floating into harbour, we sight the well-remembered kirk on the rock, and the steady weathercock which the moonlight steeps in silentness. A dissonant note is struck at once. We have left a world where prodigies were normal, and have returned to one where they are monstrous. But prodigies still pursue us with unseasonable pertinacity, and our feeling is somewhat akin to that of the Ancient Mariner himself, whose prayer is that he may either 'be awake' or may 'sleep alway'. We would fain either surrender unconditionally to reality, or remain free, as naturalised citizens of a self-governing dreamland.

If 'The Ancient Mariner' is the finest example in our literature, of purely fantastic creation – and we think it is – the First Part of 'Christabel' is not less wonderful in its power of producing an equally full and rich effect by infinitely more frugal means. In 'Christabel', there is nothing extravagant or bizarre, no mere imaginative libertinism, nothing that even most distantly suggests a riot of fancy. The glamour, everywhere present, is delicate, elusive, impalpable, curiously insidious – the glamour of 'en-chantments drear, where more is meant than meets the ear.' Acute critics seem to have felt from the first that the very essence of the unique attraction exercised by this poem lay in its obscurity, its enigmatical character, – that its fascination was pre-eminently the fascination of the impenetrable. Charles Lamb dreaded a 'continuation' which should solve the riddle – and break the spell: which should light up – and destroy – this costly and fault-less fabric of mystery. His fears (he was eventually reconciled to the 'continuation' by the inimitable passage on divided friend-ship) were only too well justified. In the Second Part, Coleridge does not actually vulgarise his shadowland by letting in common-place daylight; but he distinctly goes some little way in that direction. It is not merely a falling-off in the quality of the work-manship – (although there *is* a falling off of that sort, the poetry, as such, is still very fine) – but the whole basis, environment, and atmosphere of the First Part were magical, – and were homo-geneous. The conditions of time and place were purely ideal; there was no uncomfortable elbowing of Wonder by Familiarity; the clumsy foot of Fact did not once tread upon the rustling train of Romance. But we turn to the continution – we enter the second chamber of this enchanted palace – and we are met at the threshold by the dull and earthy imp, Topography. Since writing his First Part, Coleridge has removed to Keswick, and so, forsooth, when he resumes his story, we hear of Borrowdale and Langdale, of Bratha-Head and Dungeon-Ghyll. The subtlest part of the illusion is gone: the incursion of accidents has commenced, and the empire of fantasy is threatened. The notable thing is, that the point where the air of the fine strangeness and aloofness ceases to be sustained, is precisely the point where the impression of *mere unreality* begins to make itself obtrusively felt. There has been conceded to us just that foothold in *terra firma* which affords a basis for the leisurely delimitation of *terra incognita*. And, truth to tell, the poet has not really taken up again his abandoned thread. How could he? It was a filament of fairy gossamer, and he has endeavoured to piece it with what is, after all, only the very finest silk from the reel.

SOURCE: 'Coleridge's Supernaturalism', *Excursions in Criticism* (1893).

PART THREE

Modern Critical Studies

Mark L. Reed

WORDSWORTH, COLERIDGE, AND THE 'PLAN' OF THE *LYRICAL BALLADS* (1965)

Most longer recent studies of William Wordsworth and Samuel Taylor Coleridge have contributed one way or another to clearer discernment of the varied and complex personal forces, the tides obedient and currents self-determined, that were interacting in the progress of the friendship of the poets. One fact increasingly well understood is, that however much at some time the two men may have considered themselves 'twins almost in genius and in mind', there were at work from the outset of their association individual elements of thought and personality making emergence of doubts and hesitations in each about the ideas or even character of the other a matter only of time. It also is becoming increasingly evident that the formation of the first great monument of their friendship, *Lyrical Ballads*, and their early theoretical justifications of the volume offer a touchstone by which the dynamics of several problems latent in their relationship as a whole can be understood. Professor Parrish, for example, has explained many of Wordsworth's probable artistic goals in his early contributions to *Lyrical Ballads*, and indicated the degree to which his intentions failed to coincide with the preoccupations and assumptions of Coleridge. In a recent provocative essay Professor Buchan has examined certain aspects of the poets' early companionship in terms of the needs of the personalities of both men, and has offered suggestions as to how and why Wordsworth (with a dominance characteristic of him throughout the relationship as a whole) apparently appropriated to himself the entire joint project of *Lyrical Ballads* – as early as 30 April 1798, in fact, Dorothy was announcing that her brother was 'about to publish some poems' – and how and why Coleridge in equally typical fashion evidently accepted without hesitation a secondary role in the historic venture, too quickly ignoring distinct differences in aim and attitude between himself and his admired companion.[1]

Professor Parrish's remarks would no doubt lend support to the latter views, although they offer no conjecture about the precise nature of the original plans for the *Lyrical Ballads* and, indeed, assume that the poets had argued to some extent from early in their friendship on topics relevant to its aesthetics. Recollecttions by no means dim and faint of such arguments turn up in later remarks of Coleridge's like 'To the faults and defects [of Wordsworth's poems] I have been far more alive than his detractors, even from the first publication of the Lyrical Ballads tho' for a long course of years my opinions were sacred to his own ear.'[2] The doubts about Wordsworth's matter-of-factness that he expressed to Hazlitt during his 1798 visit to Nether Stowey, later recorded by Hazlitt in *My First Acquaintance with Poets*, indicate that some of his opinions might on occasion have reached another ear, but as to what he may have told Wordsworth himself a greater problem remains. One still wonders why not even slight contemporary evidence remains of conscious direct disagreement between the poets on this kind of subject before and during at least the first two editions of *Lyrical Ballads*, and why Coleridge, whatever his later views, was in 1800 stating that Wordsworth's Preface contained his and Wordsworth's 'joint opinions on Poetry' or, in 1802, that (in regard to the Preface) with few exceptions we could scarcely either of us perhaps positively say, which first started any particular Thought.'[3]

Increased insight into deeper levels of the early relationship of the two men amplifies problems of approach to both, for it demands clearer perception of traits in each possibly inseparable from their genius, but in any case decidedly deficient from the standpoint of attractiveness. One must acknowledge the unbending, unremitting, almost entirely humourless determination of Wordsworth's search for permanent truths about man, nature, and human life, and for a means of expressing those truths in art, that led him to devour, digest – but too seldom acknowledge – the loyalty and contributions of his small, diversely gifted group of satellites. His intolerance towards the personal weaknesses of

Coleridge and his limited overt recognition of his debt to that great intellect are perhaps the most unforgivable of his failures in this respect. One must acknowledge Coleridge's regrettable but also distressing, and finally tiresome, unsteadiness of will, his nearly infantile dependence on Wordsworth's abiding strength of personality, his decline into increasing self-doubt and self-pity as his friend failed properly to understand or endorse his own thoughts and achievements. Such traits no doubt deprived his world and ours of a sizable quantity of important literary achievement. Awareness of difficulties like these hardly brings with it a temptation to devalue the fruits of the creative activity of the poets, but it nevertheless obliges admirers to place some curb on their affections. It can very easily also encourage a committed student consciously or unconsciously to take sides for or against one of the poets – a dangerous course where the values to be gained from study of both are so great, and where a deep understanding of either cannot be hoped for without an intimate knowledge of the other. What follows perhaps does not attain impartiality, but it may be a fair suggestion at this point that with regard to the early history of *Lyrical Ballads*, as with all the early history of the relationship, one tends to find Wordsworth's appearance of callousness toward Coleridge somewhat more disturbing (that the fault was unconscious hardly improves matters) than Coleridge's generous weakness, or weakliness, towards Wordsworth.

The main points of the problem as far as *Lyrical Ballads* is concerned look reasonably clear. The older man was more fortunate in the composition of poems in accordance with a joint plan, described later by both poets in slightly varying terms, which in some sense represented a stated or unstated agreement freeing each writer to follow the peculiar bent of his own talent. Wordsworth, however, failing now as later to understand much of the unique quality and value of the intellect of his friend, soon began to consider the developing volume his own, and, when explanations of its philosophical bases were required, did his explaining on his own terms from the start. His exposition of his views may well eventually in turn have helped Coleridge toward his disappointing and perhaps demoralizing realizations of the broader differences that lay between himself and Wordsworth in more

areas than poetic theory and practice alone. Dorothy, as mentioned already, spoke of the poems as her brother's at the outset. On 30 April he was 'about to publish some poems'; 'William,'
she continued on 31 May, 'now has some poems in the Bristol
Press.' The result of the joint plan, Coleridge said, was 'presented' by Wordsworth 'as an experiment' in treating in the
'language of ordinary life' 'subjects . . . that rejected the usual
ornaments.'[4] The Preface of 1800 carried on the work of Wordsworth's presentation in a manner that Coleridge himself realized increasingly – especially after the 1802 verson – did not present a synthesis of his and Wordsworth's views but rather an
over-elaborate defence of a theory in several essential points entirely Wordsworth's own. After Coleridge had expended immense
effort on 'Christabel' for the *Lyrical Ballads* of 1800, Wordsworth decided not to use the poem and in an obtuse and un-
gracious note publicized his belief that he was showing no negli-
gible tolerance in allowing the perplexing 'Ancient Mariner' to
remain; nor did he make any real acknowledgment at all of
Coleridge's extensive assistance in preparing the edition of 1800.
'The Ancient Mariner' and Coleridge's other contributions became simply 'the assistance of a friend', whom Wordsworth had
called upon on account of a rhetorically modest 'need of variety'
and consciousness of 'his own weakness'. Coleridge's comment
to Wrangham of 19 December 1800 typifies his own attitude
toward the volume : '[Wordsworth] is a great, a true Poet – I am
only a kind of a Metaphysician. – He has even now sent off the
last sheet of a second Volume of his Lyrical Ballads –.'[5]

So the main points look. The evidence taken in its entirety, however, appears to indicate that more factors probably acted in
creating these attitudes and events than Coleridge's lack of
strength and certain of those personal qualities in Wordsworth
that made him so noticeably (in his great friend's phrase)
'all man' – characteristics like his single-minded pursuit of
only his own goals, his lack of sympathy (especially for weakness), his tendency, despite occasional compliments to others, toward habitual assumption that his creation, thought, and achievement were in most ways that mattered the result of his own inde-
pendent powers interacting with what he often called Nature. Not
much account seems, for instance, to have been taken of the fact

that the only really plain indications by the authors that a volume like the 1798 *Lyrical Ballads* was brought into being as the result of a jointly held aesthetic plan come from Coleridge nearly two decades, and from Wordsworth over four decades, after the volume was published. As Coleridge recalled in the *Biographia Literaria*: 'The thought suggested itself (to which of us I do not recollect) that a series of poems might be composed of two sorts. . . . In this idea originated the plan of the *Lyrical Ballads*. . . .' Wordsworth's much later memory in the long Fenwick note to 'We Are Seven' was: 'The Ancient Mariner grew and grew till it became too important for our first object, . . . and we began to talk of a Volume. . . . Accordingly I wrote The Idiot Boy, Her eyes are wild, etc., We are seven, The Thorn, and some others.' A main problem about the earliest stage of that joint effort which Wordsworth apparently so hastily began regarding as his own has been the determination of which of the poets' descriptions of the project (Coleridge speaks of a plan for poems of 'two sorts', natural and supernatural; Wordsworth mentions poetry of mainly one sort, 'Poems chiefly on natural subjects taken from common life, but looked at, as much as might be, through an imaginative medium') is the more correct. A secondary question, and one usually handled with more care, is that of when the plan was formed. While the ground has been covered often before, it will perhaps not be superfluous to recall at this time a few elements of the broader personal inter-relationships from which the volume and its plan grew.

The more significant events in the first stages of the friendship are easily remembered: Wordsworth's introduction to Coleridge in Bristol, probably in September 1795; the deep impression made on Coleridge then or in early 1796 by Wordsworth's most mature long poem to date, 'Salisbury Plain'; Wordsworth's visit to Coleridge in late March or early April 1797; Coleridge's visit to the Wordsworths at Racedown in June 1797 (with his short-cut over the gate and across the field on arrival); Wordsworth's and his household's removal to Nether Stowey a month later in order to be near Coleridge; the Wordsworths' residence for the next year at Alfoxden. Coleridge had known Wordsworth's poetry as early as the summer of 1793, and was discussing it with Christopher Wordsworth at Cambridge by autumn of that year;[6]

Wordsworth probably had taken no decided note, quite possibly had heard only little of Coleridge before his visit to Bristol in 1795. In considering the events of the early years following the meeting of the two it is important to keep in mind the degree to which (no matter what the latent potential for disagreement) the actions of both men acknowledged the immensely satisfying nature of the gifts which each brought the other. Wordsworth, however much Coleridge may from the first of their acquaintance have felt in him a personality 'strong in himself, and powerful to give strength', showed little tendency indeed, even unconscious, to dominate his friend. The older poet had been eager to be better known to Coleridge months before they wrote each other; he was asking Cottle in January 1796 to tell him that 'I wish much to hear from him.' It was Wordsworth who paid the first visit later in the year, prolonging his journey from Bristol to Racedown to call on Coleridge at Nether Stowey; far from being 'absorbed', as had been suggested, 'in his own dream of poetic fame'⁷ when in early 1796 he failed to give unreserved praise to Coleridge's 'Religious Musings', a poem that in no way deserves unreserved praise, he was then, 'dead to deeper hope', suffering through probably the worst period of self-doubt in his career. Again, it was Wordsworth who, with hardly any other possible warrant than a brief visit to Nether Stowey and Coleridge's arguments and personality, left his residence at Racedown to follow Coleridge to the Quantocks. These early years were not merely a period of discovery by Coleridge of the stature of 'The Giant Wordsworth', gifted with a strength and dynamism that he felt wanting in himself, but a time of dawning awareness on the part of both men of the marvellous extent to which each stimulated and gratified the other's intellectual and emotional needs. Nor does Wordsworth's behaviour to Coleridge appear, by any normal standards, so far as it can be traced, the outgrowth of remissness in acknowledgment of someone else's powers.

In the rich intercommunication of great thought and deep response that characterized the lives of Coleridge and Wordsworth during the residence of the latter at Alfoxden lie the grounds for rewarding scholarly interpretations about a host of subjects. But even the most objective study of the feelings of the poets during this time may still produce a sense of pathos. Fundamentally different as they were in so many respects, the two men now to no small extent saw each other enveloped by a light that never was. It may smack of shallow utilitarianism to suggest that their sense of pleasure in this case 'overcomes every consideration, or rather obliterates all consideration' because it was responsible directly or indirectly for several of our great poems and for a seed-time in which were germinated major forces in the re-formation of modern poetry. But it is hardly justifiable to find pathos in a situation where no one was deceived or self-deceived, either consciously or unconsciously; and it might be well to try to determine as exactly as possible the degree to which the latter quality could characterize the poets' early attitudes towards *Lyrical Ballads* and its theories. Relevant evidence lies in scattered comments, many of them quite casual and offering poor enough ground for scrupulous analysis. But one source of difficulty in the subject under discussion can, I think, be found to be that Wordsworth and Coleridge have helped complicate later students' responses to the facts of the matter by an attempt to adjust and clarify their own attitudes towards them. Their efforts to present, to themselves as well as the public, a fairer picture of the complete environment, emotional and intellectual, from which the achievement of *Lyrical Ballads* and its Preface had arisen than had existed in their minds near the time of the composition itself – efforts that came after a long period of silent or overt tensions in which balanced interpretations by either had been virtually impossible – have almost surely led to a certain number of misplaced emphases and an unnecessary amount of uneasiness.

Dorothy's remarks of 20 November 1797 are the well-known first indication of the birth of a plan to publish a joint volume. Wordsworth and Coleridge have decided, she says, to publish 'The Ancient Mariner' together with 'some pieces of William's'.[8] Her comments imply that the plan for 'The Ancient Mariner' was evolved on 13 November and the project of the volume either then or shortly after, and certainly by 20 November. What 'some pieces' included is not clear; 'Salisbury Plain', the future 'Guilt and Sorrow', is a possibility, or some version of 'The Ruined Cottage', or both. No evidence points, anyhow, to Wordsworth's having composed any short poems during the past few months, although various pieces of a slightly earlier date, like his work on 'The Old Cumberland Beggar', 'Old Man Travelling', or 'Lines, Left upon a Seat in a Yew Tree', may, perhaps, have been in mind also. In any event, nothing resembling the joint aesthetic plan described in *Biographia Literaria* or the 'We Are Seven' note had been motivating their efforts up till now. Nor, indeed, did any such plan occupy their thought or energy to any discernible extent during the rest of the winter. Wordsworth was visiting London most of the time between 20 November 1797 and 3 January 1798, and his composition there must have been largely confined to revision of *The Borderers* in his unsuccessful attempt to fit it for the stage. Coleridge was in his turn absent from the Stowey–Alfoxden area from early January until 9 February. He had, in fact, been contemplating separate sale of 'The Ancient Mariner' on 6 January, a fairly plain proof that fulfillment of the joint plan was not at that time a serious goal. During the late winter, of course, Wordsworth was undeniably preoccupied with the furtherance of one plan definitely of joint birth, the 'philosophical poem', 'The Recluse'. His own description of himself at this time as 'tolerably industrious' amounts to understatement; he was writing an extensive quantity of narrative, descriptive, and meditative blank verse, most of it almost certainly towards this goal.[9] But as far as surviving MS. evidence offers a clue, 'A Night Piece' and some work on 'The Old Cumberland Beggar' seem to be the only short compositions on which he worked before 5 March – and certainly neither of these is the sort of poem that Wordsworth later said he wrote on account of the plan that produced *Lyrical Ballads*.[10]

Had that plan, then, one wonders, attained prominence in their minds by the time that Wordsworth was offering 'his poems' to Cottle through Coleridge about 13 March?[11] If so, the offer might point to an early instance of Coleridge's neglect of his own achievement and talents in the face of his companion's 'outdistancing' of him in the fulfillment of the project. The outdistancing would, however, have had to occur with astonishing rapidity, for the poems that Coleridge stated that he was offering Cottle were 'Salisbury Plain', 'The Ruined Cottage', and 'a few others'. The last phrase would hardly be used to describe works which had resulted from an aesthetic concept of any importance and originality, and there appears little real likelihood that *Lyrical Ballads* written from the plan were among them. A volume of poems was indeed a goal, of course; still another 'plan' beyond that referred to in the last paragraph had now arisen, that of an extended visit to Germany, and such a trip required money. But there is even at this time no indication that either poet considered himself engaged in a joint venture with the other along pre-established aesthetic lines.

To leave the sort of object just mentioned aside for a moment, it seems, on the other hand, quite clear that Wordsworth was himself deeply concerned from early March about some kind of new aim besides those of either the philosophical poem or the trip to Germany. At least from around that time he was 'adding rapidly to his stock of poetry';[12] and such poems of his as can be given dates between then and late May, when most of the Lyrical Ballads went to Bristol with Cottle, do not at all resemble *The Recluse*, but are written in stanzas, and in a diction decidedly simpler than that of the blank verse of 'The Ruined Cottage' or 'The Old Cumberland Beggar'. With the exception of 'The Idiot Boy' and 'Peter Bell', they are, further, all short poems. The following more specific chronological suggestions and evidence can be briefly noted : 'Lines Written in Early Spring' would not date before early March, and most probably was composed in early April, when primroses and periwinkles began to bloom (Dorothy's *Journal*). 'To My Sister' most likely dates from early March, especially 6, 8, or 9 March (Dorothy's *Journal*). 'Goody Blake and Harry Gill' probably dates from March (*Early Letters*, 169; Moorman, *William Wordsworth*, 284; Coleridge, *Letters*, I 399n.). 'The Thorn' was probably begun 19 March (Dorothy's *Journal*; note to *The Thorn*; [J. R. Dix,] *Pen and Ink Sketches of Poets, Preachers, and Politicians* (London, 1846) p. 123). 'Anecdote for Fathers' can be supposed, from its spring-like setting, to have been composed between early April and Cottle's departure in late May. 'Peter Bell' was begun 20 April and probably finished in some form by late May (Dorothy's *Journal*; Hazlitt's *My First Acquaintance with Poets*). 'Expostulation and Reply' and 'The Tables Turned' would not date before Hazlitt's visit of late May, since Hazlitt almost surely prompted the works.

The abundance of such poems seems to leave little doubt that, over and above the financial requirements of the trip to Germany, an aesthetic plan of some kind was spurring the older poet in his work, and that this plan included not only some philosophy of subject matter but of language and character presentation as well – the latter aspects of his thought containing elements that Coleridge was later to deny ever having approved of. The evidence of content and Fenwick notes implies that 'Complaint of the Forsaken Indian Woman', 'The Last of the Flock', and most probably 'We Are Seven' and 'Simon Lee' must also have been the results of Wordsworth's 'plan'. It remains a remarkable circumstance that of the poems to which fairly exact dates can be assigned, only one can be placed with any probability before the letter which Coleridge wrote to Cottle about 13 March. No absolute proof exists, at last, that several of these works were not composed before that date, but the extent of the blank verse which Wordsworth wrote during the winter and his excitement in early May about his 'new plan' suggest strongly that few of these poems could have existed before. Conjecture, then, that Coleridge was in any sense becoming overpowered any time around early March by the spectacle of Wordsworth's superior productivity seems groundless. The ample extent and variety of the younger man's own composition presents equally little basis for assumption that his energies were being sapped by anything at all – as they also provoke some conjecture about the degree of his commitment to a major literary plan.

Those compositions of Coleridge's which may date at least in part from spring 1798 and could be supposed, if so, to have particular relevance to the joint plan are 'The Ancient Mariner', 'Christabel', some possible work towards a poem concerning 'The Dark Ladie', and 'The Three Graves'. Coleridge speaks in *Biographia Literaria* of having written the first, and having been preparing the next two, for the joint volume. A substantial portion of 'The Ancient Mariner' was begun and an appreciable part almost certainly written, as an abundance of comment by both poets makes clear, well before the spring, and therefore before a joint volume of the kind under discussion became a pressing ambition. If any work was in fact done on 'The Dark Ladie' at this time, a matter of considerable doubt, it probably amounted to very little; Coleridge's comment in the *Biographia* that he was preparing the poem contemporaneously with 'Christabel' (the date of which itself is by no means certain) cannot be confirmed by any other evidence. 'The Three Graves' was not begun for any sort of joint effort, for a portion of the MS. is in the hand of Mary Hutchinson, who left Racedown on 4 June 1797 just before Coleridge's arrival, and only one section, lines 470–517, seems very likely to date from spring of 1798. The real problem in regard to the last poem is that it in any case does not correspond to the description of Coleridge's end of the plan in *Biographia Literaria*, for its events are basically 'natural', even if in the realm of abnormal psychology.[13] Of 'Christabel', finally, if the date of that work is spring 1798, the poet's first later relevant comment was that it was 'in direct opposition to the very purpose for which the *Lyrical Ballads* were published', that purpose being 'an experiment to see how far those passions, which alone give any value to extraordinary Incidents, were capable of interesting, in & for themselves, in the incidents of common Life' – nearly as Wordsworth was then describing the matter in the Preface.[14] Coleridge does not appear to be aiming at great exactitude in his phrasing here, but if a distinction is being implied between 'written' and 'published', the question arises of why he later said that this very volume came into being (regardless of Wordsworth's 'presentation') as the result of a joint plan that fits the volume, in terms of our common thinking about it, quite neatly? If no such distinction is intended, it is strange that he should have expended such poetic energy at this time towards an object contrary in purpose to the book on which he and his friend were at work.

Coleridge's other poems of the spring (some of them plainly written with an eye towards the *Morning Post*, some most probably not) are distinguished from those just discussed at the outset by the fact that most of them can be dated with some certainty. As readily remarkable is their decidedly diverse range of style and tone. They include: his inconsequential compliment in five-line stanzas, 'To a Young Lady . . . on Her Recovery from a Fever'; his 'Circassian' transformation of schoolboy octosyllabics of Wordsworth's into 'Lewti'; his lengthy blank verse meditation 'Fears in Solitude' (dated on the same day that Wordsworth began the radical 'Peter Bell'); the shorter, beautiful blank verse meditation 'The Nightingale'; possibly also some work towards the political satire 'Recantation', a product of the same political climate that produced 'Fears in Solitude'. One could hardly maintain that Wordsworth's 'Lines Written in Early Spring' and 'Goody Blake and Harry Gill' present an identical functioning of tone, diction, and rhetoric, but the production of the older man during this period in any case shows a distinct homogeneity when compared to that of Coleridge.

The first two allusions by either poet to an effort to present the world with a joint volume are both made by Coleridge in late May or early June 1798, after Cottle had departed from Alfoxden with 'The Ancient Mariner' and most of Wordsworth's contributions to the project. One is in a letter from Coleridge to Cottle: 'We deem that the volumes offered to you are to a certain degree *one work, in kind tho' not in degree,* as an Ode is one work – & that our different poems are as stanzas, good relatively rather than absolutely : – Mark you, I say *in kind* tho' not in degree.'[15] The terms he employs are poetic rather than analytic. His figure of speech perhaps expresses the mutual confidence of each poet in the congruence of his thought and aims with the other's, or their mutual fears about their appearance before the public in such a pronounced attempt at financial profit, or perhaps their pleasure in having succeeded at discovering a practical means (not necessarily long before) of creating a literary monument to their friendship – an object in which previously they had, even if good-humouredly, failed – but they offer little distinct indication either of a deliberate joint plan, or the aesthetics of such a plan.

Another comment by Coleridge, made within a few days of this one, during his and Hazlitt's walking trip to Linton (see Hazlitt's description in *My First Acquaintance with Poets*), is much clearer: 'He said the *Lyrical Ballads* were an experiment about to be tried by him and Wordsworth, to see how far the public taste would endure poetry written in a more natural and simple style than had hitherto been attempted; totally discarding the artifices of poetic diction, and making use only of such words as had probably been common in the most ordinary language since the days of Henry II.' Hazlitt's memory was possibly coloured by later comments by both poets, and his recollection does not constitute a solid enough basis for extended discussion from an aesthetic standpoint; but it can be observed that subject matter is not referred to at all, and that the view of style and language expressed comes extremely close indeed to the manner in which Coleridge much later stated – how carefully is not clear – that his friend had 'presented' the volume. As far as Coleridge's poems are concerned, 'The Foster-mother's Tale' and 'The Dungeon', both excerpts from the earlier *Osorio*, are in blank verse not remarkably plainer than 'hitherto attempted'. The blank verse of 'The Nightingale' develops in the easy meditative style which Coleridge had mastered by the end of 1795. If 'Lewti' was ever intended to represent an effort at conscious simplicity, it fails conspicuously at that goal. In fact, 'The Ancient Mariner' seems the only one of Coleridge's contributions written with self-conscious linguistic objectives; and although the language of the poem is defended in the 'Advertisement', Coleridge was to make great numbers of changes in just this regard, especially by modernizing the original version's numerous archaisms, in the 1800 edition. 'The Ancient Mariner', then, appears the single work of Coleridge's in the volume even part of the composition of which could have been governed by the conception of an 'experiment' of the sort he described to Hazlitt. By 1800, however, what he says of the experimental purpose of the volume is oriented, as already noted, towards the 'passions' dealt with in the poems; and his future remarks avoid association of himself in partnership with any of Wordsworth's early linguistic views.

Joseph Cottle, finally, makes a well-known statement that the format of *Lyrical Ballads* was determined during his visit of late May. His phrasing regarding the solution then of the problems of whether two volumes rather than one should be published and of whether 'The Ancient Mariner' was to be included remains, to say the least, ambiguous, and the letter already mentioned from Coleridge to the publisher indicates that the mind of at least the latter had not in fact been resolved in this respect when he departed, his statements to the contrary notwithstanding. Coleridge remarks that he hopes for an early opportunity to come and 'reason with' Cottle on these subjects. The poet himself still speaks of 'the volumes' rather than a single volume.[16]

Plans on plans were rolling over in the mind of the arch-planner Coleridge during that spring. His letters show his concern with the problem of obtaining money for the German trip.

He had been much occupied rationally and emotionally during the late winter with helping Wordsworth form plans ('I believe partly suggested by me' was his modest later recollection) for the work that had succeeded his own 'Brook', *The Recluse*; Wordsworth's shorter poems were always, to his mind, objects of inferior significance, and the efforts that went into them expended in neglect of the philosophical poem in which he felt such a strong proprietary interest.[17] And plans for a joint volume had, of course, been talked over the previous autumn. Although certainties are impossible, it seems reasonable to suggest that the idea of such a venture probably lay dormant until around early March, but that near the latter date some renewed talk, now enriched by current or recent discussion of various philosophical principles concerning a similar volume may well have arisen again in the poets' conversation. To understand the events of the future it is necessary to observe, however, that the plain indication of the available facts is that regardless of whatever exact artistic orientations may have influenced any example or aspect of the work of each from March on, Coleridge's preoccupation with such matters during this period, and his feeling of their importance to him in any respect other than financial, were weak and ill-defined compared to Wordsworth's. There is in fact no sign that a lasting plan for a truly joint volume with such exact goals as both later described was for any length of time a powerful motivating principle in the consciousness of either; whereas certain far from indistinct aesthetic aims of intense personal meaning (whatever the catalyst that precipitated their birth) undoubtedly formed a motion and spirit impelling the objects of Wordsworth's own poetic thought. His present composition, in turn, produced his first significant lyrical poems; its purposes were, furthermore, responsible for all but two of the really important works in the volume that was finally published.

Despite the certain cheerfulness of the poets in response to the actuality of publication, the fact is that *Lyrical Ballads* as it appeared in the late summer was the upshot of a late decision among a variety of choices that they had been exploring. The bulk of the contents were the older poet's and written in pursuit of the strongly-felt goals that had prompted virtually all, if not, indeed, all, of his work of the spring. Wordsworth was thus stating in 1800 what would have appeared – and was – only a plain fact in his remark that Coleridge's contributions represented 'the assistance of a friend'. Both men were nonetheless increasingly to understand the degree to which the volume and Wordsworth's efforts to explain it marked a watershed in the history of their own relationship and the history of English poetry. Their later comments reflect a growing assumption, conscious or unconscious, that the extent of the meaning of the volume in terms of the full range of preoccupations occupying their thoughts while it had been produced over-rode the necessity – or possibility – of exactness about the precise factual details of its birth.

Whether Wordsworth wrote the early theoretical explanations of the volume willingly is uncertain; he in fact later repeatedly made such complaints, as Professor Griggs has noted, as that the Preface was written 'at the request of Mr Coleridge out of sheer good nature' or 'solely' to gratify Coleridge.[18] Entering, briefly in 1798 and then at length in 1800, on his task of explaining the aesthetic bases of the poems, Wordsworth, who was never comfortable in direct philosophical discourse anyhow, attempted to define what seemed the basic elements in his own 'plan', simply because it had been, even if no doubt logically incomplete in some respects, the only plan effectually operative in the production of most of the volume which he was describing. His imperfections as a handler of dialectical nuance now and later prevented his elaboration of a completely integrated and cohesive description of the poems. Increasingly aware, however, of the importance of the poems themselves, the commencement of his own mature lyrical career, as a focal point in the development of modern verse, and bearing the burden of the attack on a theory which he had perhaps not been especially anxious in the first place to define exactly, he never thought of altering the too minute principles he had laboriously set forth.

On the other hand, later remarks show his growing willingness, especially as self-justification becomes a less urgent requirement, to acknowledge at least indirectly the abiding truth that regardless of immediate details, Coleridge had been in emotional and intellectual respects without number as much a partner and a guide in the first *Lyrical Ballads* as if he had deliberately written fully half of its poems. As early as 1805, when Wordsworth speaks in *The Prelude* of Coleridge's early recitations of 'The Ancient Mariner' and 'Christabel' 'on Quantock's grassy hills', he describes himself in an ambiguous but cordial phrase as 'associate with such labour' (xiii, ll. 393–9). Mary Wordsworth, addressing, probably, Sara Hutchinson, tells something of the feelings of her household on 29 September 1814: 'Mary [Monkhouse Hutchinson] says that one of your vols I of the Lyrical Ballads is lost – I am grieved at this for your dress copy is now the only one that is amongst us – which is a shame. We shall have no copy of Coleridge's share of these Pomes [*sic*].'[19] At the conclusion of the 1815 Preface Wordsworth expresses his regret for the 'necessity of separating [his] compositions from some beautiful Poems' of Coleridge's with which they had 'long been associated in publication'. He does not speak directly of a plan, but goes on to remark that the 'feelings with which that joint publication was made, have been gratified'. In 1836 – two years following Coleridge's death – he was compressing various events not closely related into a suggestion of extended co-operation towards a somewhat carefully projected joint volume: '['The Ancient Mariner'] was to have been a joint work,' Crabb Robinson records from comments of the poet. 'But Wordsworth left the execution to Coleridge after [making various suggestions] . . . Wordsworth at the same time wrote many of his *Lyrical Ballads* – Coleridge wrote the first four lines of 'We are Seven'.[20] By the early 1840s Wordsworth, in the Fenwick note on 'We Are Seven', was finally speaking of, and confirming (if not in exact detail) the existence of the joint plan of which 'Mr Coleridge has told the world'.

The role of business assistant, secretary, and minor contributor to *Lyrical Ballads* would not at first have seemed a particularly inappropriate one, at any level of consciousness whatever, to Coleridge, whose real interests in the volume were at the outset of a different quality entirely from Wordsworth's. The primary labour of the composition of the poems and the writings of the theory were in fact mostly the older poet's. Confident enough in the main, about 1800, of the congruence of his and his friend's thought and feeling, the younger man, with his personal views not well defined, could unhesitatingly endorse Wordsworth's opinions as his own. But Coleridge was a committed philosopher,

and continually, seriously interested in many ways that Wordsworth was not in the theory and practice of every aspect of the
creative process; he was to become increasingly aware of failures
in sympathy on the part of Wordsworth as his own needs for
that sympathy took on greater urgency, to become increasingly
curious about the details of Wordsworth's theoretical proposi-
tions, and like his friend to become increasingly aware of the
historical importance of *Lyrical Ballads*. He thus grew conscious
much earlier than Wordsworth of the extent to which the Preface – and the volume as well – had been in fact (details of
actual writing again aside) 'half a child of [his] own Brain,'[21] and
he grew – altogether justly – anxious to be given his share in the
achievement, to define the divisive issues that, formerly little
noticed if at all, had lain nascent in *Lyrical Ballads* and its
theories. His recollection of argument and disagreement from
the early days of the companionship becomes more and more
certain with the passage of years. In 1802 he and Wordsworth
were just 'beginning' to suspect a radical difference in their
opinions. By 1811 he was pondering writing a preface 'relative to
the principles of Poetry, which I have ever held'. By 1815 he was
claiming only to be doing his duty, in the MS. of *Biographia
Literaria*, in 'compleatly subverting the Theory'. More important,
the publication of *Biographia Literaria* in 1817 made known for
the first time his recollection of the 'plan' which contemporary
facts appear to confirm, at least in the manner he described it,
to so small a degree. To the latter year belongs also his remark,
noted above, that he had been 'far more alive' than Wordsworth's detractors 'to the faults and defects' of his poetry 'even
from the first publication of the Lyrical Ballads – tho' for a long
course of years my opinions were sacred to his own ear'.[22]

While the plan of which both spoke in their later lives could
hardly have been a major force in the production of the small
volume that was to have such effect on our literary history,
neither man's memory could help being influenced by the metaphoric appropriateness of such a description for the pivotal
achievement which it represented. For if their recollections tend
to confuse or mis-emphasize precise details, they nevertheless represent an acknowledgment, however indirect, by both poets that
the primary source of *Lyrical Ballads* and all that it later came

to mean was the complete physical, emotional, and spiritual context of those splendid thirteen months that began in early June, 1797, when Coleridge leaped over the gate to greet his friends at Racedown.

SOURCE : *University of Toronto Quarterly*, xxxiv, No. 3 (April 1965).

NOTES

1. Stephen M. Parrish, 'The Wordsworth-Coleridge Controversy', *PMLA*, LXXIII (1958) 367–74; Parrish, 'Dramatic Technique in the *Lyrical Ballads*,' *PMLA*, LXXIV (1959) 85–98; A. M. Buchan, 'The Influence of Wordsworth on Coleridge (1795–1800)', *UTQ*, XXXII (1963) 346–66 (see pp. 136–59 below); *Early Letters of William and Dorothy Wordsworth*, ed. Ernest de Selincourt (Oxford, 1935), p. 191.

2. *Collected Letters of Samuel Taylor Coleridge,* ed. E. L. Griggs (Oxford, 1956–71) IV 780.

3. Coleridge, *Letters,* I 627; II 830.

4. *Early Letters,* 191, 192. *Biographia Literaria,* ed. J. Shawcross (Oxford, 1958) II 6.

5. Coleridge, *Letters,* I 658.

6. Christopher Wordsworth, *Social Life at the English Universities* (Cambridge, 1874) p. 589.

7. Buchan, p. 347 (see p. 137 below).

8. *Early Letters,* p. 174.

9. Coleridge, *Letters,* I 368–9, 383–5; *Early Letters,* pp. 188, 190.

10. A detailed analysis of the chronological evidence about Wordsworth's poetic production of the first two months of 1798 is beyond the limits of this paper. Suffice it to say that the MSS. that can be conjectured to have received Wordsworth's attention between 'A Night Piece' (probably January 25 1798) and March 5, when Dorothy began an extensive copy of parts of 'The Ruined Cottage' in a letter to Mary Hutchinson, include only the Alfoxden and Christabel Notebooks (see *The Prelude,* ed. Ernest de Selincourt and Helen Darbishire (Oxford, 1959) xxv–xxvii) and 'The Ruined Cottage' MS. B. In the Alfoxden NB, all work preceding the drafts on 'The Thorn' (probably begun 19 March) is in blank verse; and while placement in a NB is not always reliable evidence in dating Wordsworth MSS., the appearance of the entries and the fact that work on 'Night Piece' (indicated by a stub; not mentioned *Pre-*

lude) and 'Ruined Cottage' work definitely preceding the March 5 letter are among them tend to place this work before March 5. The only 'Christabel' Notebook work that can in fact be shown definitely to belong to the Alfoxden period at all is composition toward 'The Ruined Cottage' that precedes the March 5 letter. (I am grateful to the Trustees of Dove Cottage for permitting me to examine the MSS. in question.)

De Selincourt (*Prelude*, p. xlvi) suggests that even the revision of 'The Old Cumberland Beggar' that appears in the Alfoxden NB is toward 'The Recluse', but this conjecture seems somewhat doubtful.

11. Coleridge, *Letters*, I 399–400.

12. *Early Letters*, p. 190.

13. *Early Letters*, pp. 167–8. (De Selincourt does not note that Wordsworth's 'June 5th' is an impossible date for the Sunday on which he was writing.) Racedown Notebook, Dove Cottage Papers; see the spring entries of Dorothy Wordsworth's *Journal* and Mary Moorman, *William Wordsworth, A Biography, The Early Years* (Oxford, 1957) pp. 389–90; Ernest de Selincourt, *The Early Wordsworth* (Oxford, 1936) p. 28.

14. Coleridge, *Letters*, I 631.

15. Coleridge, *Letters*, I 412.

16. Joseph Cottle, *Reminiscences of Samuel Taylor Coleridge and Robert Southey* (London, 1848) pp. 178–80.

17. *Specimens of the Table Talk of the Late Samuel Taylor Coleridge*, ed. H. N. Coleridge (London, 1835) II 70–1; *Biographia Literaria*, I 128–9; Wordsworth, *The River Duddon*, Fenwick note; Coleridge, *Letters*, I 527.

18. MS. comments by Wordsworth in Barron Field's 'Memoirs of Wordsworth', B.M. Add. MS. 41,325; *The Letters of William and Dorothy Wordsworth, The Later Years*, ed. Ernest de Selincourt, III 1248–9. See *The Later Years*, I 537; II 910; also Coleridge, *Letters*, I 628n.

19. *The Letters of Mary Wordsworth 1800–55*, ed. Mary E. Burton (Oxford, 1958) p. 15.

20. *Henry Crabb Robinson on Books and their Writers*, ed. E. J. Morley (London, 1938) II 481.

21. Coleridge, *Letters*, II 830.

22. Coleridge, *Letters*, II 812; III 324; IV 579, 780.

A. M. Buchan

THE INFLUENCE OF WORDSWORTH ON COLERIDGE, 1795-1800 (1963)

Some time in the autumn of 1795 Wordsworth and Coleridge met, apparently for the first time, in Bristol. Both young men were at a parting of the ways. Wordsworth was in happier mood than he had been in almost two years, because he had come to Bristol to take occupancy of Racedown in Dorset as a free gift from a friend, John Pinney, and saw an end to his aimless, jobless wandering. Coleridge was sadly breaking away from the illusion of the Susquehanna and from Southey and was preparing for his marriage to Sara Fricker. While they were together in town, Southey was still on friendly terms, Wordsworth acknowledging his contribution of the best two lines of a piece of translation from Juvenal,[1] but the rift was opening and by November Southey set sail for Lisbon. The three men talked, as was inevitable, about their common interest in writing, and Wordsworth, on the lookout for a publisher for some recent verses, was introduced to Joseph Cottle.

To Racedown, therefore, after the visiting B.A. of St John's, Cambridge, as he had pompously signed himself in the quarto editions of *The Evening Walk* and *Descriptive Sketches*, there went from the always generous and vain publisher a copy of Southey's *Joan of Arc*. As Wordsworth read the Preface, he had the impression that the author was a 'coxcomb'.[2] A little later, he received a copy of Coleridge's *Poems*, issued in April of 1796. For Cottle's approval he had a fair copy made of 'Guilt and Sorrow, or Incidents upon Salisbury Plain', a new kind of poetry he had been experimenting with, and Coleridge, though he was busy and despondent winding up the affairs of *The Watchman*, found leisure at Cottle's request for a careful editorial job of interleaving the manuscript and jotting down his comments on it. He was already familiar with *The Evening Walk*, and probably also the *Descriptive Sketches*, and he had quoted a phrase and inserted a footnote in the *Poems* referring to Wordsworth as: '. . . a Poet, whose versification is occasionally harsh and his diction too frequently obscure, but whom I deem unrivalled among the writers of the present day in manly sentiment, novel imagery, and vivid colouring.'[3] The claim that Wordsworth was the best poet of his age was repeated in a letter to John Thelwall, although Wordsworth's comment on Coleridge's *Poems* was a back-handed one in which he praised two short passages in the 'Religious Musings' as being worth all the rest of the volume.[4]

In this first encounter may be traced, lightly as yet but with a firm and clear outline by and by, every characteristic of the relationship between the two poets: Wordsworth, so absorbed in his own dream of poetic fame as to pass over with the hint of a compliment the hard-wrought accomplishment of his friend; Coleridge, in need of comfort and another man to worship, laying himself prostrate before one more assured in his priestlike ways and aims than he. The northern man, tossed between blind faith in himself and twinges of a true humility, asking somebody else's approval to back his own high judgement of his work. The more volatile Coleridge, convinced of his own insight and yet always unsure of the next step, looking for security where it was least to be found in a place other than his own mind. Wordsworth, the single-thoughted follower of a path he chose early and trod all his days; Coleridge, lured along many paths and yet always ready to open one up, with interest and labour, for a colleague.

It is still hard to guess why Coleridge, from reading Wordsworth's early works, came to the opinion that his as yet little-known partner in writing had the makings of a great poet. *The Evening Walk*, in the rhymed heroics that both men came to detest, was little more than an exercise in the sentimental, bucolic manner of James Thomson. A cock, a swan, and the shades of evening furnished the local and conventionally decorative colour required for a fashionable excursion in the picturesque, and the old female beggar with her children asked for the sympathy with the poor and downtrodden that Wordsworth was to elevate afterwards into a philosophy of the worth of rustic life. As yet, how-

ever, it was a young man's remote and superior feeling for the
'wretched many' about whom Coleridge, too, lamented in
'Religious Musings'. A similar and equally experimental liking
for the picturesque accompanied Wordsworth through the
Descriptive Sketches, and neither the lakes of Switzerland nor
the Simplon, as he described them for his walking companion,
Robert Jones, awakened in him more than the startled outcry
of the tourist. Through this poem, it is true, ran a clear thread
of Rousseauite doctrine woven of simpler words than Coleridge
had found for it in his verses. The difference may be noticed in
two brief passages, Wordsworth's an English version of
Rousseau's opening thought in the *Contrat Social*,

> One man entirely free, alone and wild,
>   Was bless'd as free – for he was Nature's child.[5]

The thought is Rousseau's, the simple melodious lines are Wordsworth's own. This sort of plain statement of a great truism always baffled Coleridge, as his version in the 'Musings' showed :

> In the primeval age a dateless while
> The vacant shepherd wander'd with his flock,
> Pitching his tent where'er the green grass waved.[6]

Try as he might, Coleridge was unable to record effectively
in verse the kind of spiritual commonplace that surprised Wordsworth into his finest passages of poetry, perhaps because he
was by nature incapable of seeing a spiritual belief bare of its
many and harsh complexities. If Wordsworth was aware of
them, the knowledge did not hamper the lucid flow of his line, as
his friend could not help perceiving.

Through the merely picturesque, too, of the Wordsworth
poems Coleridge might have noticed a quality in the man that he
came to envy even when he argued against its dominance. The
cock and the swan described by the country poet were sugared
over with the epithets of *The Seasons*, but underneath the diction
lay, even as early as this in Wordsworth's career, a vivid sense
of the creature outside him. The animal was a real animal and
no mere symbol for a notion in his mind. The old beggar woman
whose children played with the glowworms

> . . . while on the ground
> Small circles of green radiance gleam around

was a real beggar and not one of the old women of the 'Musings' :

> O aged Women! ye who weekly catch
> The morsel tossed by law-forced charity
> And die so slowly, none call it murder.

In Wordsworth he found a mind much closer than his own to the brute facts of the earth around. For himself this hard, resistless world of things was only too often an intrusion on the world he preferred, a world of image and idea that made of the objects of experience only symbols to express its own meaning. In this inner world Wordsworth, too, could walk with some confidence but often with a distrust of its insubstantiality. Traditional as the couplets of *The Evening Walk* might be, they held a word-substance descriptive of places and things that the poet knew well. Though the two poems were almost equally redolent of a young man's desire that Freedom should conquer Avarice, Pride, Oppression, Ambition, and all the other personified evils of the new political doctrine, *Descriptive Sketches* had behind it, as Coleridge's poem did not, an actual tour through France, Switzerland, and Italy, and the facts spoke through the conventional diction their own clear and definite message.

This concreteness of impression and free movement of lines of verse were still more marked in the 'Guilt and Sorrow' on which Coleridge made editorial comments for his friend. As Herbert Read has pointed out, Wordsworth had already in his new kind of composition moved away from the artificial manner of the earlier publications. The language was occasionally 'simple to the verge of triteness',[7] and by this almost casual ordering of common words the feelings of simple folk, also trite and a trifle dull, were in a strange way effectively conveyed. The author was in the presence of 'flesh and blood', and yet he was able to suggest, if he could not in this simple speech completely express, attitudes towards life and its experiences that seemed to be of great significance. He was, in fact, though a 'Republican and at least a semi-Atheist',[8] as Coleridge described him to Thelwall, successfully producing the kind of metaphysical poetry which Coleridge had tried in the *Musings* but with far less success.

For the author of the *Musings*, then, with his innate belief in the immediate relationship between the work and the man, the

conclusion was unavoidable. Such a writer as Wordsworth must
be a person of sterling worth and everything he did must partake
of the excellence beginning to appear, if only fragmentarily, in his
verse. It is this type of reverence that glowed through every comment he made about Wordsworth as he induced him to leave
Racedown and take over Alfoxden near his own cottage in
Nether Stowey. They had met again, after a long separation, in
Bristol or Nether Stowey. The idyll of Coleridge's stay in a cottage was harshly interrupted by a recurrence of Lloyd's epilepsy,
seizure upon seizure followed by delirious intervals that always
preyed on Coleridge's own fears. Lloyd had to be moved to town,
and there, probably, with Poole along to help care for the frac-
tious patient, the two poets came together. Talking to Wordsworth helped to relieve the misery and kindled again the hopes
of poetic fame that always went glimmering when anxieties
pressed too hard. So, two months later, Coleridge, who was busily
at work on the play *Osorio*, took the unfinished manuscript over
to Racedown to read it to William and Dorothy, and his letter
of ecstatic praise of his hosts, written to Cottle in Bristol, has
become a classic:

Wordsworth admires my Tragedy – which gives me great hopes.
Wordsworth has written a Tragedy himself. I speak with heart-felt
sincerity & (I think) unblinded judgment, when I tell you, that I
feel myself *a little man by his* side; & yet do not think myself the
less man, than I formerly thought myself. – His Drama is absolutely
wonderful. You know, I do not commonly speak in such abrupt &
unmingled phrases – & therefore will the more readily believe me . . .
in Wordsworth there are no *inequalities*. T. Poole's opinion of
Wordsworth is – that he is the greatest Man, he ever knew – I coincide.[9]

Such ardour of language is for everybody except the user one of
hyperbole. One doubts, indeed, whether the level-headed Tom
Poole ever remarked that Wordsworth was the greatest man
he ever knew; if he did, he recovered rapidly from his illusion.
Coleridge would settle for nothing less than to bring the two
Wordsworths to Nether Stowey, and, through the practical efforts
of Poole, to have them occupy the gentleman's seat of Alfoxden
three miles away. In a letter to Southey announcing their arrival,
the same abundance of superlatives brimmed over:

Wordsworth is a very great man – the only man, to whom *at all times* & in *all modes of excellence* I feel myself inferior – the only one, I mean, whom *I have yet met with* – for the London Literati appear to me to be very much like little Potatoes – i.e. *no great Things* – a compost of Nullity & Dullity. –[10]

Even those who are willing to accept Wordsworth's greatness as a poet and his essential integrity as a man – in spite of his difficulties with Annette Vallon and his sister – must recognize that praise of this sort is not given to a man but to an idea of a man built up in another's mind. It is an emotion akin to the young man's feeling that his is the only girl, or to the parent's for a child, or to the child's – and this is the essence of Coleridge's situation – for a father. It sets the one person apart from all other human beings, not because he is a perfect creature, but because he satisfies in some way a passionate need in the one who loves and admires him to this extent.

What has to be asked, therefore, is not so much the factual question as to whether Wordsworth really was the great man of Coleridge's eulogies, but what were the needs in Coleridge that Wordsworth by his presence during the months around Stowey satisfied in his admiring friend and neighbour. The others who lived there and who came to visit were not overcome with admiration of the taciturn poet and his wild-eyed and devoted sister. Southey and Wordsworth were slow to make friends, even after they came to live as neighbours in the Lake Country. Very soon Poole began to caution Coleridge against his reverence, and Cottle's welcome to the northern visitor lacked the heartiness he had shown towards his earlier poetical protégés. Even Coleridge himself, under the different circumstances of the trip to Germany, learned that it might be convenient and not too restrictive to be separated from his less sociable companions. As he contemplated his return to England, it was to Poole he wanted to flee rather than to go north with the Wordsworths. How was it, then, that for this moment he discovered in William and Dorothy a comfort that he needed and to which he paid tribute in glowing words of adulation?

It is not enough to respect, with M. Légouis, the 'self-denying anxiety of Coleridge to undeceive his own admirers and to make them bow down like himself before the great man he had discovered.'[11] This submission, as much as any other circumstance, may be in part responsible for the waywardness of his future career and his abandonment of poetry. By sheer mischance or perhaps the fatality of his temperament, he discovered and clung to the man who, at the most critical moment of his life as he embarked on a course of his own, had the ability to offer competition in the one activity in which both were beginning to excel. Yet the stranger was too self-absorbed to be able to reciprocate in that mood of faith and encouragement of which Coleridge was so lavish and Wordsworth so penurious. In the language of the psychiatrist, Coleridge had attracted to himself a 'father' against whom it was dangerous to compete, and his besetting weakness, to turn his back on the prospect of success, found in William Wordsworth its most effective stimulant. The acolyte might not be in competition with his god.

After the fiasco of the year 1796, with the failure of *The Watchman*, the break with Southey, and marriage to Sara, he found in Tom Poole the kind of friend and companion he needed. From their first meeting Poole had faith in his protégé's genius and realized that for its development some protective shelter from the pressures of ordinary life might be necessary for a while. With his friend in the Stowey cottage, this shelter could be readily and unobtrusively provided – a few friends for Sara, too, so she would not be a burden on her husband, the provision of food and the daily needs, quietness in which writing could be carried on, and a willing audience to the talk in which Coleridge unburdened and shaped his conceptions. With uncanny shrewdness Poole furnished all these and more, though with never a hint of rivalry in the area of mental activity that he wanted his guest to cultivate. He saw in him that combination of thought and poetic fire that together might produce works in which great human truths would in course of time find a fit and powerful expression. While he might not have thought of it in precisely these terms, he was offering his young visitor the opportunity that Milton had chosen during the Horton years to read and meditate in preparation for great writing to come.

Unhappily, a year before, Coleridge had met a man who was already moving successfully in the direction he wanted to take, and the chance meeting in Bristol in March of 1796 put him in touch with William Wordsworth again. Here was a being a little lower than the angels who had made his choice of the truths he wanted to proclaim, such as the flight from political theory and its elysiums back to the common heart of man, the certitude of a vision of truth gained in solitude and exemplified in the common incidents of every day. In this direction Coleridge himself had been turning as more and more the shifts in international affairs and his own inner struggle with the creeds made him unhappy about France and England and Godwin and Hartley and the Church Establishment. By the merest chance or fatality he discovered in Wordsworth a person who had taken the same journey and felt he had devised a way out. Not only a way and a goal but also a form of simple poetic utterance new to this kind of investigation, couched in deceptively common words and unadorned with the familiar trappings of verse. With such a poet moving confidently towards the consideration of man, nature, and the soul, why need he compete?

He recognized, too, the superior advantages of his new companion. Though he was not by nature a stable individual, Wordsworth's quiet, inexpressive manner effectively concealed from most of his intimates the fires banked within, and they saw in him a rock of strength and purpose. Because he was recovering from his love for a French girl whom he could not marry and had an admiring sister to care for his daily needs, he was free to devote himself with a whole heart to the career of thought and poetry he desired. While not asking for too much, he had been blessed with things coming his way, a gift of money from Raisley Calvert and a temporary gift of a house at Racedown. He was in possession of that 'unanxious seclusion' which Coleridge continued to long for, in vain, as a necessary provision for his best work. With a different temperament and the burden on his shoulders that it had created, Coleridge had largely separated himself from peace of mind and ease of circumstance. Because he had spent money unwisely in college and had suffered for his extravagance, he was inordinately sensitive to the need for money and would yet spend it heedlessly when he had it. The bare, self-denying provision that Dorothy made for her brother would not have long contented Coleridge who, as he confessed to Sara, had a liking for good food, pleasant company, and the niceties of living.[12]

During his troubles in 1795, friends and relatives had been generous with their help, but being in debt had become such a habit with him that money he received was usually spent in meeting old obligations, and the need for more haunted him daily. As steadily oppressive as any other load was the presence of Sara and their first child, Hartley. In his expansive way he loved both of them, having laid aside for the time being the suspicion that he and Sara had been dragooned into a marriage, but he could expect no sympathy in Sara for his poetic aspirations if there was no income, and in his moods of depression he saw her and the child staring at him with accusing eyes for his lack of practical sense. For more than a year before he came to Stowey he had felt driven by fate and his own temperament, beating always into the east wind of calamity, while his more manly friend and poetic companion, after a year or two of love, regret, and wandering, seemed to have landed in a secure haven.

What he needed and was beginning to find alongside Tom Poole was a sense of 'family', a house to go to in which he would be made welcome and a more experienced man than himself to handle his affairs. The frequency of his dreams about Christ's Hospital indicated the loneliness and terror he had suffered while living there. He and his brothers were strangers to one another in spite of their practical willingness to aid him. During the trouble in Cambridge they had done their utmost to meet his debts but had disturbed him dreadfully by the suggestion that he must be mad to have done as he did. The breach was widened by the emigration scheme which they took as a sign that he belonged to the odious class of democrats and repudiated the conventional religious and social position on which the family prided itself. He willingly forgot to communicate with his brothers and visited them and his mother only as a duty. At Poole's request he would send his brothers a letter and he accepted Cottle's proposal to dedicate the second edition of his *Poems* to George, but a note he attached to a copy of the volume tells how the honour was received:

If this volume should ever be delivered according to its direction, i.e. to Posterity, let it be known that the Reverend George Coleridge was displeased and thought his character endangered by the Dedication.[13]

His way and his brothers' ran widely apart, and the account of the relationship which he gave soon after his return from Germany revealed what his feelings had been for a number of years:

I have three Brothers/ that is to say, Relations by Gore – two are Parsons and one is a Colonel – George and the Colonel good men as times go – very good men; but, alas! we have neither Tastes or feelings in common.[14]

In his restless wanderings from place to place, he searched for a home and a father, deluding himself now and then that he had found what he sought, as in the Evans home when he was an undergraduate. He came close to his desire in the months at Stowey where he could depend on Poole without thinking of him as a rival. And then Wordsworth came, offering in his simple, happy housekeeping at Racedown and Alfoxden another vision of home, but one from which Coleridge was excluded by almost every circumstance of his married life.

However this need may be interpreted, it was through its lens that Coleridge viewed Wordsworth and saw him magnified. For some time he saw everything about his new associate in larger than human dimensions. *The Borderers* was 'absolutely wonderful' and contained 'those *profound* touches of the human heart, which I find three or four times in "The Robbers" of Schiller, & often in Shakespeare'. Some early lines of blank verse were transcribed for Mr Estlin as sure to please. Dorothy was his idol's 'exquisite Sister', worthy of lines written about Joan of Arc, a woman of perfect taste and sensitiveness.[15] Compared with this unprepossessing young man from the north the men of letters in London were 'no great things'. Among the chief benefits of the Wedgwood annuity was the opportunity it gave to spend the spring and summer with the Wordsworths, and clear through the spring and summer the worshipful attitude persisted:

– The Giant Wordsworth – God love him! even when I speak in the terms due to his intellect, I fear lest tho[se] terms should keep out of sight the amiableness of his manners – he has written near 1200 lines of blank verse, superior, I hesitate not to aver, to any thing in our language which any way resembles it. Poole . . . thinks of it as likely to benefit mankind much more than any thing Wordsworth has yet written –[16]

A plan was formed for Cottle to publish *Osorio* and *The Borderers* together, and, though it was cancelled when a high enough price was not available, it brought the publisher a letter comparing the two dramas: 'My tragedy employed and strained all my thoughts and faculties for six or seven months: Wordsworth consumed far more time, and far more thought, and far more genius.'[17] When the expiry of the lease of Alfoxden came around and William and Dorothy were threatened with eviction, Coleridge lamented their going as a major disaster:

. . . whether we shall be able to procure him a house and furniture near Stowey, we know not, and yet we must : for the hills, and the woods, and the streams, and the sea, and the shores would break forth into reproaches against us, if we did not strain every nerve, to keep their Poet among them. Without joking, and in serious sadness, Poole and I cannot endure to think of losing him.[18]

Even if Wordsworth's religious views were unorthodox, he was a 'tried good man', with intellectual powers of which his friend stood in increasing awe as the months went by. No wonder that when the plan was mooted for an excursion into Germany, agreement was enthusiastic, and at the cost of leaving Sara at home with two children, one a four-month-old baby, Coleridge was not to be separated – not yet – from his god. No wonder that around this friendship grew the legend, fostered by the romantic imagination of a number of the people who saw it develop, of the immense benefit to both poets of their association together. As they looked back on this time from the chillier vantage-point of less loving years, memory bathed the scenery and the incidents in a magical mist.

For Wordsworth, undoubtedly, the stay in Alfoxden was the seedtime of his finest poetry. A sufficient time had elapsed for the memory of the year with Annette to become dim, the ardour of his attachment to cool, and the difficulties in the way of seeing her again to lessen his sense of remorse for having left her behind. Once again as in his adolescence, he could look around on the face of the countryside and recognize in the objects he saw, the sounds he heard, and the very motion of the air, a company less demanding than human nature and an agency of healing for his human hurt. After long uncertainty he had been persuaded by his own aimlessness and the encouragement of Dorothy to accept his poetic vocation, and she was as willing as he to put up with frugality and the disapproval of relatives as a small price to pay for freedom to think and write. Out of the turmoil of the years since he had left France he had won a position on which to stand; if certain moral questions had to be given up in despair, they could be examined again from a different viewpoint with some hope of comfort. From the wreckage of his revolutionary beliefs he had salvaged a trust in the goodness of the common man and a supposition that he began to put in practice in his verse that the speech of the common man might be a more appropriate language for the poet than the high-flown, gaudy phraseology that poets had borrowed from rhetoric and philosophy.

With Coleridge, too, as a magnet to attract visitors, he had an audience, few but fit. Tom Poole, though the owner and manager of his own tannery, was really a common man of the kind described in 'Michael',[19] so that his approval of *The Borderers* and the 'Female Vagrant' was a guarantee of their authenticity. There came also to Stowey the notorious John Thelwall, a democrat at odds with political theory and anxious to settle down; Charles Lamb, the London clerk with an uncanny instinct for the best in literature; Charles Lloyd, an unstable young man with a curious sentimental mind; Cottle, the worshipful publisher, who could be most helpful and generous in a pinch; and, in May of 1798, for a three-week visit, William Hazlitt, whose ardour for poetry, metaphysics and Coleridge, made him a stimulating, if unprepossessing, companion. Best of all was the adoring Coleridge, throwing out ideas with full hands and holding to a sublime faith in a poet's worth. Between the visits of friends and their ardent talk were the blessed hours of loneliness, with Dorothy alongside, in which to brood over the suggestion that Coleridge had made about a great poem on 'man, nature, and the human soul', in which he could leap across his recent troubles into the dear memories of his childhood. All around, reawakening the memories, were the trees and fields of Alfoxden, the combes and glens enclosing them, and within an hour's walk, the sea.

It ought to have been equally stimulating for Coleridge, but the circumstances played against him. By the time he brought the Wordsworth to Stowey, he seems to have pulled himself away from the dependence on laudanum that had coloured his mood during the pre-Stowey months in Bristol, but the origin of 'Kubla 'Khan'[20] and several flighty letters suggest that the drug was too ready a remedy for any ache or pain. Already he feared it and yet argued for its necessity. The life in a cottage, too, that had appeared so wonderful in prospect, was quite grim during the winter months. The small house was damp, so much so that Wordsworth came to be afraid for the safety of his few belongings stored there,[21] and its facilities too narrow and primitive for decent comfort. Sara, going about her housekeeping, and Hartley, the little boy, were always under foot, and Coleridge escaped from them as often as he could to Poole's windy parlour and then to the ample accommodation of Alfoxden. There seems little doubt that the writing of *Osorio* and the editorial work on the second edition of the *Poems* were largely done in Poole's house. The interval at first was fruitful and a change from the distractions of the town of Bristol but the chances against its continuing happy and productive were very great.

More depressing than the environment was his bitter acceptance of regret that the hope he had shared with Southey, when first they worked in Bristol, of making a name for himself as a poet and a living as a writer must now be given up. He had been despondent before he came to Stowey, having argued with Poole that he needed a more secure livelihood than writing provided:

. . . But literature, tho' I shall never abandon it, will always be a secondary Object with me – my poetic Vanity & my political Furore have been exhaled; and I would rather be an expert, self-maintaining Gardener than a Milton, if I could not unite both.[22]

In the shadow of Poole's faith in him, he pulled out of this dejected mood and was busily concentrating on the play for Sheridan when the Wordsworths arrived. Almost at once he had confirmation of what he had suspected since reading 'Guilt and Sorrow', that, in William Wordsworth he had met a man much more capable than he of doing what his own friends had encouraged him to do, write a grand philosophical poem embodying the new ferment of ideas stirred up by the startling events in the world around. This had been Poole's hope from the beginning of their friendship. Charles Lamb had written encouraging him to make a start, and he himself had believed that he might be able to do in the Miltonic manner what Southey could never do because he lacked the philosophic mind. The intimacy with Wordsworth effectively shattered this belief. As he walked and talked with William and Dorothy, he recognized how little he had of the single-track devotion to poetry that these two displayed. As he listened to his friend's brooding tones bring out the deep emotion that coursed through the simple language of the pieces that were to appear in the *Lyrical Ballads* and watched the agonies of his composition, he knew that his own efforts in this kind had been lightly experienced, made out of his head more than his heart, not poetry at all as Wordsworth tried to make it.

His own testimony was perfectly clear and honest, though it came after the trip to Germany reconciled him somewhat to the study of philosophy as a second-best. To Thelwall, who received many of his comments about his plans, he wrote : 'As to Poetry, I have altogèther abandoned it, being convinced that I never had the essentials of Poetic Genius, & that I mistook a strong desire for original power.'[23] Two days later, he gave Francis Wrangham, Wordsworth's former companion in London, the reason why :

As to our literary occupations they are still more distant than our residences – He is a great, a true Poet – I am only a kind of a Metaphysician. – He has even now sent off the last sheet of a second volume of his Lyrical Ballads.[24]

When the two volumes of this edition came out, Coleridge announced them to William Godwin and wrote his own poetic epitaph :

Have you seen the second volume of the Lyrical Ballads, & the Preface prefixed to the First? – I shall judge of a man's Heart, and Intellect, precisely according to the degree & intensity of the admiration, with which he read those Poems – . . . If I die, and the Booksellers will give you any thing for my Life, be sure to say – 'Wordsworth descended on him, like the Γνῶθι σεαυτόν from Heaven; by showing him what true Poetry was, he made him know, that he himself was no poet'.[25]

On the evidence, therefore, it seems that the familiar notion that the presence of the Wordsworths stimulated Coleridge to write poetry may have to be laid aside. As both of them recalled, they did much talking about the nature and purpose of poetry, and on their walks between Nether Stowey and Alfoxden they took notice of aspects of the moon, the trees, and the clouds which found their way into Dorothy's Journal and into the poetry of both men. If we may judge from the verse they wrote a little later, Wordsworth in Goslar and Coleridge in Greta Hall, they held a running debate on the influence of Nature on the human mind, Wordsworth insisting that good came to man through his senses and Coleridge arguing that 'we receive but what we give,' Nature itself being impersonal and the mind its own interpreter of the objects of earth. They were good company for one another, Wordsworth gratified to receive the homage of a fairly well-known writer and Coleridge at peace with himself, as far as it was possible, because he walked with a man stronger and more self-directed than he. But the poetry of both men had already been flowing from sources deeper than could be affected by their talk and argument and regular association.

Out of a common need for a sum of money they devised a plan, towards the end of 1797, for a partnership in composition similar to Coleridge's earlier co-operation with Southey, Lamb, and Charles Lloyd. Coleridge was always proposing plans of the sort calling for verse almost on demand, because he worked at one time with Southey who could turn out lines with a mechanical and appalling fluency. This time his partner in the enterprise of writing about John Cruikshank's dream backed away very soon, and Coleridge found himself under duress to do the piece alone. In a sense he was the natural choice for a ballad about a dream with a 'Gothic' strangeness to it. His *Osorio*, just about finished, was a Gothic play in character and incident, though he had tried '. . . to have few sentences which *might not* be spoken in conversation, avoiding those that are *commonly* used in conversations –'[26] tried, that is to say, on his own, to produce a dramatic speech as natural as Wordsworth's new diction in verse. Whether in preparation for his play or just as a check on it and a reviewing task, he had been reading Lewis's *Monk* and was due to read *The Castle Spectre* before 'The

Ancient Mariner' was completed. Southey was doing well for himself by writing ballads, and of a considerable number he turned out for the *Morning Post*, Coleridge had given approval to 'Rudiger' and 'Mary, the Maid of the Inn', chiefly because the diction was colloquial.[27] A ballad had the appearance of being a simple, straightforward piece of narrative uncluttered with 'lofty thoughts' and making one prime demand on its writer that the incidents be made to appear credible and the sentiments natural.

What Coleridge overlooked in his willingness to publish something alongside the verses of Wordsworth was that, as soon as he forgot lofty and abstract thoughts and relied on the free run of reverie, the objects he wrote about were no longer, for him, the simple materials of narrative but highly explosive symbols arising from deep in his mind. It was hardly possible for him to compose a ballad in Southey's efficient and rather offhand manner as an exercise in verse précis faithful to incidents of a tale read or heard about. The realm of strange occurrences to which the dream of the spectre-ship belonged already occupied a congenial part of his own mind, where each object and act and incident had gathered to itself colour and meaning as remote from the original story as his mind was different from Cruickshank's or from Wordsworth's. After his youthful experimentation, Wordsworth was now able to look around on sea or land and 'add' the gleam which was his interpretation of what he saw. In this kind of fanciful exercise Coleridge saw less clearly than his friend, and the 'moral' he discovered was apt to be a bookish one, less intensely felt than Wordsworth's. On the other hand, when he moved into the world of fantasy towards which his neighbour's dream lured him, he found stirring into vivid imaginative life a Virgil's Hades of ghostly shapes, quite like those his friend heard 'murmuring in Glaramara's inmost cave',[28] only more intensely seen and intimately experienced. Under the highly individual pressures of temperament and experience, the two writers had reached the point of seeing the world outside and the world within very differently, and they would never agree on the relationship between them. In the process of creation there was little that one could do to help the other – in fact the help he gave might easily be a hindrance.

In essence they moved towards the same imaginative end, a

sharper and more sensitive understanding of the human mind in
its complex dealings with the universe of alien things around it,
but the ingredients with which they worked were almost totally
unlike. In the trivial, commonplace events of the Alfoxden neighbourhood, such as an old huntsman's gratitude or the rumour
of a dead child buried under a thorn tree, Wordsworth guessed
at large truths about human gratitude and sorrow. But a strange
sailor on a forlorn ship, a dim forest where an innocent girl en-
countered a woman of evil beauty, a meandering river and a
soundless sea, were phantasms that had no need of Nether Stowey
to call them to life, though they hinted at an evil, a fear, and a
mystery in which every village shared.

It was, indeed, one of those collisions of chance and destiny
that placed the Cruickshank dream in Coleridge's hands at precisely the right moment. Before the Wordsworths came, he had
filled *Osorio* with fragments of dream lore and reverie, and to one
manuscript had attached a note commenting on the frequent use
of dreams in tragedy and the possibility that the vague figures
and vivid feelings of the dream-world had both truth and value
for poetry. As his notebooks show, he had already set out on an
inquiry he kept up for years on the massive influence on the
mind of the 'dark' ideas,[29] moving under the surface of the logical
intelligence. He speculated on whether poetry itself ought not to
be considered as a 'thing of nature' to be felt deeply and not perfectly understood. In writing the sketches of his early years for
Poole, this whole area of his mind had been stimulated afresh,
as he recalled the dreams of his childhood and his father's prophetic dream of dying. Under the influence of the laudanum he
had recently used in Bristol to dull the pains of neuralgia, the
now-familiar and terrifying activity of this subconscious part of
his mind had been renewed and was threatening to become a
regular symptom of his periods of anxiety. However the interest
was kindled, it dominated almost every long speech of the play,
and 'swarthy figures', weird music, crawling esurient worms, the
phantoms and dim noises of dream are more real than the characters – Maria, Velez, Alhadra, Albert, Osorio, Ferdinand, and
Ferdinand's three-year-old son – who are the people dreaming.

Wordsworth, too, was aware of this activity within himself
but fled away from it. For months after he left Annette in France,

his dreams were miserable and the mood of wretchedness they cast over him persisted through the day :

> I scarcely had one night of quiet sleep
> Such ghastly visions had I of despair
> And tyranny, and implements of death,
> And long orations which in dream I pleaded
> Before unjust Tribunals, with a voice
> Labouring, a brain confounded, and a sense
> Of treachery and desertion in the place
> The holiest that I knew of, my own soul.[30]

But it was his peculiarity and strength that he could turn from these ugly terrors of mind and conscience to the more comfortable forms of Nature. Instead of being able to run away, Coleridge plunged headlong into the phantom world, encouraging the dark objects to come from the shadows and listening to the weird sounds. He suspected there might be more meaning in this disturbed underworld of the mind than in the cataracts and mountains that haunted his friend like a passion.

There was not much, then, that either man could do to sway the poetic drift of the other. From the beginning they had to come to an agreement about their totally different contributions to the *Lyrical Ballads*, and the two Wordsworths were calmly convinced that Coleridge's share was a minor, and perhaps not a helpful, one. They linked 'The Ancient Mariner' and 'Christabel' with the popular ballad craze as a kind of concession to the public that would help to sell the volume in spite of William's less appetizing verses. In all her announcements to friends about the project, Dorothy referred to the contents as 'William's poems',[31] and in one of his first letters to Cottle inquiring about the volume Wordsworth already considered leaving 'The Ancient Mariner' out of any other edition. Worrying quite foolishly about sales which were going very well, he suspected that the Coleridge poem had been hurtful :

From what I can gather it seems that The Ancyent Marinere has upon the whole been an injury to the volume. I mean that the old words and the strangeness of it have deterred readers from going on. If the volume should come to a second edition I could put in its place some little things which would be more likely to suit the common taste.[32]

'The strangeness of it!' Surely not the comment of a man who could have been helpful in bringing the poem into being.

During the preparation for the second edition, it was still clearer that Wordsworth looked on Coleridge's contributions as little more than a sop to popular taste and a lure to find readers for his own more valuable verses. Since the first edition had exhausted itself in a year, he put his own name on its successor with a note that a 'Friend' had also contributed. 'The Ancient Mariner' was allowed to remain, changed indeed because many of the 'old words' were altered to conform to the current ballad fashion and with an apology that the poem had defects and 'that many persons had been much displeased with it'. It had been the intention, too, to include 'Christabel', the second part of which was written especially for this edition, but at the last moment it was excluded in spite of Wordsworth's professed admiration for it. Coleridge gave the account to Humphry Davy :

. . . he thought it indelicate to print two Volumes with *his name* in which so much of another man's was included – & which was of more consequence – the poem was in direct opposition to the very purpose for which the Lyrical Ballads were published – viz – an experiment to see how far those passions, which alone give any value to extraordinary Incidents, were capable of interesting, in & for themselves, in the incidents of common Life.

Even if Wordsworth claimed to admire 'Christabel', there was a diffidence in his praise that communicated itself to the writer :

– I assure you, I think very differently of 'CHRISTABEL'. – I would rather have written Ruth, and Nature's Lady than a million such poems/ but why do I calumniate my own spirit by saying, *I* would rather – God knows – it is as delightful to me that they *are* written – I *know*, that at present . . . my mind has disciplined itself into a willing exertion of it's powers . . .[33]

What had happened appears perfectly clear. Wordsworth's new-found insistence on the supreme worth for poetry of incidents of common life and of the kinds of emotion he discovered there had stiffened his innate suspicion of the type of poetry Coleridge had been practising off and on ever since he came to Stowey. If guilt and fear and sorrow and remorse were the fit material for a poet, they were to be discovered and traced only in the incidents he heard about or in the happier experiences of his childhood. There seemed to be no sense in delving into the dark abyss of human consciousness. In those inner places guilt and remorse spoke in a highly intimate and personal voice and upset the belief that Nature and man's heart never betrayed themselves. Certainly both 'The Ancient Mariner' and 'Christabel' were alien poems, but not only to the purpose of the *Lyrical Ballads*. They disturbed Wordsworth's hard-found serenity of mind, raising questions that had no easy answer, drawing the outlines of a face of Evil from which there was no running away. The very brilliance of their colouring gave them a fearsome reality. With such questions and such a picture he could not be comfortable for a moment because they, and not the city of Paris as he had imagined, constituted the haunted place of fear

> Defenceless as a wood where tigers roam[34]

into which he was no longer willing to venture.

The exclusion of 'Christabel' from the *Lyrical Ballads* might have been due to its opposition to the purpose for which the volumes were published, and its bright picture of sexual evil was one sign of the opposition. By the unaccountable workings of Coleridge's fancy, the poem's setting had moved from Nether Stowey to the neighbourhood of Windermere, and, inadvertently or not, Christabel's plea to her father

> And would'st thou wrong thy only child,
> Her child and thine?

had too poignant a ring as Wordsworth remembered Caroline across the Straits and made plans to marry another woman than her mother. It hinted at a topic too delicate for a letter,[35] even, and to give it place in a book of poems signed by William Wordsworth might lead to conclusions that he and Dorothy were anxious to conceal. In any event, it was safer to consider 'Christabel' and 'The Ancient Mariner' as simple ballads like Southey's with no more meaning than the surface tale.

Its rejection and the failure of the substitute plan of publishing it with 'The Recluse' were not happy events for the author. He

made apologies for delaying the appearance of the second volume
because he found it hard to complete 'Christabel'; possibly the
real story behind it was a continuing one that he had brought
up-to-date in Part II and could not take further :

The delay in Copy has been owing in part to me, as the writer of
Christabel – Every line has been produced by me with labor-pangs.
I abandon Poetry altogether – I leave the higher & deeper kinds to
Wordsworth, the delightful, popular & simply dignified to Southey;
& reserve for myself the honorable attempt to make others feel
and understand their writings, as they deserve to be felt & understood.[36]

Composing out of deep layers of feeling, he was ill and asked
Humphry Davy about some work on pain done by a well-known
surgeon : '. . . My eyes have been inflamed . . . and . . . the act of
poetic composition, as I lay in bed, perceptibly affected them, and
my voluntary ideas were every minute passing, more or less trans-
formed into vivid spectra.'[37] The vivid spectra were the all-too-
familiar shapes that he had toyed with in *Osorio* and 'The Ancient
Mariner', the ghosts that shadowed him as he tumbled on (to use
his own phrase) 'through sands and swamps of Evil' on the un-
hallowed ground of dream. All of the fantasy seemed, in the light
of common sense, to be far less significant than the comfortable
moral lessons read by Wordsworth into the tale of 'Michael',
the poem that took the place of 'Christabel', yet, as he wrote to
Poole, there might be more meaning in those dim parts of the
mind through which he groped than had as yet been discovered.
The traveller through these sands and swamps, like Christian in
the Slough of Despond, fared roughly because of the burden on
his back, but it might be part of the purpose of the imagination
to see what the burden was and so take a little of its weight off
man's shoulders.

At all events he had written part of a ballad, and even if
Wordsworth did not implement his approval by allowing it to be
printed, the hard job was done. Because his friend did so much
better than he the reflective type of poem, he had long ago given
up the hope of setting his 'lofty thoughts' to verse. Now that the
same friend was cool about the ballads, it might be sensible to
let Southey have that field to himself. Both of these writers had

that 'great confidence in their own powers'[38] which was one of the marks of ability, and the success of their poetic effort meant much more to them than the publication of 'Christabel' to himself. He would be content for a year or two more with his worship of Wordsworth, persuading himself that the widening recognition of his friend more than made up for what had been destroyed in his own heart.

He remonstrated with Sara about her dislike of William and Dorothy. She saw more faults and imperfections in them than he did, the most galling being their attitude of condescension towards her ways of looking after house and children. She was not happy that they lured her husband away from home even if he believed that much ought to be forgiven in the service of Wordsworth's genius. Now and then he confessed that his friend and companion might be too snugly wrapped around in a cocoon of his own complacency and the adoration of Dorothy, at first, and then of Mary, too; but it was only to an intimate like Poole that Coleridge, for a number of years, would breathe such an impious thought:

I owe it to Truth and Justice, as well as to myself to say, that the concern, which I have felt in this instance, and one or two other more *crying* instances, of Self-involution in Wordsworth, has been almost wholly a Feeling of friendly Regret, & disinterested Apprehension – I saw him more and more benetted in hypochondriacal Fancies, living wholly among Devotees – having every the minutest Thing, almost his very Eating, & Drinking, done for him by his Sister, or Wife – & I trembled, lest a Film should rise, and thicken on his moral Eye.[39]

This comment came later as a kind of belated acknowledgment of the truth of Poole's warning not to prostrate himself before the other man's genius. There was no hint of an accusation for what had happened to 'Christabel', three years before, except the cryptic entry in a notebook that A had 'been himself deeply wounded by B's selfishness', and that 'A had been long, long idle owing perhaps in part to his Idolatry of B'.[40] There were other reasons for the long idleness, but one of the chief Coleridge slowly and reluctantly began to recognize, was that Wordsworth, being as he was a glutton of praise with little to spare for another, had been greatly instrumental in suspending the 'shaping spirit of Imagination' in the friend to whom he owed so much.

SOURCE: *University of Toronto Quarterly*, XXXII, No. 4 (July 1963).

NOTES

1. *The Early Letters of William and Dorothy Wordsworth*, ed. E. de Selincourt (Oxford, 1935) 144; 20 Nov. 1795.
2. Ibid., p. 155.
3. *Poems on Various Subjects* (London, 1796) pp. 185–6.
4. *Letters of Samuel Taylor Coleridge*, ed. E. L. Griggs (Oxford, 1956) I 215–16 and note 216.
5. *The Poetical Works of William Wordsworth*, ed. E. de Selincourt (Oxford, 1940) I 116.
6. *Poetical Works of Samuel Taylor Coleridge*, ed. E. H. Coleridge (Oxford, 1912) I 116.
7. Herbert Read, *Wordsworth* (London, 1949) p. 100.
8. *Letters*, I 216.
9. Ibid., I 325.
10. Ibid., I 334.
11. Emile Légouis, *The Early Life of William Wordsworth* (London, 1921) p. 340.
12. *Letters*, II 881.
13. Ibid., I 324, also headnote to Letter 189.
14. Ibid., I 528.
15. Ibid., I 330.
16. Ibid., I 391.
17. Ibid., I 402.
18. Ibid., I 403.
19. *Early Letters of William and Dorothy Wordsworth*, pp. 266–7. Wordsworth asked Poole's opinion of 'Michael': '. . . in writing it, I had your character often before my eyes, and sometimes thought I was delineating such a man as you yourself would have been under the same circumstance.'
20. Elisabeth Schneider, in her *Coleridge, Opium and 'Kubla Khan'* (Chicago, 1953) offers a plausible argument for dating 'Kubla Khan' after Coleridge's return from Germany. She also brings together the evidence for an early dependence on opium, so that, if Coleridge's own datings of the poem as composed in the summer or autumn of 1797 are mistaken, the statement about the drug remains true.

21. *Early Letters of William and Dorothy Wordsworth*, p. 201.

22. *Letters*, I 275.

23. Ibid., I 656.

24. Ibid., I 658.

25. Ibid., I 714.

26. Ibid., I 356.

27. Ibid., I 334.

28. *Poetical Works of Wordsworth*, II 210, 'Yew Trees in Borrowdale'.

29. *The Notebooks of Samuel Taylor Coleridge*, ed. K. Coburn (New York, 1957) I v notes 95, 136, 138, 152, 178, 188, 194, 198, 205, etc.

30. *The Prelude* (text of 1805) ed. E. de Selincourt (London, 1949) X 374–81.

31. Hazlitt's famous essay, 'My First Acquaintance With Poets', was written twenty-five years after the events in Shrewsbury and Stowey which it records, and, while the details are coloured in memory, an interesting item is the visit of Coleridge and Hazlitt to Alfoxden. Dorothy was alone, William being absent on a visit to Bristol. The visitors '. . . had free access to her brother's poems, the *Lyrical Ballads*, which were still in manuscript', and the poems read aloud were Wordsworth's. (See pp. 51–6 above.)

32. *Early Letters of William and Dorothy Wordsworth*, p. 226.

33. *Letters*, I 631–2.

34. *The Prelude*, ed. E. de Selincourt, p. 179.

35. *Letters*, II 849. The phrase, under heavy inking in a letter from Coleridge to Sarah Hutchinson, has been deciphered by the editor.

36. Ibid., I 623.

37. Ibid., I 648.

38. Ibid., II 863.

39. Ibid., II 1013.

40. *Notebooks*, I note 1606.

George Whalley

THE MARINER AND THE
ALBATROSS (1946–7)

For me, I was never so affected with any human Tale. After first reading it, I was totally possessed with it for many days – I dislike all the miraculous part of it, but the feelings of the man under the operation of such scenery dragged me along like Tom Piper's magic whistle.[1]

In these words, in a letter to Wordsworth dated 30 January 1801, Charles Lamb spoke of Coleridge's 'The Rime of the Ancient Mariner.' Some readers continue to echo Mrs Barbauld's complaints that the poem is improbable and has an inadequate or distasteful moral. But these are mental reservations: poetry of the order of 'The Ancient Mariner' does not work its magic upon the mind alone; and mental afterthoughts are of little use in explaining, least of all in explaining away, the profound spiritual and emotional effect of this poem. For every sympathetic reader since Lamb has been similarly possessed and haunted by 'The Ancient Mariner.'

Lamb's criticism is remarkable in a contemporary. The incisiveness of his comment, however, lies not so much in his sensitivity to the fascination of the poem as in his immediate recognition of human feeling as being central in it. Lamb understood and loved Coleridge, and was never to free himself of the fascination of the man: 'the rogue has given me potions to make me love him';[2] ' 'tis enough to be within the whiff and wind of his genius, for us not to possess our souls in quiet.'[3] Unfortunately we have not the means of knowing that 'provocative and baffling personality' as Lamb did. But a close and sympathetic reading of the 'Rime' will bring us much nearer to the essential Coleridge than one would expect in a poem that is professedly 'a work of pure imagination.'

'The Rime of the Ancient Mariner' is less 'a fantasticall imagination and a drowsie dreame' than 'a continued allegory, and a darke conceit.' There is an important letter of Coleridge's which confirms the allegorical interpretation of the poem : 'I have often thought, within the last five or six years, that if ever I should feel once again the genial warmth and stir of the poetic impulse, and referred to my own experiences, I should venture on a yet stranger & wilder Allegory than of yore–. . . .' It is difficult to see how the missing factor in the comparative could be anything but 'The Ancient Mariner'; and the opinion is confirmed by the associated idea that follows : 'that I would *allegorize* myself, as a Rock with it's summit just raised above the surface of some Bay or Strait in the Arctic Sea. . . .'[4] Although the early action of the poem and the killing of the albatross take place in the Antarctic Sea, the details derive from the literature of Arctic travel, as Lowes has shown and as Coleridge would certainly remember.

I wish to examine the poem (*a*) to show how and to what extent Coleridge's inner life is revealed in the 'Rime'; and (*b*) to show that the albatross was for Coleridge, whether consciously or unconsciously, a symbol with profound personal significance.

I

The aesthetic and poetic qualities of 'The Ancient Mariner' are impressive. Other writers have examined in the poem the elements of colour and drama, the moral, the truth and accuracy of the detail, the supple and sensitive versification. But the haunting quality of the poem does not, and cannot, grow from any of these elements, whether taken singly or in any combination. Coleridge's creative imagination has fused all these elements into a completely unified organism to express his fundamental meaning; a meaning of whose full significance he was probably unconscious at the time of composition.

Without in any way detracting from the value of 'The Rime' as a poem, I wish to show that the 'haunting quality' grows from our intimate experience in the poem of the most intense personal suffering, perplexity, loneliness, longing, horror, fear. This experience brings us, with Coleridge, to the fringes of madness and death, and carries us to that nightmare land that Coleridge inhabited, the realm of Life-in-Death.[5] There is no other single poem in which we come so close to the fullness of his innermost suffering. The year after the composition of 'The Ancient Mariner' he gave the self-revealing image of

> some night-wandering man whose heart was pierced
> With the remembrance of a grievous wrong,
> Or slow distemper, or neglected love,
> (And so, poor wretch! filled all things with himself,
> And made all gentle sounds tell back the tale
> Of his own sorrow).[6]

Many years later he told how 'from my very childhood I have been accustomed to *abstract* and as it were unrealize whatever of more than common interest my eyes dwelt on; and then by a sort of transference and transmission of my consciousness to identify myself with the Object –. . .'[7] Whether or not he recognised this process at the time, Coleridge enshrined in 'The Ancient Mariner' the quintessence of himself, of his suffering and dread, his sense of sin, his remorse, his powerlessness. And

> Never sadder tale was heard
> By man of woman born.[8]

For it is not only a crystallization of his personal experience up to the time of the composition of the first version, but also an appalling prophecy fulfilled to a great extent in his life and successively endorsed by his own hand as time passed.

II

Life-in-Death is a recurrent theme in Coleridge's thought. In 'The Ancient Mariner' it is luridly personified :

> *Her* lips were red, *her* looks were free,
> Her locks were yellow as gold :
> Her skin was as white as leprosy,
> The Night-mare LIFE-IN-DEATH was she,
> Who thicks man's blood with cold.

And when he summarizes his life in 1833 in his own epitaph, he beseeches the passer-by to

> lift one thought in prayer for S.T.C.;
> That he, who many a year, with toil of breath
> Found Death in Life, may here find Life in Death.[9]

Life-in-Death meant to Coleridge a mixture of remorse and loneliness. Yet 'loneliness' is perhaps too gentle and human a word;
let us say 'aloneness.' It is precisely this combination of remorse
and aloneness with which the Mariner's experience is steeped.
Remorse is an emotion easy to find in the poem. It is also broad-
cast throughout Coleridge's letters and later poems, and requires
no detailed consideration here.

The Mariner's aloneness is directly stated :

> Alone, alone, all, all alone,
> Alone on a wide wide sea !
> And never a saint took pity on[10]
> My soul in agony.

It is thrown into relief by contrast with multiplicity :

> The many men, so beautiful !
> And they all dead did lie :
> And a thousand thousand slimy things
> Lived on; and so did I.

And it culminates in the horror of utter solitude :

> O Wedding-Guest ! this soul hath been
> Alone on a wide wide sea :
> So lonely 'twas, that God himself
> Scarce seemed there to be.

The same theme recurs in smaller details. When the spirits leave
the shipmates' bodies, it is with the sound of birds and 'like
a *lonely* flute.' The 'Spirit from the south pole' is a *lonesome* spirit;
and, even though there is an air of self-sufficiency in the phrase
'who bideth by himself,' like so many solitary people – like Coleridge, like Dorothy Wordsworth – he loves birds : [11]

> He loved the bird that loved the man
> Who shot him with his bow.

When the spectre-bark has sailed away and the Mariner has snap-
ped the spell of the dead seamen's eyes, he looks out over the
ocean and feels a sense of foreboding

> Like one, that on a *lonesome* road
> Doth walk in fear and dread.

These details have a cumulative effect in heightening the direct statement of the mariner's desolation.

The Mariner's isolation is not 'the wages of sin' so much as the state of sin.

> I looked to heaven, and tried to pray;
> But or ever a prayer had gusht,
> A wicked whisper came, and made
> My heart as dry as dust.

Or again :

> The pang, the curse, with which they died,
> Had never passed away :
> I could not draw my eyes from theirs,
> Nor turn them up to pray.

The same aloneness haunted Coleridge and echoes like doom through his other poems, his letters, the Notebooks. And in the passionate eloquence of his morbid remorse, he is constantly and restlessly seeking the sin at the root of the desolation; finding as alternative sins his indolence, 'abstruse research,' the failure of his marriage, the opium habit.

The 'Moon gloss' forges a powerful link between the Mariner and Coleridge.

In his *loneliness and fixedness* he yearneth towards the journeying *Moon*, and the stars that still sojourn, yet still move onward; and every where the *blue sky* belongs to them, and is their appointed rest, and their *native country* and their own *natural homes*, which they enter unannounced, as lords that are certainly expected and yet there is a *silent joy at their arrival.*[12]

The gloss was written some time between 1806 and 1817, and may have been under revision until the completion of the 1829 collection.[13] It is Coleridge's personal and mature comment upon 'The Ancient Mariner.' The 'Moon gloss' itself contains the essence of his loneliness and homelessness, feelings which were acutely present long before the composition of 'The Ancient Mariner.'

In 'Frost at Midnight' (1798) Coleridge recalls the sense of isolation he felt as an orphan at Christ's Hospital :[14]

> if the door half opened, and I snatched
> A hasty glance, and still my heart leaped up,
> For still I hoped to see the *stranger's* face,
> Townsman, or aunt, or sister more beloved. . . .
>   For I was reared
> In the great city, pent 'mid cloisters dim,
> And saw nought lovely but the sky and stars.

In January 1796, we find him writing to the Reverend T. Edwards :

I have got among all the first families in Nottingham, and am marvellously caressed, but to tell you the truth I am quite home-sick – owing to this long long absence from Bristol. I was at the *Ball,* last night – and saw the most numerous collection of handsome men and women, that I ever did in one place; but alas! the faces of strangers are but moving Portraits – . . . I feel as if I were in the long damp gallery of some Nobleman's House, amused with the beauty and variety of the Paintings, but shivering from cold, and melancholy from loneliness.[15]

Six months before the composition of the 'Rime,' we find him telling his brother that

>   at times
> My soul is sad, that I have roamed through life
> Still most a stranger, most with naked heart
> At mine own home and birth-place.[16]

And in January 1798, he wrote : 'The first sunny morning that I walk out, at Shrewsbury, will make my heart die away within me – for I shall be in a *land of Strangers*!'[17] With the last important recrudescence of his creative genius, he was to write in 1802 a curious echo of the watersnake passage :

> All this long eve, so balmy and serene,
> Have I been gazing on the western sky,
>   And its peculiar tint of yellow green :
> And still I gaze – and with how blank an eye !
> And those thin clouds above, in flakes and bars,

That give away their motion to the *stars*;
.Those stars, that glide behind them or between,
Now sparkling, now bedimmed, but always seen :
Yon crescent *Moon,* as fixed as if it grew
In its own cloudless, starless lake of *blue,*
I see them all so excellently fair,
I see, not feel, how beautiful they are![18]

It is important to notice in the 'Moon gloss' the association of the Moon, the blue sky, and home. Elsewhere the same combination of symbols, sometimes with the addition of tree(s), is associated with the thought of home, friendship and love, or their absence.

Practically speaking Coleridge was homeless for the greater part of his life. Remembering the number of times he must have exhausted the patience of his hosts to the point of serious misunderstanding and even the breach of friendship, the last part of the 'Moon gloss' is given pathetic personal significance by comparison with 'Youth and Age' (1823–32).

Where no hope is, life's a warning
That only serves to make us grieve,
                When we are old :

That only serves to make us grieve
With oft and tedious taking-leave,
Like some poor nigh-related guest,
That may not rudely be dismist;
.   *Yet hath outstayed his welcome while,*
And tells the jest without the smile.[19]

In thinking of nature as a healer, he notes (1811) the fate of the desolate man : again his thought turns to home, and the parallel with the 'Moon gloss' is again striking.

—and even when all men have seemed to desert us & the Friend of our heart has passed on with one glance from his 'cold disliking eye', yet even then the *blue Heaven* spreads it out & bends over us, & the little Tree still shelters us under its plumage as a second Cope, a *domestic Firmament,* and the low creeping Gale will sigh in the Heath-plant and soothe us by sound of Sympathy till the lulled Grief lose itself in *fixed gaze* on the purple Heath-blossom, till the present beauty becomes a Vision of Memory.[20]

And in October 1803, he is trying to account for his aloneness. 'But yet . . . the greater & perhaps nobler certainly all the subtler parts of one's nature, must be solitary—Man exists herein to himself & to God alone,—yea, in how much only to God—how much lies *below* his own Consciousness!'[21]

Let us see how this sense of homelessness is imaged in the 'Mariner.' When the ship finally reaches port he cries:

> Oh! dream of joy! is this indeed
> The light-house top I see?
> Is this the hill? is this the kirk?
> Is this mine own countree?

This utterance is charged with the deep thankfulness of the sea-farer returned. In many a page of his travel books Coleridge had read of the emotions aroused by sighting the home port after a long voyage; and he is able to reproduce the feeling, mingled joy and pathos and fear, because he has experienced it imaginatively. In December 1796, he had anticipated in a striking manner the Mariner's return: 'The Sailor, who has borne cheerily a circumnavigation, may be allowed to feel a little like a coward, when within sight of his expected and wished for port.'[22] Although the Mariner is returning to his 'own countree,' one feels sure that he does not expect anybody to be waiting for him.

> The Pilot and the Pilot's boy,
> I heard them coming fast:
> Dear Lord in Heaven! it was a joy
> The dead men could not blast.

Returned from the dead, Lazarus-fashion, he is overjoyed to see living people, to hear their voices. But there is a characteristic note of homelessness when he says

> O sweeter than the marriage-feast,
> 'Tis sweeter far to me,
> To walk together to the kirk
> With a goodly company! –

> To walk together to the kirk,
> And all together pray,
> While each to his great Father bends,
> Old men, and babes, and loving friends
> And youths and maidens gay!

It is an impersonal picture, pregnant with the sense of isolation. There are 'loving friends' but they do not seem to be his; the 'old men' are not his brothers or his father, the 'youths and maidens gay' are not his children. We catch an overtone of words spoken by him on a grimmer occasion :

> O happy living things ! no tongue
> Their beauty might declare :

words uttered with the same sense of isolation in which Coleridge wrote some twenty-five years later

> And I the while, the sole unbusy thing,
> Nor honey make, nor pair, nor build, nor sing.[23]

Not only are the Mariner's spiritual and emotional experiences similar to, if not identical with, those we know Coleridge to have suffered, but there is rather more than a hint that the drawing of the Mariner is a self-portrait. The Mariner's two salient characteristics are his glittering mesmeric eyes, and his passivity.[24] The Mariner says,

> I move like night from land to land,
> I have strange power of speech.

The first line is not only a reflection of Coleridge's isolation, but also a vivid metaphoric description of his imaginative wanderings while reading 'like a cormorant' before composing 'The Ancient Mariner.' We have Lamb's evidence for Coleridge's 'strange power of speech' even at school. 'How have I seen the casual passer through the Cloisters stand still, entranced with admiration (while he weighed the disproportion between the *speech* and the *garb* of the young Mirandula), to hear thee unfold, in thy deep and sweet intonations, the mysteries of Jamblichus, or Plotinus . . . , or reciting Homer in his Greek, or Pindar— . . .'[25] Even the hostile Hazlitt could write, in 1818 : 'That spell is broke; that time is gone for ever; that voice is heard no more : but still the recollection comes rushing by with thoughts of long-past years, and rings in my ears with never-dying sound.'

The Mariner's passivity is Coleridge's too; and the significance of that word (as of 'pathos,' 'patience,' 'sympathy') is rooted, in more than the etymological sense, in suffering. In those deeply moving observations of the night sky noted in early November 1803,[26] all written at about two o'clock in the morning, the elements of passivity, suffering, and the moon meet; while finally, in a similar entry made in Malta six months later, all combine with the longing for home and for Asra: 'the glorious evening [star] coasted the moon, and at length absolutely crested its upper tip ... It was the most singular at the same time beautiful Sight, I ever beheld/O that it could have appeared the same in England/at Grasmere—'[27] In these entries we see a man who is waiting, capable still of feeling; and he is driving down the intolerable suffering only by the *fixedness* with which he gazes on the sky.[28] Sometimes there must have shaped in his mind the blasphemy that he expunged from the 'Rime' after 1798: that 'Christ would take no pity on My soul in agony.'[29] And the Mariner's prayer must often have been repeated in those long nights:

> O let me be awake, my God!
> Or let me sleep alway.

At the height of the Mariner's suffering and loneliness, sleep and dream become central ideas. It is noticeable that the Mariner, like Coleridge, does not regard them as necessary concomitants. The Mariner, it is true, hears the 'two voices in the air' while he is asleep; but he recognizes them as being merely voices so that the tempo of the verse does not race as it did when he sighted the spectre-bark. His prayer on entering harbour shows that the whole voyage has been, in a real and horrible sense, a dream; when he hears the Pilot approaching his pulse quickens because the dream of the voyage is broken by a breath of solid human reality. Coleridge conceived sleep to be, in its essence, dreamless. We have his own evidence for the fact that his life (like the Mariner's voyage) passed in a state of dream;[30] and that there were times, *after* the composition of 'The Ancient Mariner,' when the dream, the thing imagined, was more solid and terrible than 'the normal realities of life.'

While I am awake, by patience, employment, effort of mind, and walking I can keep the fiend at Arm's length; but the Night is my Hell, Sleep my tormenting Angel. Three nights out of four I fall asleep, struggling to lie awake – and my frequent Night-screams have almost made me a nuisance in my own House. *Dreams with*

*me are no Shadows, but the very Substances and foot-thick Cala-
mities of my Life.*[31]

It is the dreams which accompany his sleep that are the torment
and horror. Remove the dreams from his sleep and he would
not 'fall asleep, struggling to lie awake.'[32] And the Mariner's
craving and prayer for sleep are paralleled by Coleridge before
1802, and are more insistently repeated after that date.

The first version of 'The Ancient Mariner' was completed for
publication in *Lyrical Ballads* in 1798. In 1801 Coleridge wrote,
'The Poet is dead in me.'[33] Successive revisions of the 'Rime' were
not complete until 1815;[34] the gloss, though first published in
1817, had not achieved its final and complete form until the
edition of 1829; and, although no important changes can be
assigned to a later date than 1817, the poem was again revised
in small points of detail for the collection of 1834. The revisions
of the poem resulted in a tightening of the texture, the omission
of unnecessary archaisms, the removal of elements of horror
which he recognized as gratuitous and ephemeral in their appeal,
and the abbreviation of certain passages whose length endangered the balance and emphasis of their setting. But no fundamental change was made in the plan or direction of the poem.
Beyond these revisions the gloss, valuable more as profound meditation than as an argument, was added. That the poem was of
real personal importance to Coleridge is shown, not so much by his
careful revision of the text, as by the additions to and revisions of
the gloss. The final version of 'The Ancient Mariner' is the outcome of at least twenty years of reflection, no matter how sporadic
the reflection may have been. That can only mean that the poem
continued to hold for him the personal significance with which it
was charged at its creation.[35]

In the course of revision the symbolism has been sharpened, not
least of all by the gloss; the personal context has been clarified;
and, most important of all, the whole poem has been confirmed in
the light of his later life.

III

It is misleading to think of Coleridge's life as falling into three
distinct phases: one of turbulent preparation, one of cloudless

creation, and one of disappointment and broken imagination. The brief creative period, 1797–9, emerges from a mind more hopeful than in the later period; but it is essentially the same mind – restless, mercurial, morbid, remorseful, fearful. For a short time he was lifted up (though on no constant wings) by his marriage, by the birth of Hartley, by his intimacy with William and Dorothy Wordsworth. But even such 'fecundating' happiness, a happiness ominously stressed in the letters of the period, was not able to change the thing that was Coleridge. The early period foreshadows the later. In 1796 he had written: 'There is one Ghost that I *am* afraid of; with that I should be perpetually haunted in this same cursed Acton, the hideous Ghost of departed Hope.'[36] In the same year he observed that

> Such a green mountain 'twere most sweet to climb,
> E'en while the bosom ached with loneliness –. . . .[37]

In the spring of 1797 he told Cottle: 'On the Saturday, the Sunday, and the ten days after my arrival at Stowey I felt a depression too dreadful to be described. . . . Wordsworth's conversation, &c., roused me somewhat; but even now I am not the man I have been – and I think never shall. A sort of calm hopelessness diffuses itself over my heart.'[38] Early in 1797 he had anticipated 'The Ancient Mariner' by telling his brother George that 'I have roamed through life Still most a stranger,' and that 'To me the Eternal Wisdom hath dispensed A different fortune and more different mind.'[39] As early as 1795 he had referred to the taking of drugs;[40] and in the spring of 1798 'Kubla Khan' was conceived 'in a profound sleep, at least of the external senses.' All the elements of the later broken Coleridge are noticeably present by 1797. Coleridge was too intelligent and introspective a man to fail to notice them and understand, at least dimly, their import.

Before the date of the composition of 'The Ancient Mariner' the sense of personal doom was present to Coleridge, even though at times, and for lengthy periods, he was able to 'keep the fiend at Arm's length.' It has been shown that the acute consciousness of his aloneness and homelessness was already present, foreshadowing the 'Moon gloss' and the pitiful threnody 'Youth and Age.' The 'Rime' is the projection of his own suffering, of his sense of

personal danger, his passivity, his perplexity. At first he projected himself unconsciously into the poem by the intensity with
which he imaginatively experienced the Mariner's situation.
During the voyage from Gibraltar to Malta he had an opportunity
not only to verify his 'observations' of the sea, but also to know
what it was to pass '55 days of literal Horror almost daily expecting and wishing to die.' The time in Malta was a critical, desolate
period; and I believe that in Malta Coleridge realized more
vividly than ever before that he trembled on the brink of in-
activity, of dream, of fatal procrastination, of creative impotence.
It is this realization that he projects into the 1817 version of 'The
Ancient Mariner': the personal allegory is sharpened by the
gloss, and the addition of important details relates the Mariner's
experience more intimately with Coleridge's experience of
opium.[41]

Fundamentally it is the personal quality of the poem that
accounts for its vivid haunting fascination. And that effect is
much heightened when we recognize the prophetic power of the
poem; when we know that Coleridge himself in later life recognized the poem for a personal allegory and endorsed its prophecy
by a life of wandering loneliness and suffering.

IV

The central figure of the albatross remains to be considered; for
'the albatross . . . binds inseparably together the three structural
principles of the poem: the voyage, and the supernatural
machinery, and the unfolding cycle of the deed's results.'[42] Nothing
less than an intensely personal symbolism would be acceptable
against the background of such intense suffering. The albatross
must be much more than a stage property chosen at random or a
mechanical device introduced as a motive of action in the plot.[43]
The albatross is the symbol of Coleridge's creative imagination,
his eagle.[44]

It was Wordsworth, not Coleridge, who thought of the albatross.[45] Whether Wordsworth or Coleridge actually stumbled
upon the albatross, in Shelvocke or anywhere else, does not
matter. In November 1797, the final element, around which the
whole poem would crystallize, was needed. As Lowes has shown,

Coleridge, in all his diverse and obscure reading before 'The Ancient Mariner,' read with the falcon's eye 'which habitually pierced to the secret spring of poetry beneath the crust of fact' : it is as though he knew intuitively what he needed without knowing exactly what he was looking for. It would be valuable to have a verbatim record of the dialogue during that momentous walk through the Quantock Hills, rather than the retrospective and somewhat patronizing report made by Wordsworth nearly fifty years after the event.

Coleridge would notice at once that the albatross was mechanically suitable : it would fit naturally into a voyage to Antarctic regions; sailors are superstitious about birds and indeed have special superstitions about the albatross; and he may even have noticed that it was amenable to rhyming in a way that other alternatives may not have been. But apart from practical considerations of plot or versification, the albatross was exactly what Coleridge was looking for. It was a rare species of bird,[46] of exceptional size,[47] solitary, haunting a limited and strange and, for Coleridge, evocative zone, harmless yet by tradition beneficent. Some or all of these facts would, I suggest, flash through Coleridge's mind; and he at once seized upon the albatross as the right (or, at the very lowest valuation, an adequate) symbol for his purpose.

Coleridge was a confirmed symbolist. In 1815 he wrote : 'An *idea*, in the highest sense of that word, can not be conveyed but by a *symbol*.'[48] Ten years before, he had noted how

In looking at objects of Nature while I am thinking, as at yonder moon dim-glimmering through the dewy window-pane, I seem rather to be seeking, as it were *asking* for, a symbolical language for something within me that already and for ever exists, than observing anything new. Even when that latter is the case, yet still I have always an obscure feeling as if that new phænomenon were the dim Awaking of a forgotten or hidden Truth of my inner Nature/It is still interesting as a Word, a Symbol ! It is Λόγος the Creator ! and the Evolver ![49]

The process he describes here is not a newly acquired practice, but an innate and habitual attitude of mind. 'The Ancient Mariner' is what it is for the reason that Coleridge has clearly given : because in that poem he found what he was 'seeking, as it were *asking for*,' long before the date of the Notebook entry – 'a symbolical language for something within me that already and for ever exists.' Furthermore Coleridge was not the man to use words or symbols without consideration or to select them carelessly. In an entry, touched with more humility than this single sentence would suggest, he said in 1805 : 'few men, I will be bold to say, put more meaning into their words than I or choose them more deliberately & discriminatingly.'[50]

That the link between the albatross and the creative imagination grows out of the inner necessity of the poem and of the man can be verified by only one passage in the 'Rime.' The evidence is extremely nebulous, but, being possibly primary evidence, should not be overlooked. The shipmates' first judgment on the killing of the albatross was that the Mariner had

> killed the *bird*
> That made the *breeze* to blow.

Late in 1806 Coleridge connects Genius and the wind :

Tho' Genius, like the fire on the Altar, can only be kindled from Heaven, yet it will perish unless supplied with appropriate fuel to feed it—or if it meet not with the virtues, whose society alone can reconcile it to earth, it will return whence it came, or at least lie hid as beneath embers, till some sudden & awakening Gust of regenerating Grace, ἀναζωπυρεῖ, rekindles and reveals it anew.[51]

And the symbol of the imagination, or of inspiration, is frequently, outside Coleridge's writing,[52] a bird.

Far more important is Coleridge's reply to the celebrated strictures of Mrs Barbauld. 'The Ancient Mariner,' he said, 'ought to have had no more moral than the Arabian Nights' tale of the merchant's sitting down to eat dates by the side of a well, and throwing the shells aside, and lo ! a geni starts up, and says he *must* kill the aforesaid merchant, *because* one of the date-shells had, it seems, put out the eye of the geni's son.'[53] The tone of the retort is jocular. If the 'Rime' had for Coleridge the personal significance that I believe it had, it would be difficult for him to reply other than jocularly. About seven years before the reply to Mrs Barbauld, he tells a correspondent exactly how he reacts to a situation of that kind.

My sentiments on the nature of all intrusions into private Life, & of
mere private *personalities* in all shapes I have given at large in the
Friend, and yet more pointedly in the Literary Life. . . . These you
know; but you cannot know, my dear Sir! . . . how many causes
accumulating thro' a long series of years, and acting perhaps on
constitutional predisposition, have combined to make me shrink
from all occasions that threaten to force my thoughts back on *myself* personally – as soon as any thing of this sort is on the point
of being talked of, I feel uneasy till I have turned the conversation,
or fairly slunk out of the room . . .[54]

Coleridge's facetiousness in speaking of the moral of 'The Ancient
Mariner' was misleading, as it was intended to be; but it both
hides and contains the clue we are looking for.

The nature of the Mariner's crime is thrown into high relief by
Coleridge's italics (*must, because*): and with it, the nature of
Coleridge's personal 'crime' – for so he regarded it in later life.
The identity is then complete.

The crime was at the same time wanton and unintentional.[55]
The Mariner shoots 'the *harmless* albatross,' and '*inhospitably*
killeth the pious bird of good omen,' having no conception of the
implications of his deed. The Mariner *could* have withheld his
arrow, the merchant his date-shell; but neither saw any reason for
doing so. Certainly the Mariner learned a sharp lesson about
killing birds before the voyage was done; but that lesson was of no
service to him when, in a moment of idleness or boredom, he
aimed his cross-bow at the albatross. 'But so it is! Experience,
like the stern lanthorn of a Ship, casts it's light only on the *Wake*
– on the Track already past.'[56] There is the sternness and in-
exorability of Greek tragedy in the paradox that an act committed in ignorance of the laws governing albatrosses and genii
must be punished in the most severe manner.

That Coleridge regarded his own suffering in precisely this
light is clear from a poem written as early as 1803.

> Such punishments, I said, were due
> To natures deepliest stained with sin, –
> For aye entempesting anew
> The unfathomable hell within,
> The horror of their deeds to view,
> To know and loathe, yet wish and do !
> *Such griefs with such men well agree,*
> *But wherefore, wherefore fall on me?*[57]

'The Pains of Sleep' is saturated with the same confusion and perplexity that the Mariner experienced. The sin from which the suffering arose was committed in the same way: 'Tho' before God I dare not lift up my eyelids, & only do not despair of his Mercy because to despair would be adding crime to crime; yet to my fellow-men I may say, that I was seduced into the ACCURSED Habit ignorantly.'[58] Even though he may have suspected, when it was too late, what would be the outcome of his struggle with 'this body that does me most grievous wrong,' Coleridge did not know, when the process began, that he was killing his eagle. The act was wanton: yes, in the sense that it was unnecessary, that it could have been avoided. And it is that very knowledge – afterwards – that the act could, perhaps easily, have been avoided, if at the very beginning he had understood the implications of his action, that makes stark tragedy both in Coleridge's life and in the Mariner's voyage.

O had I health and youth, and were what I once was – but I played the fool, and cut the throat of my Happiness, of my genius, of my utility, in compliment to the nearest phantom of overstrained Honor! –[59]

Well would it have been for me perhaps had I never relapsed into the same mental disease; if I had continued to pluck the flowers and reap the harvest from the cultivated surface, instead of delving in the unwholesome quicksilver mines of metaphysic lore. And if in after-time I have sought a refuge from bodily pain and mismanaged sensibility in abstruse researches, which exercised the strength and subtilty of the understanding without awakening the feelings of the heart; still there was a long and blessed interval, during which my natural faculties were allowed to expand, and my original tendencies to develop themselves; – my fancy, and the love of nature, and the sense of beauty in forms and sounds.[60]

The interval was a good deal shorter and less blessed than he was prepared to remember in 1815. And there was a great deal more in the two apparently naïve verses of moral than Mrs Barbauld could have guessed, more even than Coleridge was willing to remember when, long after their writing, he was asked for an explanation.

When the process of the atrophy of his creative imagination, foreshadowed in 'The Ancient Mariner,' was far advanced and

Coleridge felt that his life was sinking 'in tumult to a lifeless sea,' he wrote his comment upon that process. The lines are some of the most desolate ever written.

> But now afflictions bow me down to earth :
> Nor care I that they rob me of my mirth ;
>   But oh ! each visitation
> Suspends what nature gave me at my birth,
>   My shaping spirit of Imagination.
> For not to think of what I needs must feel,
>   But to be still and patient, all I can ;
> And haply by abstruse research to steal
>   From my own nature all the natural man —
> This was my sole resource, my only plan :
> Till that which suits a part infects the whole,
> And now is almost grown the habit of my soul.[61]

V

'The Ancient Mariner,' in addition to its other unique qualities, is both an unconscious projection of Coleridge's early sufferings and a vivid prophecy of the sufferings that were to follow. The poem was probably not originally intended to be a personal allegory : but that is what, in Coleridge's eyes, it became later as the prophecy was slowly, inexorably, and lingeringly fulfilled.

As far as I know 'The Ancient Mariner' has never been interpreted as a personal allegory. To do so (and the evidence for it is weighty) not only gives a clue to the source of the poem's intensity but also explains beyond cavil its moral implications. 'The Ancient Mariner' is, however, of primary importance *as a poem*; and no specialized interest – moral, biographical, or allegorical – can be allowed to assail the integrity to which, as a poem, it is entitled. But the interpretation I have suggested does bring the reader into intimate contact with Coleridge the man. Even to attempt to understand him will induce sympathy, and from sympathy some understanding can grow.

Carlyle's judgment of Coleridge is harsh and grossly unsympathetic : 'To steal into heaven . . . is forever forbidden. High treason is the name of that attempt; and it continues to be punished as such.'[62] Yet Coleridge had written :

I dare affirm, that few men have ever felt or regretted their own infirmities, more deeply than myself – they have in truth preyed *too* deeply on my mind, & the hauntings of Regret have injured me more than the things to be regretted—.[63]

. . . for years the anguish of my spirit has been indescribable, the sense of my danger *staring*, but the conscience of my GUILT worse, far far worse than all!—I have prayed with drops of agony on my Brow, trembling not only before the Justice of my Maker, but even before the Mercy of my Redeemer. 'I gave thee so many Talents. What hast thou done with them?'[64]

. . . and as to what *people* in *general* think about me, my mind and spirit are too awfully occupied with the concerns of another Tribunal, before which I stand momently, to be much affected by it one way or other.[65]

Carlyle's judgment overlooks the quantity and quality of the work Coleridge did complete; overlooks the fact that Coleridge throughout his life was dogged by physical disease; overlooks the fact that Coleridge became a man tormented and haunted, at times beyond the capacities of desire or effort, by the knowledge that the eagle had visited him, that he had inhospitably killed 'the pious bird of good omen,' and that it might well have been otherwise.

SOURCE: *University of Toronto Quarterly*, XVI (1946–7).

NOTES

1. *Letters of Charles and Mary Lamb*, ed. E.V. Lucas (London, 1935) I 240.
2. Ibid., I 185.
3. Ibid., II 191.
4. *Collected Letters of Samuel Taylor Coleridge*, ed. E. L. Griggs (Oxford 1956–71) hereafter referred to as *CL* – IV 975 [? Nov. 1819]. Coleridge may be thinking of his 'Allegoric Vision' (*The Complete Poetical Works of Samuel Taylor Coleridge*, ed. E. H. Coleridge (Oxford, 1912) II 1091–6). This prose allegory, written August 1795, was successively used for an attack on the Church of

England, for an attack on the Church of Rome, and in the introduction to *A Lay Sermon: Addressed to the Higher and Middle Classes*. In the 'Allegoric Vision' Coleridge does not in any sense allegorize himself.

5. For a consideration of the place of opium as inducing Coleridge's 'Bad most shocking Dreams,' as an element in the composition of 'The Ancient Mariner,' and specifically as a factor in the image of Life-in-Death, see R. C. Bald, 'Coleridge and "The Ancient Mariner"' in *Nineteenth-Century Studies*, ed. H. Davis, W. C. De Vane, R. C. Bald (Ithaca 1940).

6. 'The Nightingale : A Conversation Poem.' April 1798.

7. *CL* IV 974–5. This passage immediately precedes the passage quoted above (note 4).

8. 1798 version. Unless otherwise indicated, quotations from the poem follow the 1834 version.

9. See *CL* VI 963; cf. 970, 973, and *Poetical Works* I 492.

10. Cf. 1798 version : 'And Christ would take no pity on.'

11. For Coleridge on birds, see note 46 below.

12. My italics [G.W.].

13. Too little is known of the date of composition of the gloss, and of the process of revision. For the date of important revisions to 'The Ancient Mariner' see J. L. Lowes, *The Road to Xanadu* (Boston and New York, rev. ed., 1930) pp. 475–6. For successive changes in the 'Courts of the Sun' gloss, see ibid., 164 ff.

14. Cf. Edmund Blunden in *Coleridge: Ssudies by Several Hands on the Hundredth Anniversary of His Death*, ed. E. Blunden and E. L. Griggs (London, 1934) p. 66 : 'I sometimes wonder whether, germinally, the "Ancient Mariner" altogether is not one of his Christ's Hospital poems. I mean . . . that he had to travel through a long period of haunted solitariness.'

15. *CL* I 178–9 [29 Jan. 1796].

16. 'To the Rev. George Coleridge'; composed 26 May 1797.

17. *CL* I 369 [6 Jan. 1798]. Cf. *The Notebooks of Samuel Taylor Coleridge*, ed. Kathleen Coburn (New York and London, 1957–72), hereafter referred to as *CN*, III 3324 : '. . . when I am in company with Mr Sharp [et al.] . . . I feel like a Child – nay, rather like an Inhabitant of another Planet – their very faces all act upon me, sometimes, as if they were Ghosts, but more often as if I were a Ghost among them – at all times, as if we were not *consubstantial*.'

18 'Dejection : An Ode'; composed 4 April 1802. My italics [G. W.].

19. Cf. *CL* II 959; dated 1 August 1803. He speaks of himself as 'an involuntary Impostor.' The whole letter is of importance for

the statements which lead to the conclusion : 'This on my honor is as fair a statement of my habitual Haunting, as I could give before the Tribunal of Heaven/ How it arose in me, I have but lately discovered.'

20. *CN* III 4040. My italics [G. W.].

21. *CN* I 1554.

22. *CN* I 263. *CN* II shows that the voyage to Malta, Coleridge's loneliness there and the establishment of the opium addiction, and also the circumstances of his return to England, provide again fulfilment of the prophecy of 'The Ancient Mariner.'

23. 'Work without Hope'; composed 21 February 1825.

24. Lamb's critical comment is again of interest : 'The Ancient Marinere undergoes such Trials, as overwhelm and bury all individuality or memory of what he was, like the state of a man in a Bad dream, one terrible peculiarity of which is : that all consciousness of personality is gone' (*Letters of Charles and Mary Lamb*, I 240). Cf. *CN* I 1834.

25. 'Christ's Hospital Five and Thirty Years Ago.'

26. *CN* I 1622, 1624, 1625, 1627, 1628, 1635, 1648, 1649, 1650.

27. *CN* II 2139.

28. Cf. an amusing parallel in *CL* I 658. 'In truth, my Glass being opposite to the Window, I seldom shave without cutting myself. Some Mountain or Peak is rising out of the Mist, or some slanting Column of misty Sunlight is sailing across me/so that I offer up soap & blood daily, as an Eye-servant of the Goddess Nature.'

29. Cf. *CL* II 1202 : '55 days of literal Horror [at sea], almost daily expecting and wishing to die'; and *CL* IV 673 : 'I longed for Death with an intensity that I have never seen expresst but in the Book of Job – '.

30. See the dream-epitaph in *CL* II 992 :
> Here sleeps at length poor Col, & without Screaming,
> Who died, as he had always liv'd, a dreaming :
> Shot dead, while sleeping, by the Gout within,
> Alone, and all unknown, at E'nbro' in an Inn.

31. *CL* II 991. Many other of his letters voice the same theme.

32. Opium is certainly responsible for the horror of these dreams. Coleridge's interest in the nature of his nightmares and reveries, and the acuteness of his introspective analysis of dream phenomena, are to be seen in *CL* II *passim* and elsewhere in his writing. Bald, pp. 29–35, examines closely the responsibility for opium in Coleridge's dreams of horror; and at pp. 40–3 he considers Coleridge's distinction between dream, reverie, and nightmare.

33. *CL* II 714; to Godwin, 25 March 1801. Cf. *CL* II 831; July 1802 : 'All my poetic Genius . . . is gone. . . .'

34. The MS. of *Sibylline Leaves*, including 'The Ancient Mariner,' seems to have gone to the printer in August or September 1815.

35. This conclusion would be less tenable if the poet were almost anybody except Coleridge. In this respect 'The Ancient Mariner' stands in sharp contrast to 'Christabel.' 'Christabel' was left in a fragmentary state even though Coleridge 'had the whole present to my mind, with the wholeness, no less than the liveliness of a vision.' The passage on broken friendship is almost the only clear personal trace of Coleridge in 'Christabel.' 'Christabel' was far more 'a work of pure imagination' than 'The Ancient Mariner' : it had so little personal significance for him that he was unable to overcome the practical difficulties of completing it.

36. *CL* I 272. [This refers to a suggestion that Coleridge might move from Stowey to 'cursed Acton'.]

37. 'To a Young Friend.'

38. *CL* I 320.

39. 'To the Rev. George Coleridge.'

40. The earliest reference to the use of opium, *CL* I 188 of 1791, implies earlier medicinal use; cf. *CL* I 186 of 12 March 1796.

41. See Bald, pp. 33 ff.

42. Lowes, *The Road to Xanadu,* p. 221.

43. Cf ibid., p. 303. Lowes emphasizes the *triviality* of the deed and suggests that Coleridge required a trivial deed to set the punishment in motion.

44. Cf. T. S. Eliot, *The Use of Poetry and the Use of Criticism* (London, 1933) p. 69, where the eagle is used as the symbol of the creative imagination. Coleridge also seems to be using the symbol in an epigram of 1807 in reply to Poole's encouragement : 'Let Eagle bid the Tortoise sunward rise – As vainly Strength speaks to a broken mind' (*Complete Poetical Works,* ed. E. H. Coleridge, II 1001). Cf. Shelley's description of Coleridge as 'a hooded eagle among blinking owls.'

45. *The Poetical Works of William Wordsworth,* ed. E. de Selincourt and Helen Darbishire (Oxford, 1940–9) I 360–1.

46. Coleridge's keen interest in birds is shown by his footnote to 'This Lime-Tree Bower,' and by a MS. note in a copy of Gilbert White's *Works* : 'I have myself made & collected a better table of characters of Flight and Motion [of birds].' See also *CN* II 3182, 3184; III 3314, 3359.

47. The giant albatross probably would occur to Coleridge's mind. Notice Wordsworth's mention of 'wingspan of 12 or 13 feet.' But

see Lowes, *The Road to Xanadu*, 226–7 and 529, for the 'feasible' species; and *CN* ii 1957 : 'Saw a . . . Boy running up to the Main top with a large Leg of Mutton swung, Albatross-fashion about his neck.'

48. *Biographia Literaria*, ch. ix.

49. *CN* ii 2546; dated 14 Apr. 1805. See also *CN* iii 3762 : '. . . words are not mere symbols of things & thoughts, but themselves things—and . . . any harmony in the things symbolized will perforce be presented to us more easily as well as with additional beauty by a correspondent harmony of the Symbols with each other.'

50. *CN* i 2372.

51. *CN* ii 3136. This parallel is offered with caution.

52. But see note 44 above for an example in Coleridge's writing. *CN* ii 3182 is also of interest : 'The moulting Peacock, with only two of his long tail-feathers remaining, & those sadly in tatters, yet proudly as ever spreads out his ruined fan in the Sun & Breeze.' This may be a direct observation; but it is also one of several instances of Coleridge using a bird as a self-image.

53. *Table Talk*, 31 May 1830. Henry Nelson Coleridge, in his review of the *Poetical Works* 1834, observed : 'It was a sad mistake in the able artist – Mr Scott, we believe – who in his engravings has made the ancient mariner an old decrepit man. That is not the true image; no ! he should have been a growthless, decayless being, impassive to time or season, a silent cloud – the wandering Jew.' The remark is made on the authority of an unpublished entry in the MS. of *Table Talk*.

54. *CL* v 125–6.

55. Bald (pp. 39 ff.), in interpreting this passage, is concerned to explain the *amoral* attitude as a characteristic of opium reverie. Lamb notes the same quality in the mariner without reference to opium.

56. *CL* v 478. E. H. Coleridge noted the first appearance of this recurrent stock sentence in the *Morning Post* of 2 January 1800. (*Essays on his Own Times*, i 197–8).

57. 'The Pains of Sleep.'

58. *CL* iii 476 : Coleridge, here replying to Joseph Cottle's harsh accusations, is thinking specifically of the opium habit, but he recognized it as a symptom and did not regard it as the 'sin' itself.

59. *CL* iii 73–4; 17 February 1808.

60. *Biographia Literaria*, ch. i. See also *CL* v 125–6.

61. 'Dejection,' ll. 82–93. 'Dejection' is echoed in 'To William Wordsworth' (1807).

62. Thomas Carlyle, *The Life of John Sterling;* in *Complete*

Works of Thomas Carlyle (New York, 1853) **xx** 60.

   63. *CL* III 337 [12 Oct 1811].

   64. *CL* III 476; 26 April 1814.

   65. *CL* VI 770–1; 9 November 1828.

Edward E. Bostetter

THE NIGHTMARE WORLD OF 'THE ANCIENT MARINER' (1962)

Probably the most influential modern interpretation of 'The Rime of the Ancient Mariner' is Robert Penn Warren's essay, 'A Poem of Pure Imagination: An Experiment in Reading'.[1] Undoubtedly, as Mr Pottle has recently said,[2] it is 'the most elaborate and learned critique' the poem has ever received, as thoroughgoing in scholarship as it is provocative in criticism. The notes alone provide a useful guide to important critical and scholarly comments on 'The Rime', an erudite commentary on Coleridge's philosophical and critical theories, and exhaustive cross references to pertinent essays, letters, and poems. In the essay itself Warren has cogently argued the case for a symbolic interpretation of the poem and backed it up by an elaborate and impressive analysis in terms of what he calls the primary theme of the sacramental vision or the 'One Life', and the secondary theme of the imagination. It is little wonder that students of the poem, awed by so massive a reading, look upon it as a model of criticism and often appear to prefer it to the poem itself.

Yet it is in many ways a questionable interpretation. It superimposes upon the poem a rigid and consistent pattern of meaning which can only be maintained by forcing certain key episodes into conformity with the pattern and ignoring others. This practice is particularly noticeable in the interpretation of the moon–sun imagery. Warren sees the good events taking place under the aegis of the moon, the bad under that of the sun. The moon he identifies with the imagination, the sun with the understanding which is the reflective faculty that partakes of death. These symbolic identifications, he insists, hold constant through the poem, and he is forced into some tortuous twistings of the text, particularly in the latter half of the poem, in order to demonstrate his contentions. Various critics have protested the rigidity of this symbolic interpretation, but it remained for two recent critics – J. B. Beer and Elliott B. Gose, Jr. – to show in detail how vulnerable it is.[3] Warren had quoted extensively from other writings of Coleridge in justification of his identifications; these critics quote just as extensively to refute him. Specifically, they show convincingly that Coleridge more often than not used the sun in its traditional identification with God; and they argue persuasively for such an identification in 'The Rime'. In his zeal, Gose goes on to equate the moon with mutable nature, and is led in his turn into an interpretation which reads almost like a parody of Warren's. Beer takes the most convincing approach to the symbolic problem when he points out how for Coleridge all natural phenomena were symbols of Deity and functioned ambiguously – now benignly, now malignly – as instruments of punishment and salvation.

But both these critics – and the majority of other critics who have written since Warren – are quite content to accept his interpretation of the primary theme of the 'sacramental vision'. Yet this interpretation is certainly as questionable as the other. In his opposition to such critics as Griggs, who feels that no moral meaning should be sought in the poem, and Lowes, who contends that 'the "moral" of the poem, *outside the poem*, will not hold water,'[4] Warren insists that the poem presents symbolically a view of the world and man's relation to it which is as valid outside the poem as within. It is a view which, Warren argues, is 'thoroughly consistent with Coleridge's basic theological and philosophical views as given to us in sober prose'. As Warren interprets it, the poem dramatizes fundamentally Christian statements of sin, punishment, repentance, and redemption.

The Mariner shoots the bird; suffers various pains, the greatest of which is loneliness and spiritual anguish; upon recognizing the beauty of the foul sea snakes experiences a gush of love for them and is able to pray; is returned miraculously to his home port, where he discovers the joy of human communion in God, and utters the moral, 'He prayeth best who loveth best, etc.' We arrive at the notion of a universal charity . . . the sense of the 'One Life' in which all creation participates and which Coleridge perhaps derived from his neo-Platonic studies and which he had already celebrated, and was to celebrate, in other and more discursive poems.[5]

The term, 'One Life', appears most prominently in 'The Eolian Harp', in lines appended to the poem in 1817 :

> O ! the one Life within us and abroad,
> Which meets all motion and becomes its soul,
> A light in sound, a sound-like power in light,
> Rhythm in all thought, and joyance everywhere—.

Now these lines undoubtedly embody the conception of a benevolent harmonious universe in which Coleridge publicly proclaimed his belief throughout his life and which he made the cornerstone of his philosophical and critical theories. What Warren does is to define the moral tag (as it easily can be defined if lifted from context) in terms of his conception and then to superimpose the definition back upon the universe of the poem, thus apparently reconciling Christian values and the vague pantheism of eighteenth-century sentimentalism. He is able to do this by interpreting the universe of the poem as one of fundamentally benevolent order and law, in which the events proceed according to a clearly demonstrable logic for the purpose of discovering to the Mariner 'the sacramental view of the universe'. When the Mariner in the end accepts this view, 'his will is released from its state of "utmost abstraction" and gains the state of "immanence" in wisdom and love.'[6]

But if we look at the poem with the moral tag removed (or put out of mind as much as possible), we see that the view of the universe presented is by no means so simple or so easily resolved as Warren would suggest. He has achieved the 'sacramental vision' by rationalizing those portions of the poem in which the powers of the universe are presented as sternly authoritarian and punitive, and ignoring those in which they are revealed as capricious and irrational.

The universe which is jarred into revealing itself by the Mariner's act is a grim and forbidding one in which the punishment of violation is swift, severe, sustained. Insofar as it is a Christian universe, it has little or nothing in common with the necessitarian benevolence of Hartley and Priestley, on the one hand; or the idealism of Berkeley and the Neoplatonists, on the other. Its most striking affinity is with medieval Catholicism, seventeenth-century Puritanism, or the lurid Calvinism of the extreme Evangelicals of Coleridge's own age. The Mariner's blessing of the snakes is like the evangelistic moment of conversion :

> A spring of love gushed from my heart,
> And I blessed them unaware.

Furthermore this act, though it reveals the Mariner as one of the Elect and promises his ultimate salvation, does not free him from pain and penance. He remains subject, like an Evangelical, to an unrelenting sense of guilt, the compulsion to confession, the uncertainty as to when if ever penance will end. We are reminded of the nightmarish experiences of Cowper.

But the most disturbing characteristic of this universe is the caprice that lies at the heart of it; the precise punishment of the Mariner and his shipmates depends upon chance. The spectre crew of Death and Life-in-Death gamble for them :

> The naked hulk alongside came
> And the twain were casting dice;
> 'The game is done ! I've won ! I've won !'
> Quoth she, and whistles thrice.

Now certainly these are loaded dice. As in a dream in which chance enters, we have no doubt of the outcome, indeed we know what the outcome will be, so here we as readers accept the outcome of the throw as inevitable. As a matter of fact, most critics including Warren are so accustomed to taking for granted the relentless logic of crime and punishment that they pass over without comment the implications of the dice game. Surely it knocks out any attempt to impose a systematic philosophical or religious interpretation, be it necessitarian, Christian, or Platonic, upon the poem. Whether we consider it as part of the ideological symbolism, or as the Mariner's interpretation of the fact that the men died and he lived on (a product of his delirium, as it were), or simply as dramatic machinery, the dice game makes chance the decisive factor in the Mariner's punish-

ment. It throws into question the moral and intellectual respon-
sibilities of the rulers of the universe. To the extent that the
Mariner's act of pride and capricious sadism sets in motion retri-
butory forces of the same nature, the question is inevitably raised :
how responsible is he ultimately for his act of evil? How much
is his act simply the reflex of a universal pattern of action?

More or less because the dice game is ignored, the question
of the justification of the crew's death has provoked much
solemn debate. Most recent critics seem willing to accept Warren's
argument that the men have 'duplicated the Mariner's own
crime of pride' and 'have violated the sacramental conception of
the universe, by making man's convenience the measure of an
act, by isolating him from Nature and the "One Life" '.[7] But this
is a specious argument which further points up the absurdity of
trying to impose upon the poem a rigidly logical religious interpretation. The men are guilty of no more than the usual human
frailty. True, by acquiescing they become accomplices but there is
a vast difference in degree if not in kind between passive ignor-
ant acquiescence and the Mariner's violent act. And what of the
rulers of the universe? They are revealed as holding the same contempt for human life that the Mariner held for the bird's life, by
finding the crew equally guilty and deserving of the same punishment as the Mariner : whether they live or die depends upon
the throw of the dice. The moral conception here is primitive and
savage – utterly arbitrary in its ruthlessness. Even as Warren sees
it, it is the Old Testament morality of the avenging Jehovah.
In suggesting that the moral implications are to be taken as relevant or meaningful beyond the limits of the poem, he seems, therefore, to be sanctioning and would have Coleridge sanction the
most intolerant and merciless morality as the law of the universe
– and man. Carried to its ultimate bitter implications, this
morality would today find entire nations deserving of destruction
because their people have acquiesced in the actions of their
rulers.

From this point on, the sacramental vision is of a hierarchal
universe. When the Mariner blesses the snakes unaware, but
through a power superior to himself ('Sure my kind saint took
pity on me'), he is heard by the Holy Mother who sends 'the
gentle sleep from Heaven' and the rain which refreshes him when

he awakes. And 'by the invocation of the guardian saint' the angelic spirits enter the bodies of the ship's crew. The 'lonesome spirit from the south-pole', who is certainly less a Neoplatonic daemon than a kind of primitive totem-force, is subservient to the angelic forces, and is pressed into carrying the ship as far as the line. But he has power enough to demand and receive penance 'long and heavy' for the Mariner. However we look at it, there is something arbitrary and less than merciful in the way in which the higher powers defer to the Polar spirit; particularly is this inconsistent with the view of the poem as a 'tract on universal benevolism and the religion of nature', as Fairchild calls it.[8] Fairchild tries to draw a distinction between the hierarchal body of the poem, which he dismisses as mere dramatic machinery, and what he calls the allegory. Even Warren, who sees the poem as an integrated whole, glosses over the ambiguous implications of the hierarchal action. Yet if we concede that meaning is implicit in the poem, we have no justification for interpreting the moral other than in terms of the total symbolic action – or indeed for deciding that part of the poem is allegorical and part not – or for deciding that certain action is meaningful and ignoring other action. As Warren himself says, 'Insofar as the poem is truly the poet's, insofar as it ultimately expresses him, it involves his own view of the world, his own values'.[9] We must assume, therefore, unless we have evidence to the contrary, that the organization and manipulation of the hierarchal action in this way rather than another reveals significant attitudes of the author.

At any rate, the arbitrary exhibition of supernatural power continues in the sinking of the ship, and in the woeful agony that wrenches the Mariner when he asks the Hermit to shrieve him. The Hermit is powerless to give absolution to the Mariner, to forgive him in the name of the Church or God. Instead, as the gloss says omniously, 'the penance of life falls upon' the Mariner from above. The conclusion of the poem is oppressively puritanical. The Mariner passes 'like night from land to land'; he tells the Wedding-Guest that it is sweeter far than the marriage feast with a goodly company 'to walk together to the kirk' and pray; he leaves his listener because the 'little vesper bell' bids him to prayer; and the Wedding-Guest turning from the bridegroom's door

went like one that hath been stunned,
And is of sense forlorn :
A sadder and a wiser man,
He rose the morrow morn.

Instead of the 'One Life' we are confronted at the end of the
poem by the eternally alienated Mariner alienating in his turn
the Wedding-Guest, for the Guest is robbed of his happiness
and the spontaneous participation in the marriage feast (which
is really the 'one life') and forced to share the disillusioned wisdom and guilt of the Mariner.[10] In the lurid light of his tale the
Mariner's pious moral becomes inescapably ironic :

He prayeth best, who loveth best
All things both great and small;
For the dear God who loveth us,
He made and loveth all.

The last lines lifted from context as they generally are become
the statement of a universal love and charity, of which the
Mariner is the recipient and in which he shares. It implies, as
we have said, the benevolent, vaguely pantheistic and egalitarian
universe of the eighteenth-century sentimentalists. This is the
'One Life' which Warren presumably sees as prevailing throughout the poem and which the Mariner comes to recognize by way
of his experience, so that in the end he 'discovers the joy of human
communion in God' and gains 'the state of "immanence" in wisdom and love'. But by the moral principles of such a universe, the
punishment of the Mariner should have been unthinkable. The
God who loved man as well as bird should have been merciful
and forgiving. The God of the poem, however, is a jealous God;
and in context the moral tag carried the concealed threat that
even the most trivial violation of his love will bring ruthless and
prolonged punishment. The way to avoid conscious or unconscious sin is to withdraw from active life to humble ourselves in
prayer. At best, the 'love' of God is the love of the benevolent
despot, the paternal tyrant, the 'great Father' to whom each bends.
We love not through joy and spontaneous participation in the
'One Life' but through fear and enforced obedience. The little
moral tag has the same ambiguous implications as Geraldine's

remarks in Part I of 'Christabel' which are the prelude to the enslavement of Christabel:

> All they who live in the upper sky,
> Do love you, holy Christabel!

It is because of the ambiguous and terrifying implications of the Mariner's experience that critics like Lowes have denied that the moral statement of the poem is valid outside the magic circle of the voyage and preferred simply to view the poem as a dream, a literary fairy tale, or an old wives' tale. They are uncomfortably aware not only that the whole tenor of the poem runs counter to the sentimental implications of the moral tag but also that if taken seriously as philosophical or religious statement it becomes unacceptable to the modern mind. The magical world and its values are contradicted by all our knowledge and experience. In a narrower sense, this world is subversive of the Romantic world view and *its* values. It runs counter to the clichés of Romantic faith. Indeed, it seems irreconcilable with Coleridge's own religious pronouncements.

In their efforts to cope with the problem of belief, Lowes and Warren are led into opposite mistakes. Neither can bring himself to face head on the total implications of the poem; or to believe that Coleridge intended the world he had created. In order to make the poem palatable, Lowes argues that Coleridge uses the ethical background only to give the illusion of inevitable sequence to superb inconsequence, but this suggests unfortunately a kind of manipulation, a fundamental insincerity or disingenuousness. In his reaction against Lowes, Warren himself manipulates the poem by imposing a more or less orthodox sacramental pattern upon it in an effort to make it 'thoroughly consistent with Coleridge's basic theological and philosophical views as given to us in sober prose'. Though both Lowes and Warren recognize the dream quality in the poem, they tend for different reasons to minimize its importance as a means of resolving the dilemma of meaning. Lowes, refusing to admit that dreams reveal anything about dreamers or indeed have any relevance to waking life, uses the dream characteristics as further evidence of the poem's 'inconsequence'. Warren, admitting the significance of dreams to Coleridge, goes so far in the opposite direction as to see them as confirming and shoring up the sacramental vision.

But neither Lowes nor Warren takes into consideration the fact that a poem may be the expression of complex attitudes which are not necessarily consistent with the poet's formal philosophy and indeed may contradict it. The discrepancy between the way in which the poet is sometimes led by his experience, needs, and fears to look at the world, and the way in which he says or thinks he is looking at it may be great. Ordinarily the poet proceeding from the perspective of his reasoned beliefs holds the discrepancy to a minimum, as Coleridge does for example in his conversational poems. But occasionally a situation or symbol releases deeply felt and usually repressed attitudes which in turn shape and determine the symbolic action of the poem. This I think is what happens in 'The Rime'. It could happen because of the dramatic structure of the poem, which provided an objective correlative dissociated from the poet, so that Coleridge felt free to indulge these attitudes.[11] The clue to the significance of the poem may lie in the subtitle Coleridge affixed in 1800 : 'A Poet's Reverie'. 'Reverie' meant for Coleridge a waking dream in which the mind though remaining aware relaxed its monitoring and allowed the imagination to roam freely in a 'streamy' process of association.[12] The way in which he described the 'fiendish' dreams in the notebooks indicates that they were usually reveries. With reference to 'Kubla Khan', which in a note to the Crewe manuscript he said was 'composed in a sort of reverie', Miss Schneider has suggested that 'Coleridge's original inclination towards daydreaming, encouraged by the use of half-stupefying doses of opium, had combined with his introspective habit of observing his own mental processes and with his interest in Hartleyan psychology to make him consciously capture and use in both his poetry and prose the content and perhaps one might say the "technique" of the day dream'.[13] She has vividly demonstrated that 'Kubla Khan' expresses a perfectly meaningful attitude, similar to attitudes projected in the notebook dreams. The poem focuses on an act of power, the godlike creation of the pleasure-dome; and in the end the poet envisions himself as one who could emulate this act in his art if he could 'revive within' him the symphony and song of the Abyssinian maid, and who would then be reverenced and feared by all as divinely inspired.

In the same way, 'The Rime' focuses on an act of power, a trivial act of destruction rather than a grandiose act of construction, but nevertheless god-defying and god-attracting. Thereafter the poem is the morbidly self-obsessed account of a man who through his act has become the center of universal attention. The supernatural powers who control the world concentrate upon his punishment and redemption. Two hundred men drop dead because of his act; but he is condemned – and privileged – to live on. As seen through the eyes of the Mariner, the outcome of the dice game can never be in doubt. The crew have no identity apart from him; they are not important enough to be condemned to life-in-death. The reader has no awareness of them as human beings; he watches their deaths without surprise and without feeling except as they affect the Mariner. When, dying, the men fix their eyes upon the Mariner, the effect is not only to intensify his sense of guilt but to emphasize his importance. He has become, as the wedding-guest's outcry at this point indicates, a figure to be feared in his own right.

When he blesses the water snakes, he becomes again the object of universal action. The Albatross falls. It rains. The angels and the Polar spirit are impressed into service to bring him home. And in the end, in order to perform his penance, he himself is given superhuman powers. He passes like night from land to land; he has strange powers of speech; he is apparently immortal. As Warren points out, he can be seen among other things as the *Poète Maudit,* accursed and alienated; but as such he has what Coleridge longed for all his life and achieved as poet only through writing 'The Rime' – power to tell his tale and to force the world to listen. The moral is given an additional ironic twist in being presented by this figure of power and wish fulfillment. The Mariner's act may have been a sin, but it made him important to God and men alike; in this sense he was rewarded rather than punished.

Only within the universe of the poem, however, can the Mariner's fate be seen as partial triumph. Given such a universe, the best that can be hoped for is the partial redemption from horror, the compensatory power of speech which he is granted. Like the Mariner's experience, the universe is the projection not of reasoned beliefs but of irrational fears and guilt feelings. Coleridge has created the kind of universe which his own inexplicable sins and their consequences might have suggested to him. His fear of dreadful consequences began early in life, encompassed a wide range of sinful acts, and finally focused upon his opium addiction. Even in 1798 much of his sense of impotence could have come from his efforts to break the habit. As 'The Pains of Sleep' reveals, it was hard for him, consumed by so great a desire to live righteously, not to see himself as a helpless victim of forces beyond his control, forces that were part of the universal pattern of things. What he wanted to believe in and increasingly devoted his intellectual energies to asserting was a universe of order and benevolence in which man possessed freedom of will and action to mold his own destiny; what he feared was a universe in which he was at the mercy of arbitrary and unpredictable forces. 'The Rime' envisions such a universe. The Mariner's act is a compulsive sin which strips away the illusion of freedom and reveals just how helpless he is.[14]

In terms of Coleridge's religious conflicts, the universe of 'The Rime' is the Christian universe gone mad, rising up and reaffirming itself in the face of the philosophical heresies which he hankered after. At no time in his life was Coleridge at ease in his intellectual speculations; even in the days of greatest revolutionary fervor he sought to reconcile his republican doctrine with traditional Christian dogma, as in 'Religious Musings'. His uneasiness is vividly revealed in the concluding section of 'The Eolian Harp', where ostensibly he is pacifying his wife but in reality is appeasing the Christian God

> Who with his saving mercies healèd me,
> A sinful and most miserable man.

The God who healed could as quickly punish, and Coleridge is reassuring Him that he did not mean what he said in the first part of the poem. The attitudes expressed in the wild letters to his brother George are essentially Calvinistic. In a letter in March 1798, in which he disavows his Republicanism, Coleridge melodramatically confesses,

I believe most steadfastly in original Sin; that from our mother's wombs our understandings are darkened; and even where our understandings are in the Light, that our organization is depraved, & our volitions imperfect; and we sometimes see the good without *wishing* to attain it, and oftener *wish* it without the energy that wills & performs – And for this inherent depravity, I believe, that the *Spirit* of the Gospel is the sole cure.[15]

How much this view is expressed to please George, how much it reflects Coleridge's convictions – it is certainly not in keeping with other statements of this time – is hard to say; but it reveals the state of mind which could create the universe of 'The Rime'.

Just as the poem is molded and shaped by Coleridge's fears, so it makes its appeal to the irrational fears that lurk not far beneath the surface of modern consciousness. No matter how emancipated from the magical view of the universe modern man may be intellectually, he can never free himself from it emotionally or from the values associated with it. He is never quite able to eradicate the uneasy fear that it might turn out to be true. For that matter the anthropocentric conception of the universe continues to dominate western social organization and to determine social behavior. The inexorable punishment, penance, and redemption for sin is not the law of life, but most of us are afraid that it might be (and it has been to the advantage of social mores to encourage that fear). It is that fear which 'The Rime' reflects and plays upon. It presents itself as the parable of the man who refuses to believe in the traditional cosmos and expresses his contempt and disbelief by an act that provokes the cosmos into reaffirming itself in its most outrageous and arbitrary form. Most of us find, I think, a curious satisfaction in having this cosmos so vividly reaffirmed; it allows us to indulge our superstitious fears quite shamelessly. We enjoy having the fear of God thrown into such thoughtless, happy souls as the wedding-guest. And finally our religious tradition conditions us to accept almost automatically the pious commonplaces by which the Mariner glosses over the terrifying implications of his experience – they are after all at the foundations of Christian faith – the commonplaces about God's love for man, bird, and beast; the preferability of spiritual love to sexual love; the happiness to be found in penance and prayer. For these commonplaces give an aura of sweet reasonableness and religious authority to an experience essentially negative and irrational; and satisfy the longing to believe that in spite of our fears the universe is ultimately benevolent and reasonable, and if we behave properly will leave us alone.

To a great extent, then, the success of the poem lies in the way it satisfies the impulse to see human fears and desires founded in and revealing universal truths. From its beginning the poem moves relentlessly toward the transformation of its action into moral statement, into an enunciation of universal law. In this connection it is interesting to recall Coleridge's famous statement of purpose in the *Biographia Literaria*: his endeavors he said were to be directed toward persons and characters supernatural, 'yet so as to transfer *from our inward nature a human interest and a semblance of truth* sufficient to procure for these shadows of imagination that willing suspension of disbelief for the moment, which constitutes poetic faith' (my italics: E.B.). The measure of Coleridge's success is indicated by the way in which from many critics he has procured not merely the willing suspension of disbelief, but the willing belief which constitutes religious faith. They are led into eagerly accepting the symbolic projection of our inward nature as the symbolic representation of objective reality.

The desire that a poem should mean, not be, is understandably strong among poets themselves, in spite of their present-day protestations to the contrary. They have an uneasy fear that to admit that poem is an expression of attitudes which may not be rationally defensible is to concede some fatal weakness which robs it of greatness. The need for the poet to believe that he has been granted special moral insight is almost irresistible – otherwise of what ultimate worth is his eloquence? When he turns critic, therefore, the temptation is strong to justify poetry on moral grounds. This is the temptation to which Warren succumbs. He simply cannot believe that a poem so authoritative in vision, so powerful in symbolism as 'The Rime', is not morally meaningful beyond our fears and desires. As a result, he is led ironically into imposing the moral laws of what Coleridge called the reflective faculty upon a universe of pure imagination.

SOURCE: *Studies in Romanticism*, I (1962) pp. 351–98

NOTES

1. *The Rime of the Ancient Mariner*, with an Essay by Robert Penn Warren (New York, 1946). Hereafter referred to as *Essay*. Reprinted in R. P. Warren, *Selected Essays* (New York, 1958).

2. Frederick A. Pottle, 'Modern Criticism of "The Ancient Mariner" ', in *Essays on The Teaching of English*, ed. E. J. Gordon and E. S. Noyes (New York, 1960), p. 261.

3. J. B. Beer, *Coleridge the Visionary* (London, 1959); E. B. Gose, Jr, 'Coleridge and the Luminous Gloom', *PMLA*, LXXV (June 1960) p. 238–44.

4. *The Best of Coleridge*, ed. Earl Leslie Griggs (New York, 1934) p. 687; J. L. Lowes, *The Road to Xanadu* (Boston, 1927) p. 300.

5. *Essay*, p. 78.

6. Ibid., p. 86.

7. Ibid., p. 85.

8. H. N. Fairchild, *Religious Trends in English Poetry* (New York, 1949) III 292–4.

9. *Essay*, p. 64.

10. In a long footnote (p. 144, n. 136) Warren, admitting that the contrast between marriage and religious devotion is in the poem, nevertheless argues that 'in the total poem we cannot take the fact of the contrast as being unqualified. At the level of doctrine, we do not have contrast between marriage and sacramental love, but one as image of the other. It is no accident that the Mariner stops a light-hearted reveler on the way to a marriage feast. What he tells the wedding-guest is that the human love, which you take to be an occasion for merriment, must be understood in the context of universal love and only in that context achieves its meaning. . . . In one of its aspects the poem is a prothalamion.' But in the context of the poem the marriage is pushed into the background. The wedding-guest is prevented from attending, the Mariner's tale and the marriage end simultaneously, and the guest turns 'from the bridegroom's door.' If the poem had been intended as *prothalamion*, then the Mariner should have finished his tale prior to the wedding, in time for the wedding-guest to attend with his new-learned wisdom – but no ! the Mariner puts his tale *in the place of* the wedding. The contrast at the level of doctrine seems to me inescapable.

11. Professor Lionel Stevenson (' "The Ancient Mariner" as a Dramatic Monologue', *The Personalist*, XXX [1949] 34–44) argues

that Coleridge was 'objectively depicting a mind totally unlike his own.' The poem is 'the monologue of a primitive seaman' who evolves in his delirium a logical train of events to account for the physical and mental tortures of thirst and exposure in which he alone is spared. But Professor Stevenson fails to consider the impressive evidence from Coleridge's letters and notebooks which George Whalley has brought together in 'The Mariner and the Albatross', *University of Toronto Quarterly*, XVI (1947) 381–98. Professor Whalley perhaps goes too far in calling the poem 'a personal allegory', but he is surely right in emphasizing the extent to which the Mariner's suffering, loneliness, and fears are projections of Coleridge's own feelings. (See pp. 160–83 above.) The best study of the poem as revelation of Coleridge's unconscious frustrations and conflicts is by David Beres, in 'A Dream, A Vision and a Poem : a Psychoanalytic Study of the Origins of *The Rime of the Ancient Mariner*', *International Journal of Psycho-Analysis*, XXXIII, No. 2 (1951) 97–116.

12. Coleridge in his speculations drew a distinction between 'mere' dream and nightmare, which he defined in a notebook entry as 'a species of Reverie, akin to Somnambulism, during which the Understanding & moral Sense are awake, tho' more or less confused.' (Quoted in R. C. Bald, 'Coleridge and The Ancient Mariner', in *Nineteenth-Century Studies*, ed. Davis, De Vane, Bald [Ithaca, 1940] p. 35.) For Coleridge nightmare seemed to occur most often on the fringes between waking and sleeping. It is interesting that when in 1817 he named the woman of the spectre ship for the first time he called her the 'Nightmare Life-in-Death.' For Coleridge's views on reverie, see Bald, pp. 37–41, and Elizabeth Schneider, *Coleridge, Opium and Kubla Khan* (Chicago, 1953) pp. 81–109, 325.

13. *Coleridge, Opium and Kubla Khan*, pp. 90–1.

14. A lighter aspect of this matter is suggested by the intangible but important formative influence which the superstitions associated with Pixies in Ottery St Mary brought to bear upon the mind of the young Coleridge. Professor Kathleen Coburn has called to my attention a pamphlet published on the 500th anniversary of the installation of the bell of the Church of St Mary (R. F. Delderfield, *The Pixies Revenge*, Printed by E. J. Manley, Ottery St Mary, Devon, 1954). The pamphlet relates the various efforts of the Pixies to prevent the casting and installation of the bell, 'for the ringing of a Church bell is to the little folk as Holy Water is to the Devil.' It takes no Lowes to see how important the childhood associations of

mischievous spirits and spells, and Mary as the agent of release from the spells and the giver of peace and sleep, were in shaping the central section of the poem. In fact, the Mariner's reference to the vesper bell takes on fresh significance in the light of these legends emphasizing the importance of the bell as a means of human communication and protection against isolation and avenging spirits. In other words, as Miss Coburn remarks, 'The Mariner had been, for his sins, pixillated, as naturally to Coleridge as if he had been an Ottregian.'

15. *Collected Letters of Samuel Taylor Coleridge,* ed. E. L. Griggs (Oxford, 1956) 1 396.

Humphry House

'KUBLA KHAN' AND
'CHRISTABEL' (1953)

If Coleridge had never published his Preface, who would have thought of 'Kubla Khan' as a fragment? Who would have guessed at a dream? Who, without the confession, would have supposed that 'in consequence of a slight indisposition, an anodyne had been prescribed'? Who would have thought it nothing but a 'psychological curiosity'? Who, later, would have dared to talk of its 'patchwork brilliance'?[1] Coleridge played, out of modesty, straight into the hands of critics.

Were it not for Livingston Lowes, it would hardly still be necessary to point out the poem's essential unity and the relation between its two parts. But Lowes's book has such deserved prestige for other reasons that his view may still have undeserved currency. He treats the relation between the parts as 'inconsequential'.

With utter inconsequence, as the caves of ice glance and are gone, the Abyssinian damsel with a dulcimer is there, a tantalizing phantom of a dream-remembered dream, unlocalized, without the slightest sense of unreality, in space; while the Tartar youth with flashing eyes is projected against the background of that twice phantasmal dome in air, dream-built within the dream. It is a baffling complex involution – dreams within dreams, like a nest of Oriental ivories, 'sphere in sphere'.[2]

He also talks of the 'vivid incoherence' of the second part.[3] This shows, more clearly than anything could, the prejudice under which readers labour from having been told beforehand that the poem was a dream, or the result of a dream. For it is exactly on the relationship between these two parts that the poem's character and the whole interpretation of it depend.

The 'flashing eyes and floating hair' could only have been attributed to a 'Tartar youth' by somebody who had momentarily forgotten the *Phaedrus*, say, and *A Midsummer Night's Dream*. For this is poetic frenzy, and the 'symphony and song' are the emblemised conditions of poetic creation. The unity of the poem focuses on just that transition from the first part to the second, and the pivot of all interpretation is in the lines:

> Could I revive within me
> Her symphony and song,
> To such a deep delight 'twould win me,
> That with music loud and long,
> I would build that dome in air. . . .[4]

For 'Kubla Khan' is a poem about the act of poetic creation, about the 'ecstasy in imaginative fulfilment'.[5] Interpretations have diverged to opposite poles of major meaning on the treatment of the emphasis and rhythm of that single line – 'Could I revive within me'. If a strong emphasis (and therefore necessarily also a strong metrical stress) is put upon 'could', the word can be taken to imply 'If only I could, but I can't', and the whole poem can be made to appear to be about the failure and frustration of the creative power. But if the emphasis on 'could' is slight, then the condition is an 'open' condition, like 'Could you make it Wednesday instead of Thursday, it would be easier for me'; and the matter is the very possibility of creative achievement. The word 'once' in the line 'in a vision once I saw' then also becomes a light syllable, not implying 'Once, only once and, I fear, never again', but rather indicating delight, surprise and the sense of unique privilege.

In this choice I have no hesitation in taking the second alternative; not only is it biographically relevant to point out that in 1797–8 Coleridge, so far from bemoaning the loss of creative power, was only just discovering its strength; but also the whole rhythmic character of the paragraph requires this view. The metre is light and fast; the paragraph moves from delight and surprise, through enthusiasm to ecstasy; no sensitive reader can read it otherwise. The verse is asserting, not denying, the

ecstasy. If this were a poem of frustration and failure, the movement would be slow and the stresses heavy. Another verbal detail
points the same way – 'I would build *that* dome in air'. What
dome? Of course, the dome that has been described in the first
part. And if it had not there been fully described, the music of the
singing and the dulcimer would not have any substantial and evident power. It is just because the first part presents the dome and
the river with all its setting so completely, beautifully and finally,
that we accept the authenticity of the creative impulse in the
second part, and find in the last word 'Paradise' a fact, not a forlorn hope. 'Kubla Khan' is a triumphant positive statement of the
potentialities of poetry. How great those potentialities are is revealed partly in the description of its *effects* at the ending of the
second part and partly in the very substance and content of the
first.

The precision and clarity of the opening part are the first
things to mark – even in the order of the landscape. In the centre
is the pleasure-dome with its gardens on the river bank: to one
side is the river's source in the chasm, to the other are the
'caverns measureless to man' and the 'sunless sea' into which
the river falls: Kubla in the centre can hear the '*mingled*
measure' of the fountain of the source from one side, and of the
dark caves from the other. The river winds across the whole landscape. Nobody need keep this mere geographical consistency of
the description prominently in mind as he reads (though once
established it remains clear and constant); but I suggest that if
this factual-visual consistency had been absent, and there had
been a mere random sequence or collocation of items, such as a
dream might well have provided – items which needed a symbol-
system to establish relations at all – then the absence *would* be
observed: the poem would have been quite different, and a new
kind of effort would have been needed to apprehend what unity
it might have had. Within this main landscape, too, there is a
pervasive order. The fertility of the plain is only made possible by
the mysterious energy of the source. The dome has come into
being by Kubla's decree: the dome is stately; the gardens are
girdled round with walls and towers.

It is so often said that 'Kubla Khan' achieves its effect mainly
by 'far-reaching suggestiveness', or by incantation or by much

connotation, with little denotation, that it is worth emphasizing this element of plain clear statement at the outset, statement which does particularize a series of details inter-related to each other, and deriving their relevance from their interrelation and their order. Furthermore, the use of highly emotive and suggestive proper names is proportionately no large source of the poem's effect; it is only necessary to watch the incidence of them. Xanadu, Kubla Khan and Alph occur once in that form within the poem's opening two-and-a-half lines: and none of them occurs again except for the single repetition of Kubla in line 29. Abyssinian and Mount Abora occur once each, in the three lines 39–41. There are no other proper names in the poem at all, unless we should count the final word Paradise.

Next, the mode of appraisal which relies on suggestiveness is likely to underestimate the strength and firmness of the descriptions. In particular, lines 17–24, describing the source of the river, do not in method employ 'suggestiveness' at all.

> And from this chasm, with ceaseless turmoil seething,
> As if this earth in fast thick pants were breathing,
> A mighty fountain momently was forced :
> Amid whose swift half-intermitted burst
> Huge fragments vaulted with rebounding hail,
> Or chaffy grain beneath the thresher's flail :
> And 'mid these dancing rocks at once and ever
> It flung up momently the sacred river.

We may well believe that this is based on a combination of William Bartram's description of the 'chrystal fountain' with his description of the 'Alligator Hole',[6] but he did not provide the organization of the words to convey so fully the sense of inexhaustible energy, now falling now rising, but persisting through its own pulse. We have here in verse the counterpart to such later prose descriptions as that of the starling or the 'white rose of eddy-foam'. The whole passage is full of life because the verse has both the needed energy and the needed control. The combination of energy and control in the rhythm and sound is so great, as in

> at once and ever
> It flung up momently the sacred river

that we are even in danger of missing the force of the imagery, as in 'rebounding hail' and 'dancing rocks'. If we miss it, it is our fault not Coleridge's; and it sometimes appears as if readers are blaming or underestimating him because they have improperly allowed themselves, under the influence of the rhythm, to be blind to the 'huge fragments' and 'dancing rocks' which lay another kind of weight upon it, and to be blind to the construction of the thought, which holds together the continuity and the intermission.

A different kind of clarity and precision in the first part leads us nearer to the poem's central meaning – the consistency with which the main facts of this landscape are treated, the dome and the river. The dome (apart from the biographists' concern about its oriental connection with opium – all the more important to them because Purchas did not mention it and archaeologists have found no trace) is an agreed emblem of fulfilment and satisfaction, it is breast-like, full to touch and eye, rounded and complete. In the first part it is mentioned three times, as 'a stately pleasure-dome' in line 2, as 'the dome of pleasure' in line 31, and as 'A sunny pleasure-dome' in line 36. Each time the word 'pleasure' occurs with it. So too, the word *river* is used three times in the first part, and each time, without fail, it is 'the *sacred* river': this is its constant, invariable epithet. The centre of the landscape of this part is, as we have seen, the point at which the dome and the river join:

> The shadow of the dome of pleasure
> Floated midway on the waves.

Here, without possibility of doubt, the poem presents the conjunction of pleasure and sacredness: that is the core of Part One. And in Part Two the poet who has been able to realise this fusion of pleasure and sacredness is himself regarded as a holy or sacred person, a seer acquainted with the undivided life: and this part is clinched by the emphatic and final word Paradise. The conditional form of Part Two does not annul the presentation of Paradise in Part One, though it may hold out the hope of a future fuller vision.

What is this Paradise? Those who are intent on making 'Kubla Khan' either a poem about imaginative failure or a document for the study of opium dreams, remind us that many of the sources for Coleridge's details were descriptions of false paradises; there was Aloadine's trick Mohammedan Paradise to which young men were lured and entertained with music and girls, so that they might be willing to die in battle in the hope of winning such joys for ever. There were, still more notably, the pseudo-Paradises of Milton.

> that faire field
> Of *Enna*,[7]

and the place

> where *Abassin* Kings thir issue Guard,
> Mount *Amara*, though this by som suppos'd
> True Paradise under the *Ethiop* Line
> By *Nilus* head.[8]

Of course we have in 'Kubla Khan' a fruit of Coleridge's Miltonizing ... but because the Abassin kings and Mount Amara belong with one false paradise it does not follow that the Abyssinian maid and Mount Abora belong with another.

There is only one answer to those who want to make this a false Paradise – that is, an appeal to the poem as a whole, its rhythmical development, its total effect as a poem of fulfilment, and to say 'If you still want to make that experience a spurious experience, do so: "Thy way thou canst not miss, me mine requires".' Acceptance of the Paradise, in sympathy, is the normal response, from childhood and unsophistication to criticism : to most people rejection would mean a ruinous and purposeless wrench. But what is being accepted?

Positively, it causes a distortion of the poem if we try to approximate this Paradise either to the earthly Paradise of Eden before the Fall or to the Heavenly Paradise which is the ultimate abode of the blest. It may take its imagery from Eden, but it is not Eden because Kubla Khan is not Adam. Kubla Khan himself is literally an oriental prince with his name adapted from Purchas. We may, if we persist in hankering after formal equations, incline to say he *is* the Representative Man, or Mankind in general : but what matters is not his supposed fixed and antecedent symbolic character, so much as his activity. Within the landscape treated as literal he must be of princely scope, in order to decree the dome and gardens : and it is this decree that matters, for it images the power of man over his environment and the fact that man makes his Paradise for himself. Just as the whole poem is about poetic creation at the imaginative level, so within the work of the imagination, occurs the creativeness of man at the ethical and practical levels. This is what the poet, of all men, is capable of realizing.

I have already noticed that the name Kubla is repeated only once after the first line; and the place of its repetition is significant :

> And 'mid this tumult Kubla heard from far
> Ancestral voices prophesying war !

This is essential to the full unity of the conception : the Paradise contains knowledge of the threat of its own possible destruction. It is not held as a permanent gift; the ideal life is always open to forces of evil; it must be not only created by man for himself, but also defended by him. It is not of the essence of this Paradise that it must be lost; but there is a risk that it may be lost.

About the river, again, we need not aim to be too precise and make equations. Its function in the poem is clear. The bounding energy of its source makes the fertility of the plain possible : it is the sacred given condition of human life. By using it rightly, by building on its bank, by diverting its water into his sinuous rills, Kubla achieves his perfect state of balanced living. It is an image of these non-human, holy, given conditions. It is not an allegorical river which would still flow across that plain if Kubla was not there. It is an imaginative statement of the abundant life in the universe, which begins and ends in a mystery touched with dread, but it is a statement of this life as the ground of ideal human activity.

The 'caves of ice' need special attention. Some discussions of the poem seem to imply that they belong with the 'caverns measureless to man'; but there surely can be no doubt that in the poem they belong closely and necessarily with the dome.

> It was a miracle of rare device,
> A sunny pleasure-dome, with caves of ice !

The very line shows the closeness by the antithesis, the convex against the concave, the warm against the cold. It is not necessary to invoke Coleridge's own statement of the theory of the reconciliation of opposites in art[9] ('the heat in ice' is even one of his examples) to see that it is the holding together of these two different elements in which the miracle consists. They are repeated together, also within the single line, 47, in Part Two. Lowes shows clearly how in Coleridge's memory the caves of ice came to be associated with the sacred river;[10] and in his sources the ice does not indicate terror or torment or death (as Miss Bodkin[11] seems to think Coleridge's ice does here), but rather the marvellous, and the delight which accompanies the marvellous; the ice is linked specifically to the fountains sacred to the moon. This marvellousness is present also in 'Kubla Khan', but there is more : ice is shining, clear, crystalline, hard : and here it adds greater strength and austerity to what would be otherwise the lush, soft, even sentimental, core of the poem. As it is, the miracle of rare device consists in the combination of these softer and harder elements. And when this is seen in relation to the act of poetic creation, in the light of which all Part One must be understood, its function is still plainer : such creation has this element of austerity in it.

For this is a vision of the ideal human life *as the poetic imagination can create it*. Part One only exists in the light of Part Two. There may be other Paradises, other false Paradises too : but this is the creation of the poet in his frenzy. And it is because he can create it that he deserves the ritual dread.

II

The critique of 'Christabel' is an entirely different matter : for not only is it inescapably a fragment, but the two parts differ so much from each other, that they scarcely seem to belong to the same poem. The unlikeness here would have been altogether apparent even if Coleridge had not himself, as usual, used a Preface to explain that the two parts were written in different years, with the visit to Germany between them, and even if all his letters and other comments on the business were unknown.

One of the most obvious differences between the two parts is caused by his physical move from Somerset to the Lake District. In Part I there is the castle in the woodland, with oak and moss and mistletoe, a landscape which has its function only in relation to the persons and the atmosphere. There are no proper names but those of the three main persons. In Part II we plunge straight into the detailed geography of the region; Wyndermere, Langdale Pike, Dungeon-ghyll, Borodale and the rest, organise the reader's attention as if this were matter of history rather than of imagery.

It is generally agreed that the experience of reading the First Part of 'Christabel' is more an acquaintance with an atmosphere than the apprehension of a poetic unity. This atmosphere is achieved partly through description of the setting, partly by the mystery surrounding Geraldine.

One of the familiar examples of description will illustrate also . . . the relationship between Coleridge's descriptions and Dorothy Wordsworth's.

Dorothy, 25 January 1798 :

The sky spread over with one continuous cloud, whitened by the light of the moon . . .[12]

Dorothy, 31 January :

When we left home the moon immensely large, the sky scattered over with clouds. These soon closed in, contracting the dimensions of the moon without concealing her.[13]

Coleridge, Gutch Memorandum Book :

> Behind the thin
> Grey cloud that covered but not hid the sky
> The round full moon looked small.[14]

Coleridge, 'Christabel', Part I, lines 14–19 :

> Is the night chilly and dark?
> The night is chilly, but not dark.
> The thin gray cloud is spread on high,
> It covers but not hides the sky.
> The moon is behind, and at the full;
> And yet she looks both small and dull.

We do not know whose original observation this may have been, but one thing is clear – that Coleridge did more than merely take over an existing observation of Dorothy's or his own, and transfer it straight into 'Christabel'; because he has very much modified his own first verse draft in the Gutch book. Especially by adding the moon's dullness – perhaps he even did pronounce the word 'dull' to rhyme with 'full' – he has increased the mysteriousness and vagueness of the midnight light, and has reached an effect which is altogether absent from Wordsworth's lines in 'A Night-Piece', which also belong with the same entry in Dorothy's Journal. Wordsworth wrote :

> The sky is overcast
> With a continuous cloud of texture close,
> Heavy and wan, all whitened by the Moon,
> Which through that veil is indistinctly seen,
> A dull, contracted circle, yielding light
> So feebly spread that not a shadow falls,
> Chequering the ground.[15]

The difference of atmosphere from 'Christabel' is very marked. The whole Wordsworth poem is an attempt to expand, rather in the manner of Cowper, according to a method in which rhythm has little part; to win assent to the delight by mere accumulation of circumstance and detail. But in the result there is no particularity of mood. The Coleridge lines, by contrast, suggest both by vocabulary and rhythm that cloud and moon are behaving oddly and ominously, just out of the way of ordinary behaviour, as if proportion is thrown out and normal vision perplexed. At point after point in 'Christabel' descriptions are used to heighten the mystery by such suggestions of slight distortion in behaviour, or of contrast, or surprise –

> And wildly glittered here and there
> The gems entangled in her hair.

> in moonshine cold

> The brands were flat, the brands were dying,
> Amid their own white ashes lying;
> But when the lady passed, there came

> A tongue of light, a fit of flame;
> And Christabel saw the lady's eye

> The silver lamp burns dead and dim.

But it is all fragmentary and finally unsatisfying because it leads up to a mystery which is both incomplete and clueless. The enigmatic Geraldine entirely swamps Part I. I do not propose to go into the question of how far she was a vampire or a Lamia or whether she was a victim of metempsychosis.[16] But Ernest Hartley Coleridge was surely right when he said that there are a number of indications that in Part I Geraldine is 'at the mercy of some malign influence not herself'.[17] She is in 'sore distress' and asks for pity (l. 73); 'in wretched plight' (l. 188); she first (apparently without irony) wishes Christabel's mother were there, and even after the malignant wish for the mother to be off, she will still try to requite Christabel well; she must even pray: 'for I Must pray, ere yet in bed I lie' (ll. 233–4). The critical act of revealing her bosom is approached with extreme reluctance. She acts 'drawing in her breath aloud Like one that shuddered'. Then comes the main passage on which Ernest Hartley Coleridge comments :

> Ah ! what a stricken look was hers !
> Deep from within she seems half-way
> To lift some weight with sick assay,
> And eyes the maid and seeks delay ;
> Then suddenly, as one defied,
> Collects herself in scorn and pride,
> And lay down by the Maiden's side ![18]

These lines did not occur in the original version of 1816; they were not published till 1828; and that edition is the basis of the *textus receptus*. They occur in none of the main manuscripts. Their insertion seems rather to underline what was already implied, than to declare a later change of purpose; and they were, further, a protection against the misrepresentation of critics.

The whole of this scene has unquestionably a genuine horror in it : the mitigating explanatory lines were absent from the version reviewed so malignantly in *The Examiner* (very probably by Hazlitt) on 2 June 1816 :

There is something disgusting at the bottom of his subject, which is but ill glossed over by a veil of Della Cruscan sentiment and fine writing – like moon-beams playing on a charnel-house, or flowers strewed on a dead body.

An anonymous pamphlet later 'pronounced poor Christabel "the most obscene Poem in the English Language" ' – which prompted Coleridge's comment : 'I saw an old book at Coleorton in which the Paradise Lost was described as an "obscene Poem", so I am in good company.'[19]

There are three extant accounts of how '*Christabel*' was to have been finished that are near enough to Coleridge himself to have serious claim to be considered authentic. Two come from Gillman, in whose house at Highgate Coleridge lived from 1816 till his death; the other from Coleridge's son Derwent. The shorter Gillman account is this :

The story of Christabel is partly founded on the notion, that the virtuous of this world save the wicked. The pious and good Christabel suffers and prays for
    'The weal of her lover that is far away,'
exposed to various temptations in a foreign land; and she thus defeats the power of evil represented in the person of Geraldine. This is one main object of the tale.[20]

The Derwent Coleridge account is also short and general :

The sufferings of Christabel were to have been represented as vicarious, endured for her 'lover far away'; and Geraldine, no witch or goblin, or malignant being of any kind, but a spirit, executing her appointed task with the best good will, as she herself says : –
    All they, who live in the upper sky,
    Do love you, holy Christabel, &c. (ll. 227–32).
In form this is, of course, accommodated to 'a fond superstition', in keeping with the general tenour of the piece; but that the holy and the innocent do often suffer for the faults of those they love, and are thus made the instruments to bring them back to the ways of peace, is a matter of fact, and in Coleridge's hands might have been worked up into a tale of deep and delicate pathos.[21]

The longer Gillman account of the projected third and fourth parts is this :

Over the mountains, the Bard, as directed by Sir Leoline, 'hastes' with his disciple; but in consequence of one of those inundations supposed to be common to this country, the spot only where the castle once stood is discovered, – the edifice itself being washed away. He determines to return. Geraldine being acquainted with all that is passing, like the Weird Sisters in Macbeth, vanishes. Re-appearing, however, she waits the return of the Bard, exciting in the mean time, by her wily arts, all the anger she could rouse in the Baron's breast, as well as that jealousy of which he is described to have been susceptible. The old Bard and the youth at length arrive, and therefore she can no longer personate the character of Geraldine, the daughter of Lord Roland de Vaux, but changes her appearance to that of the accepted though absent lover of Christabel. Next ensues a courtship most distressing to Christabel, who feels – she knows not why – great disgust for her once favoured knight. This coldness is very painful to the Baron, who has no more conception than herself of the supernatural transformation. She at last yields to her father's entreaties, and consents to approach the altar with this hated suitor. The real lover returning, enters at this moment, and produces the ring which she had once given him in sign of her betrothment. Thus defeated, the supernatural being Geraldine disappears. As predicted, the castle bell tolls, the mother's voice is heard, and to the exceeding great joy of the parties, the rightful marriage takes place, after which follows a reconciliation and explanation between the father and daughter.[22]

James Dykes Campbell said in his edition of the poems (1893) that he suspected and hoped Coleridge was merely quizzing Gillman with the shorter account of the ending.[23] Dante Gabriel Rossetti took the longer Gillman ending seriously.[24] In two modern American articles it has been accepted as highly probable.[25] But the chief objection against the long Gillman ending is plain – that, as it is presented, it makes the story seem like a vulgar, trivial Gothic Romance; and Donald R. Tuttle has virtually accepted the idea that it is simply as a Gothic Romance that the poem is to be read. The shorter Gillman account of the ending, and the account given by Derwent Coleridge, both agree in making Christabel the centre of the main interest; and agree moreover on the view that the primary subject of the poem was Christabel's vicarious suffering for her lover.

This leads to the one other interesting recorded remark made by Coleridge himself about the poem – that Crashaw's verses on St Theresa beginning

> Since 'tis not to be had at home,
> She'l travel to a martyrdome

were ever present to my mind whilst writing the second part of Christabel; if, indeed by some subtle process of the mind they did not suggest the first thought of the whole poem.[26]

Now since the central theme of the Crashaw poem is the desire for martyrdom, and since the traditional view of martyrdom, and of the virtue in the blood of martyrs, includes the idea of the value to others of vicarious suffering, this one remark of Coleridge's tends strongly to reinforce the evidence of Derwent Coleridge and the shorter account given by Gillman.

A. H. Nethercot, whose book *The Road to Tryermaine* contains the fullest and fairest modern attempt to interpret the poem, found himself forced in his conclusion to the belief that its theme was relatively 'simple and straightforward'. He argues that 'Christabel' was to exemplify the 'preternatural', just as 'The Ancient Mariner' was to exemplify the 'supernatural'. Coleridge used the word 'preternatural' at the beginning of his critique of *The Monk*: in 1801 he was planning to publish 'Christabel' with two essays prefixed, one on the Preternatural and one on Metre.[27] Nethercot links this to the lines on Joan of Arc in 'The Destiny of Nations', which speak of 'Beings of higher class than Man', who take on human form for their own purposes, and make

> Of transient Evil ever-during Good
> Themselves probationary, and denied
> Confess'd to view by preternatural deed
> To o'erwhelm the will, save on some fated day.[28]

Geraldine, Nethercot argues, is such a being as this, in Derwent Coleridge's words, 'a spirit, executing her appointed task with the best good will'. She is the agency through whom Christabel (whose name has 'Christ's name in 't') is to be brought to 'an abbreviated but concentrated form'[29] of martyrdom at her father's castle. By this means Christabel would make atonement for the wrongs committed by her absent lover.

This is neat, and consistent with various evidence; but, as Nethercot fully admits, it is hard to reconcile with Coleridge's overwhelming difficulties in completing the poem, his references to his 'vision' of it, all the suggestions that the theme was subtle and complicated. The underlying fact is that none of Coleridge's poems at this period can be covered by a short, neat statement of their theme, any more than 'The Ancient Mariner' is explained by quoting the epigrammatic moral at its end. In view of Coleridge's statement about the importance to him, in a 'subtle' way, of Crashaw's poem on St Theresa, there seems a strong likelihood that he was hampered by problems which belong to the psychological borderland where matters of religion overlap with matters of sex :

> Shee never undertooke to know,
> What death with love should have to doe
> Nor has shee ere yet understood
> Why to show love shee should shed blood.

In the seventeenth century such double references could be carried together in the mind without any intellectual unease, and without any moral shame or awkwardness. In 1800 that was not so. Yet Coleridge, of all Englishmen then living, was the one most likely to have had some understanding of this borderland, and to have known intimately the difficulties of using that, perhaps dim, understanding at the centre of a narrative poem. He was not writing an elementary story of Gothic horror, but was trying to explore more deeply the serious psychological areas which such stories just touched in their own trivial way.

SOURCE : *Coleridge* (London 1953) pp. 114–36.

NOTES

1. P. H. B. Lyon, *The Discovery of Poetry* (Arnold, 1930) p. 101.

2. J. L. Lowes, *The Road to Xanadu* (Boston, Mass., 1927; rev. ed. 1930) p. 409.

3. Ibid., p. 363, where it is called an attribute of dreams.

4. *The Complete Poetical Works of Samuel Taylor Coleridge*, ed. E. H. Coleridge (Oxford, 1912) I 298 (hereafter referred to as *PW*).

5. Maud Bodkin, *Archetypal Patterns in Poetry* (Oxford, 1934) p. 95.

6. Lowes, pp. 367–9; *PW*, I 297.

7. *Paradise Lost*, IV 268–9.

8. Ibid., 280–3.

9. 'On Poesy or Art', printed in *Biographia Literaria*, II 255–6; cf. *BL*, II 12.

10. Lowes, pp. 379–80.

11. *Archetypal Patterns in Poetry*, p. 135.

12. *Journals of Dorothy Wordsworth*, ed. E. de Selincourt, I 4.

13. Ibid., I 5.

14. Quoted in *Christabel*, Samuel Taylor Coleridge. Illustrated by a facsimile of the manuscript, and by Textual and Other Notes by E. H. Coleridge (London, 1907) p. 3 (hereafter referred to as *C*).

15. *Poetical Works*, ed. E. de Selincourt (Oxford) II 208.

16. For an exhausting exploration of these questions, see Arthur N. Nethercot, *The Road to Tryermaine. A Study of Coleridge's* 'Christabel' (University of Chicago Press, 1939) Bk. II.

17. *C*, p. 76 note 2. But Gillman, *The Life of Samuel Taylor Coleridge* (1838) (p. 284) calls her 'an evil being, not of this world'.

18. Lines 256–62; the earlier versions read, simply, for these lines :
> She took two paces and a stride,
> And lay down by the maiden's side.

19. *Unpublished Letters of Samuel Taylor Coleridge*, ed. E. L. Griggs (London, 1932) p. 247 To Southey, February 1819. The letter also says : 'It seems that Hazlitt from pure malignity had spread about the Report that Geraldine was a Man in disguise.'

20. Gillman, p. 283.

21. *C*, p. 52, note 1 : From *The Poems of Samuel Taylor Coleridge*, ed. Derwent and Sara Coleridge, [?] 1870. This undated issue first contained an introductory essay by Derwent Coleridge. I have not seen a copy of it, and *C* is my only authority for the quotation.

22. Gillman, pp. 301–2. (See p. 42 above.)

23. p. 604.

24. Hall Caine, *Recollections of Dante Gabriel Rossetti* (1882) p. 154.

25. *Studies in Philology*, XXXIII (July 1936); B. R. McElderry Jr, 'Coleridge's Plan for Completing *Christabel*'. *PMLA* LIII (June 1938); Donald R. Tuttle, '*Christabel* Sources in Percy's *Reliques* and the Gothic Romance'.

26. *Letters, Conversations and Recollections of S. T. Coleridge*, edited by Thomas Allsop, 3rd edn. (1864), pp. 104–5. (See pp. 40–1 above.)

27. *Collected Letters of S. T. Coleridge*, ed. E. L. Griggs, (Oxford, 1956–71), I 349 : To Thomas Poole, 16 March 1801. See Nethercot, pp. 200–1.

28. *PW*, II 136 n. The text is that included in Southey's *Joan of Arc*, 1796. See Nethercot, pp. 201–5.

29. Nethercot, p. 210.

Harold Bloom

'KUBLA KHAN' (1961)

'Kubla Khan' is a poem of self-recognition, in which the figure of the youth as virile poet is finally identified with the poem's speaker. Behind Coleridge's poem is Collins' masterpiece of a poet's incarnation, the 'Ode on the Poetical Character', and the dark fates of Collins himself, the young Chatterton, Smart, and the other doomed bards of sensibility. These are the rich-haired youths of Morn, Apollo sacrifices who precede Coleridge in his appearance with flashing eyes and floating hair in the last lines of 'Kubla Khan'. In Blake's myth such a youth is a form of the rising Orc, the fiery dawn of a new Beulah or increase in sensual fulfilment, but an Adonis as well as an Apollo, a dawn that is merely cyclic in nature, an outburst of energy in which the organic and the creative are uneasily allied. The young poets of 'Alastor' and 'Endymion', with their dark and glorious destinies, and their sense of both embodying nature and yet being imprisoned by it, are later forms of Coleridge's myth. The old poet of 'Sailing to Byzantium' with his deliberate voyage out of nature is the fitting dying fall for the Romantic tradition of tragic poetic self-recognition.

Internally, 'Kubla Khan' is no fragment but a vision of creation and destruction, each complete. It is not quite a 'poem about the act of poetic creation,' for it contains that theme as one element in a more varied unity, just as Yeats's 'Byzantium' does.

Kubla Khan and Xanadu belong to the *given* of the poem; we need to accept them without asking why *this* potentate or *this* place. Kubla has power and can command magnificence; that is enough. He builds a dome of pleasure for himself, as the rulers of Byzantium built a greater dome to honor God. But the Byzan-

tine dome, while apt for Yeats's purposes, is too theological for
Coleridge's poem. Kubla builds the dome for himself, and the poet
with his music will build a dome in air, matching and at length
overgoing the mightiest of human material power. The orthodox censor in Coleridge gives him the remote dome in Xanadu,
and avoids the issue of the poet's relative sanctity against more
than natural verities.

Kubla picks his spot with precision. A sacred river runs into
the ground at just the point where the great dome is decreed.
Beneath the dome is the underground river, running in measureless caverns down to a sunless sea. The dome rises above an
artificial paradise, ten miles in diameter, including both elaborate
gardens and ancient forests. Amid these forests is a chasm from
which a fountain suddenly bursts, part earthquake, part geyser.
'Momently' the underground river is forced up and runs five miles
above ground until it reaches the caverns again and sinks down. In
this sudden upheaval the fountain evidently comes up near the
dome, as that is at the midpoint of the enclosure.

Now it is clear that this upheaval is only a momentary affair;
Coleridge emphasizes this by saying 'momently' twice, in lines 19
and 24. And so the miracle of rare device of line 35 is only
momentary also. Just once in this upheaval, which is to Kubla
a presage of the contrary of his pleasure garden ('ancestral voices
prophesying war'), Kubla and we can visualize the following
phenomena intimately associated : the dome (with sunlight upon
it), the dome's shadow floating midway upon the waves of the
seething, forced-up river; the fountain geyser with its hurling
rocks, just next to the dome; and the exposed icy caverns beneath, from which the fountain has momentarily removed the
covering earth. The effect is apocalyptic, for what is revealed is a
natural miracle :

> It was a miracle of rare device,
> A sunny pleasure-dome with caves of ice !

The river, now raised again, is sacred. The chasm is holy and
enchanted, and is associated with waning moonlight. The river
comes up as the fountain before it settles down again, and so the
fountain is sacred too, and the fragments of earth flung up in it
take on the orderly associations of the sacred; they are dancing

rocks. The exposed caverns are icy; the dome is sunny. What is exposed is holy; what was built for exposure is representative of a perfect pleasure, the dome being necessarily a perfect hemisphere.

At the midpoint of the momentarily flung-up river we see and hear, together, the extraordinary sight of the shadow of the pleasure dome, and the mingled music of the bursting fountain and the exposed underground current. As the contraries of sun and moon, dome and cavern, light and dark, heat and ice meet, Kubla hears the voices of the dead speaking to the living within a scene of peace and prophesying war. The momentary upheaval itself is the contrary and answer of nature to Kubla's decree of the power of art. The fountain rises suddenly like Blake's wind of Beulah or Shelley's West Wind, to create and destroy, to bring sun and ice together. The very sign of the fountain's potential for destruction is also an emblem of 'chaffy grain beneath the thresher's flail,' and the sexual intimations of the poem are undeniable, though they are subordinated to and subsumed by the more general theme of creation and destruction.

Kubla had not sought the balance or reconciliation of opposites which Coleridge and Blake alike saw as the mark of the creative imagination, but momentarily his dome and the bursting fountain together do present a vision of such a balance; the landscape becomes a poem, and the imagination has its manifestation. The triumphal chant that follows is Coleridge's assertion that he as poet can build a finer dome and a more abiding paradise than Kubla's, and one that would have both convex heat and concave ice without the necessity of earthquake. Coleridge's music would be 'loud and long'; Kubla's is momentary.

The earthly paradise traditionally takes one of its alternate placings in Abyssinia. The crucial passage here is in *Paradise Lost* :

> Mount *Amara*, though this by some suppos'd
> True Paradise under the *Ethiop* Line
> By *Nilus* head, enclos'd with shining Rock. (IV 281–3)

This is Coleridge's Mount Abora, and his Abyssinian maid, in singing of it, is celebrating Paradise. Once the poet saw her in

vision; if he now revives *within* himself her song of Eden he will
enter a state of such deep delight :

> That with music loud and long,
> I would build that dome in air,
> That sunny dome ! those caves in ice !

He would rival Kubla's decreed dome, and also produce the
imaginative miracle of the juxtaposed contraries, and without
the equivocal aid of the paradoxical upheaval that simultaneously creates and threatens the destruction of the 'rare device'.
For this is the potential of the poetic imagination to create
more lastingly than even Nature and Art can do together. And
could he do this, he would be a reincarnation of the young Apollo.
Those who heard his song would *see* his visionary creation, for that
is the inventive power of poetry. And they would grant him the
awe due to the youth who has eaten the fruit and drunk the milk
of the Eden forbidden to them, or open only through vicarious
participation in the poet's vision :

> And all who heard should see them there,
> And all should cry, Beware ! Beware !
> His flashing eyes, his floating hair !
> Weave a circle round him thrice,
> And close your eyes with holy dread,
> For he on honey-dew hath fed,
> And drunk the milk of Paradise.

SOURCE: *The Visionary Company*, (New York 1961; London
1962) pp. 212–15.

George G. Watson

'KUBLA KHAN' (1966)

Before he was twenty-six years old, and before the first edition of *Lyrical Ballads* appeared, Coleridge had made himself a poet of many languages: an apprentice in many styles, and already a master of some, as 'The Ancient Mariner', 'Christabel', and 'Frost at Midnight' all variously show. He was perhaps the first European poet to set himself the task of achieving a wide diversity of styles based upon models other than classical ones; the undertaking, after all, would have seemed barbarous nonsense to an Augustan, and unthinkable to a Renaissance poet. 'Kubla Khan' is . . . difficult . . . to interpret . . . but then by the late 1790s Coleridge might be said to have earned some right to be difficult. He was ready for ingenious solutions. Perhaps ingenuity is too pale a word to describe his poetic strength at this moment, at the height of his talent; but some of his solutions, like that in the 'Mariner' of giving a medieval dress to the most modern of themes, impress above all by their calculation and their temerity.

All this prepares for the confession that some aspects of 'Kubla Khan' remain inexplicable. The metre, for a start, is like nothing at all. The matter of dating might have proved crucial here, but unfortunately it remains inconclusive, and the traditional composition-date of May 1798 (*Poetical Works*, p. 295), which would leave the poem just later than the 'Mariner' and probably later than the beginning of 'Christabel', has been challenged in favour of Coleridge's own date of 1797 and, less plausibly, in favour of 1799–1800. If the poem is later than any part of 'Christabel', then its rhythm would represent a marked reaction back towards the heavy iambic beat of traditional English verse :

> In Xanadu did Kubla Khan
> A stately pleasure-dome decree :
> Where Alph, the sacred river, ran
> Through caverns measureless to man
> > Down to a sunless sea ... (*Poetical Works,* p. 297)

The comparison with 'Christabel' is the more tempting since both poems are largely composed in four-footers; but it is impossible to explain, though easy to applaud, the strange compromise whereby 'Kubla Khan' moves in the most traditional of iambics from paragraph to paragraph in a rhyme-scheme that is always present, and yet neither stanzaic nor yet like an ode. The language of the poem is problematical too, given the bare facts that it is by Coleridge and of the 1790's. Unlike the 'Mariner' and 'Christabel', it is in contemporary English, a fact which would pose no sort of puzzle for most poems in most ages, but which is very like a suspicious circumstance here. As a matter of fact, the suspicion is justified. Coleridge's source, to which he drew attention in the preface of 1816, on first publishing the poem side by side with 'Christabel', is a source in Jacobean prose : not the richly convoluted Jacobean of Jeremy Taylor which he was to imitate in the prose gloss to the 'Mariner', but the homespun Jacobean of Hakluyt's assistant Samuel Purchas. Coleridge obligingly quotes, or rather misquotes, the passage from Purchas's *Pilgrimage* (1613) in his preface to the poem. It actually reads :

In Xaindu did Cublai Can build a stately pallace, encompassing sixteene miles of plaine ground with a wall, wherein are fertile meddowes, pleasant springs, delightfull streames, and all sorts of beasts of chase and game, and in the middest thereof a sumptuous house of pleasure ... (IV xi).

It is easy to imagine what Coleridge in another mood might have made of that. In fact he rejects from it everything that is beguilingly of its period – 'encompassing', 'beasts of chase and game', 'in the middest thereof'. The poem is arrantly modern. Much of it offers a kind of dynamic precision of language which is quite unlike the English of any age previous to Coleridge's :

...A mighty fountain momently was forced :
Amid whose swift half-intermitted burst
Huge fragments vaulted like rebounding hail,
Or chaffy grain beneath the thresher's flail.

If 'Kubla Khan' is a poem of the *annus mirabilis* of 1797–8, as
still seems likely, and late rather than early in that year, then it is a
striking inversion of Coleridgean formula. Instead of putting
on the language of another, Coleridge has in this instance stripped
it off. This is not to say that the language of the poem, or even of
the first paragraph, is merely residual. It has too much life of its
own for that. But its modernity is itself a device.

Such ingenuities ought to underline our uncertainty concerning the poet's purpose in 'Kubla Khan'. The fact is that almost
everything is known about the poem except what it is about.
Scholarship has been lavished upon the problem of dating. The
very farmhouse in Culbone, a tiny village on the Somerset coast
where the poet may have been interrupted in his composition,
as he tells us in the 1816 preface, by 'a person on business from
Porlock', has been plausibly identified. The allegedly creative
effects of opium-taking have been experimentally investigated
and on the whole discredited. But an interpretation of the poem
that is generally acceptable is no nearer than ever. Even Humphry
House in his Clark Lectures, though he called it 'a triumphant
positive statement of the potentialities of poetry',[1] fumbled in his
conclusion, narrowly missed the point of the poem, and failed to
show how its logic works.

Taking heart from the medical evidence, which discounts the
notion that opium produces either dreams in sleep or waking
hallucinations, I shall dismiss one troublesome possibility at once.
The Crewe manuscript of 1810, now in the British Museum,
announces in Coleridge's own hand that the poem was
'composed in a sort of reverie'. By 1816, in the subtitle to the
first printed version, the poem is rather bafflingly described as
'A Vision in a Dream', and the preface claims it was composed
in 'a profound sleep' of about three hours. Coleridge's own
accounts, then, are something less than self-consistent; but even
if they had been so, it would still be clear that 'Kubla Khan' is
not in any formal sense a dream-poem, however it may have
been composed. This is not to say that Coleridge's own accounts

of how it came to be written are either mendacious or mistaken, though (after a lapse of a dozen years and more) it would not be surprising or disgraceful if they proved unreliable. It is simply that the poem is not a dream-poem in the technical sense, like Chaucer's *Book of the Duchess*, or Coleridge's own poems 'The Pains of Sleep' and 'Phantom or Fact'; except in the single detail of the damsel with the dulcimer, that is, it does not purport to relate the experience of a dream. Whether it is 'dreamlike' is a matter of definition. For some unexplained reason, that word is commonly applied to the vague, shadowy or mystical, though dreams themselves hardly ever seem to be like this: *Alice in Wonderland*, which is none of these things, surely offers a much more convincing example of what they can be like. Few wide-awake readers will find Lowes's defence of Coleridge's 1816 pre-face convincing:

Nobody in his waking senses could have fabricated those amazing eighteen lines [from 'A damsel with a dulcimer . . .']. For if any-thing ever bore the infallible marks of authenticity, it is that dis-solving panorama in which fugitive hints of Aloadine's Paradise succeed each other with the vivid incoherence, and the illusion of natural and expected sequence, and the sense of an identity that yet is not identity, which are the distinctive attributes of dreams.[2]

But it is not at all obvious that the poem is incoherent. In fact it is wonderfully of a piece. Peacock saw this point at once, in an article he drafted in 1818 in reply to the reviewers within two years of its publication. 'There are very few specimens of lyrical poetry,' he argued, 'so plain, so consistent, so completely *simplex et unum* from first to last' as 'Kubla Khan'; and he dismisses the 1816 preface boldly:

as the story of its having been composed in his sleep must necessarily, by all who are acquainted with his manner of narrating matter of fact, be received with a certain degree of scepticism, its value of a psychological curiosity is nothing; and whatever value it has is in its poetic merit alone.[3]

In any case, Coleridge's own views about dreams seem to have been interpretative, more so than Lowes's phrase 'dissolving panorama' would suggest, and he may not have thought 'Kubla

Khan' any the less significant or shapely for representing 'a vision in a dream'. Dreams, like poems, seem to have had for him 'a logic of their own' :

> Call it a moment's work (and such it seems)
> This tale's a fragment from the life of dreams;
> But say that years matur'd the silent strife,
> And 'tis a record from the dream of life
> <div align="right">(<i>Poetical Works</i>, p. 485)</div>

Dreams have significance, like life itself, and demand interpretation. Certainly 'Kubla Khan' is a difficult poem, in the sense that it calls for careful exegesis based on a good deal of information about Coleridge's intellectual preoccupations. But it is not muddled. It may sound faint praise to some to call it one of the best organized of all Coleridge's works : more explicit, perhaps, to remark that it is one of those poems that seem all bones, so firm and self-assertive is the structure. It is not even, on the face of it (to continue the argument as if the troublesome preface did not exist), an emotionally intense poem, apart from the last half-dozen lines. Much of its tone is matter-of-fact, informative, even slightly technical, as if Coleridge was anxious, as he is in the opening section of the 'Mariner', to get his measurements right. And it is worth noticing at once that he does get them right. The reader is enabled and encouraged to construct a model, or draw a map, of the Khan's whole device, and it can be no accident that the figure 'five', mentioned in the sixth line, 'So twice five miles of fertile ground/With walls and towers were girdled round . . .' is repeated in l.25 : 'Five miles meandering with a mazy motion . . .'. (This is corrected from 'twice six miles' in the Crewe manuscript.) The walls are ten miles long, in fact, in order to surround the five-mile stretch of the sacred river that is above the surface of the earth. Besides, as many have noticed, there seems to be nothing fragmentary about the poem as it survives, in spite of the 1816 subtitle 'A Fragment' : it seems to say all it has to say. And the logical progression of the poem is unusually good, each of its four paragraphs being an advance upon its predecessor, and each one tightly organized within itself. All this is not to deny that Coleridge may have composed the poem in a dream, but only to insist that the dream-hypothesis is unhelpful, and even—in so far as it may encourage the reader to let down his guard and disregard what the poem is saying – something of a nuisance.

What is 'Kubla Khan' about? This is, or ought to be, an established fact of criticism : 'Kubla Khan' is a poem about poetry. It is probably the most original poem about poetry in English, and the first hint outside his notebooks and letters that a major critic lies hidden in the twenty-five-year-old Coleridge. Anyone who objects that there is not a word about poetry in it should be sent at once to the conclusion and asked, even if he has never read any Plato, what in English poetry this is like :

> Weave a circle round him thrice,
> And close your eyes with holy dread,
> For he on honey-dew hath fed,
> And drunk the milk of Paradise.

There are dozens of parallels in Renaissance English to this account of poetic inspiration, all based – though rarely at first hand – on Plato's view of poetic madness in the *Ion* or the *Phaedrus*. Shakespeare's banter about 'the poet's eye, in a fine frenzy rolling' in *A Midsummer Night's Dream* is perhaps the most famous. The 'flashing eyes' and 'floating hair' of Coleridge's poem belong to a poet in the fury of creation. Verbal resemblances to the text of Plato itself confirm that the last paragraph of the poem is a prolonged Platonic allusion. Socrates, in the *Ion*, compares lyric poets to 'Bacchic maidens who draw *milk and honey* from the rivers when under the influence of Dionysus' and adds that poets 'gather their strains from *honied fountains* out of the gardens and dells of the Muses. . . .' Ion himself, describing the effects of poetic recitation, confesses that 'when I speak of horrors, my hair stands on end. . . .' The very phrase 'holy dread' is Platonic (*Laws* 671D). That 'Kubla Khan' is in some sense a comment on Plato's theory of poetry is not really in doubt.

Given that 'Kubla Khan' is about poetry, its general direction is not difficult to discern, and real problems only arise in trying to account for detail after detail in terms of its total significance. The fifty-four lines of the poem divide clearly at line 36. The first section, often in coldly literal detail, describes the Khan's 'rare device'. Purchas's *Pilgrimage* (1613) tells us hardly more than that the Khan built a movable palace in a beautifully enclosed park. Coleridge is much more specific, and concentrates many of Purchas's details, and some others, into a closely consistent picture. The park in the poem is a mixture of the natural and the artificial, at once a wilderness and a garden, and what is man-made contains, or is contained in, the wild and uncontrollable :

> And here were forests ancient as the hills
> Enfolding sunny spots of greenery.

Though the whole design is of course artificial – an enclosed park centering upon a palace or 'stately pleasure-dome' – it contains within itself, as its unique possession, something utterly natural and uncontrollable : the sacred river itself, for the rest of its course subterranean, bursts into the light at this point and flows violently above ground before sinking back. It is evidently for this reason that the tyrant chose the site for his palace, which stands so close to the water that it casts its shadow upon it and is within earshot of the sound of the river, both above and below ground. And these two sounds harmonize :

> Where was heard the mingled measure
> From the fountain and the caves.

With full emphasis upon the effect of harmonious contrast, the first section ends.

The second begins on an apparently irrelevant note, but its relevance is justified at once : the song of an Abyssinian girl, once heard in a dream, is capable of moving such 'deep delight' that

> I would build that dome in air . . .

'In air' presumably means not substantially but as a poem, and the reader's first instinct is to say that this is just what Coleridge has done. But this is evidently wrong. The syntax makes it very clear that the project remains unfulfilled :

> And all who heard should see them there,
> And all should cry . . .

'Kubla Khan', then, is not just about poetry : it is about two kinds of poem. One of them is there in the first thirty-six lines of the poem; and though the other is nowhere to be found, we are told what it would do to the reader and what it would do to the poet. The reader would be able to visualize a palace and park he had never seen; and the poet would behave after the classic manner of poets, like a madman. This second poem, a poem that does not exist, is so evidently the real thing that it is clear that the poem of the first thirty-six lines is not – not quite a poem at all, in Coleridge's terms. And if it is asked why Coleridge in 1798 would be likely to find ll.1-36 unpoetical, the question is already answered. They are factual, detailed, matter-of-fact. It is well known precisely why Coleridge objected to 'matter-of-factness' in poetry – the very word, in his view, was his own coinage. In the *Biographia Literaria*, written nearly twenty years later, he lists this quality as the second of Wordsworth's defects as a poet:

. . . a matter-of-factness in certain poems . . . a laborious minuteness and fidelity in the representation of objects . . . (*BL* xxii).

This may sound rather remote from the twenty-five-year-old poet who wrote 'Kubla Khan'. But Hazlitt, if his evidence is to be trusted (and it may have been conditioned by a reading of this passage in the *Biographia*, which appeared in 1817), supplies the one detail to complete the case. In his essay 'My First Acquaintance with Poets', published in the third number of *The Liberal* (April 1823) he tells how Coleridge had made the same objection to some of Wordsworth's poems in a walk near Nether Stowey in June 1798, only a few weeks after the most probable date of composition of 'Kubla Khan'. Coleridge, says Hazlitt:

lamented that Wordsworth was not prone enough to believe in the traditional superstitions of the place, and that there was something corporeal, a *matter-of-fact-ness*, a clinging to the palpable, or often to the petty, in his poetry in consequence . . . He said, however (if I remember right) that this objection must be confined to his descriptive pieces, that his philosophic poetry had a grand and comprehensive spirit in it, so that his soul seemed to inhabit the universe like a palace, and to discover truth by intuition rather than by deduction.

Here are two kinds of poetry, and evidence too that this preoccupation of Coleridge's career as a critic was already present in the fertile year of 1797–8. In a sense, it is the same question that led him, in the years that followed, into the period of intense critical activity that began with *The Friend* in 1809 and culminated in the composition of the *Biographia Literaria* in 1815. How far may poetry be purely informative and descriptive? Coleridge's answer, in effect, was 'Ideally, never.' Information is not the characteristic business of poetry. Poetry may have an informative effect, may leave us 'sadder and wiser', as the Mariner's tale left the Wedding Guest. But it ought not to proceed, as some of Wordsworth's lesser poems do, by a mere aggregation of detail ('Tis three feet long and two feet wide'). This, on its simplest and most practical level, is the force of Coleridge's imagination/ fancy distinction, and there is evidence beyond Hazlitt, in Coleridge's own notebooks and letters, to show how early he hit upon it as a summary of his case for and against Wordsworth's poetry. An early letter of 15 January 1804, addressed to Richard Sharp, contains a full outline of the distinction :

Imagination, or the *modifying* power in that highest sense of the word, in which I have ventured to oppose it to fancy, or the *aggregating* power (*CL*, II 1,034).

The interrupted discussion at the end of the thirteenth chapter of the *Biographia Literaria*, where the 'essentially vital' power of imagination is contrasted with the 'fixities and definites' of fancy, fills out the account of a dozen years earlier. But the letter of 1804 is precise enough, and early enough, to make it reasonable to suppose that the young poet of 'Kubla Khan' may already have been close to such a conclusion.

There are two aspects of the imagination-fancy distinction which, obvious as they are, tend perhaps to be overlooked. The first is that it is a value-distinction. 'Imagination' is the power that writes good poems : 'fancy' writes inferior ones. There is no such thing, in Coleridgean terms, as a bad imaginative poem. If the 'shaping spirit' really has shaped, if the poem is more than a sum of its parts and more than a mere aggregate of the poet's perceptions, then it is so far good. Secondly, the distinction is an historical one : it derives from a view of the whole past of English poetry. It is the decisive innovation of the romantic poet to write imaginative poems rather than fanciful ones, just as it was the characteristic role of the Augustans to condemn themselves to a poetry 'addressed to the fancy or the intellect' (*BL* i). Wordsworth, in this view, bestrides both worlds and is pathetically capable of both, and the *Biographia* is a belated plea inviting him to recognize both his excellence and his failings. But is just here, at this confident moment of exegesis, that an embarrassing choice emerges in the interpretation of 'Kubla Khan'. Given that it is a poem about two kinds of poetry, and that Coleridge's classic distinction may have been present to him, in essence at least, as early as 1798, there is no need to resist the conclusion that its first thirty-six lines are 'fanciful' and the remainder a programme for imaginative creation. But I do not know that there is any clear reason for assigning the fancifulness of the first section of the poem to what Coleridge disliked in the aristocratic poetry of the Augustan era, or to what he disliked in some of Wordsworth's, or to what he disliked in some of his own. The orientalism of the setting of the poem masks, and perhaps deliberately, its critical purpose.

Certainly the Khan is very like a tyrannical aristocrat as seen through romantic and liberal eyes. This is an aspect of the poem that might easily have seemed too obvious, in the years around 1800, to be worth mentioning, but it needs to be emphasized in an age which finds tyrants engagingly exotic, even to the point of supposing Kubla a model of the creative artist. The very fact that he is an oriental despot would have been reason enough in the late eighteenth century to excite hostility. To this day the French retain the word *turquerie* to describe a brutal act. Beckford's *Vathek* (1786) is one of the many oriental tales of the period, French and English, that hint at the exotic vices of eastern potentates. And there is nothing improbable about identifying eighteenth-century aristocratic failings with the medieval or modern East. Cowper vents an Englishman's indignation in the fifth book of *The Task* (1785) against Catherine the Great's ingenious Palace of Ice, a 'most magnificent and mighty freak' made without saw or hammer, a 'brittle prodigy' :

> a scene
> Of evanescent glory, once a stream
> And soon to slide into a stream again . . .
> 'Twas transient in its nature, as in show

'Twas durable : as worthless, as it seem'd
Intrinsically precious; to the foot
Treach'rous and false; it smil'd, and it was cold.

Great princes have great playthings ...
But war's a game which, were their subjects wise,
Kings would not play at.

Keats in 'Sleep and Poetry' does not invoke the East to damn
what he supposed the triviality of Augustan poetry; but the
language he uses might be aptly used of the Khan. English poetry
between the Elizabethans and the moderns he sees as a sterile
interlude, 'a schism Nurtured by foppery and barbarism' :

with a puling infant's force
They sway'd about upon a rocking horse
And thought it Pegasus.

The Khan, too, may be something of a barbarous fop. And if
this seems a lofty and remote view of the East, it should be recalled that accurate orientalism is an extreme rarity in England
before the Victorians; the orientalism of the early Romantics derives from experiences like the childhood reading of the *Arabian
Nights* that Wordsworth refers to in the *Prelude* (v 482f.). It is
colourful, picturesque, and indifferent to accuracy, at once
fascinated and dismissive. Southey sums up the attitude that
Coleridge is likely to have shared in his notes and preface to
Thalaba (1801), a Moslem tale he began in 1799 in a new
metre which was to be 'The *arabesque* ornament of an Arabian
tale'. No labour, in Southey's view, could be justified in getting
oriental details right. No faithful translation from the Persian
could make Firdausi's epic readable, and the *Arabian Nights*,
which had first appeared in English in about 1705–8, were all
the better for having passed through 'the filter of a French translation'. 'A waste of ornament and labour', as Southey puts it
loftily, 'characterizes all the works of the Orientalists'. The East
is not an object of study, but a place to let the imagination run riot
in. And the chief excitement and source of horror lies in its despotism. Purchas offers rather an attractive picture of the Khan,
as well as interesting details about his enormous, if fastidious,
sexual appetite; but then Purchas was a Jacobean and took auto-

cracy for granted, and was also impressed by the fact that this Emperor of the Tartars in the 1260's had treated his European guests well and taken a sympathetic interest in Christianity. The sentence from Purchas that Coleridge scribbled in his notebook emphasizes merely his despotism :

the greatest prince in peoples, cities, and kingdoms that ever was in the world (*CN* 1,840).

The overwhelmingly important fact about the 'pleasure-dome' of the poem, with its surrounding park, is its artificiality. It is a 'miracle of rare device', despotically willed into existence as a tyrant's toy :

> In Xanadu did Kubla Khan
> A stately pleasure-dome decree . . .'

The authoritarian word 'decree' is not in Purchas, who simply says : 'In Xaindu did Cublai Can build a stately pallace . . .' And the painfully contrived quality of the tyrant's pleasure becomes clearer with every line : in the formal, though not entirely formal, gardens, and the trivial purpose to which the brute strength of the sacred river has been harnessed. The reader is meant to be left with a disagreeable image of the patron himself, congratulating himself on his facile ingenuity in degrading a matchless natural phenomenon to the service of a landscape garden—in itself a very Augustan pleasure—in order to flatter his own megalomaniac dreams :

> And 'mid this tumult Kubla heard from far
> Ancestral voices prophesying war !

In his artistic tastes, at least, he reminds one a little of the young Alexander Pope's complacent view of Windsor Park :

> Here hills and vales, the woodland and the plain,
> Here earth and water seem to strive again ;
> Not Chaos-like together crush'd and bruis'd,
> But, as the world, harmoniously confus'd.
> > *Windsor-Forest* (1713), ll. 11–14

'In perusing French tragedies,' Coleridge remarked years later, 'I have fancied two marks of admiration at the end of each line, as hieroglyphics of the author's own admiration at his own clever-ness' (*BL* i). Kubla's arrogance is much like this. If only he knew it, the poem hints, he has bitten off much more than he can chew.

For all the violence of great emotional experience survives there in the river, contained by the Khan's device much as Augustan poems seem to contain and even to sterilize the emotions of man : 'thoughts *translated* into the language of poetry', as Coleridge later complained of Pope. The vast power of the river is allowed to rise, but only 'momently', and then sinks back into silence, 'a lifeless ocean'. This is surely not the River of Life. It is the river of the poetry of imagination which, under the old literary order, had been debased into a plaything and allowed its liberty only if 'girdled round'. The passage that describes the river as it rushes above ground is dense with the imagery of the violent reshaping of dull matter, like the 'essentially vital' power of the imagination working upon objects 'essentially fixed and dead' (*BL* xiii) :

> And from this chasm, with ceaseless turmoil seething,
> As if this earth in fast thick pants were breathing,
> A mighty fountain momently was forced,
> Amid whose swift half-intermitted burst
> Huge fragments vaulted like rebounding hail,
> Or chaffy grain beneath the thresher's flail . . .

The poem is profoundly elusive in other ways, but there is some-thing uncharacteristically familiar about Coleridge's imagery here, so commonly are rivers and springs associated with poetry in classical and Renaissance poetry. The very name 'Alph' offers an easy clue in its resemblance to the Alpheus of Milton's 'Lycidas', where it is associated with the Sicilian Muse of pastoral poetry. And the river of poetry was a preoccupation of some Romantics too. In his preface to the sonnets on *The River Dud-don* (1820) Wordsworth was later to urge Coleridge to revive an old project of their Somerset year, a poem describing the course of a symbolic river to be called 'The Brook' (*BL* x). 'There is a sympathy in streams', as he put it invitingly. The sacred river is the most traditional element in a poem otherwise evasive in its sophistication.

The triumph of 'Kubla Khan', perhaps, lies in its evasions : it hints so delicately at critical truths while demonstrating them so

boldly. The contrast between the two halves of the poem, between the terrible emergence of the imaginative power in the
first, 'momently forced', and its Dionysiac victory in the second, is
bold enough to distract attention from the business at hand. So
bold, indeed, that Coleridge for once was able to dispense with
any language out of the past. It was his own poem, a manifesto.
To read it now, with the hindsight of another age, is to feel pre-
monitions of the critical achievement to come : phrases like 'Poetry
is the spontaneous overflow of powerful feelings',[4] or 'the
imagination . . . dissoves, diffuses, dissipates, in order to re-create'
(*BL* xiii), lie only a little below the surface of the poem. But the
poem is in advance, not just of these, but in all probability of any
critical statement that survives. It may be that it stands close to
the moment of discovery itself.

SOURCE : *Coleridge the Poet* (London, 1966) pp. 117–30.

NOTES

1. H. House, *Coleridge* (London, 1953) p. 116.
2. J. L. Lowes, *The Road to Xanadu* (Boston, Mass., 1927; rev.
ed. 1930) p. 363.
3. 'An Essay on Fashionable Literature', Halliford edition of
the *Works of Peacock*, edited by H. F. B. Brett-Smith and C. E.
Jones (London, 1934) VIII 291, 290.
4. Wordsworth's preface to *Lyrical Ballads* (1800), an essay in
some degree a work of collaboration between the two poets.

Charles Tomlinson

'CHRISTABEL' (1955)

I. THE CONTEXT

'Christabel' is a tale of terror. It was written, that is to say, within a certain literary convention. Although this convention was not, artistically, a particularly successful one, its nature has some bearing on our reading of the poem. The genre was a European phenomenon. It expressed, or tried to express, a contemporary state of mind reacting to profound social changes and it did so, not by dealing with them directly, but by appearing to ignore these changes. Walpole said that he wrote *Otranto* 'glad to think of anything rather than politics'. But the politics, or rather the feelings 'which the external events gave rise, reappeared on the plane of fantasy in the combined expression of nostalgia for, yet fear of, the past.

One modern writer, M. André Breton, in his essay 'Limits not Frontiers of Surrealism',[1] has traced the significance, in this light, of the ubiquitous ruins, the inevitable ghost and the subterranean passages of the convention and suggests even that 'in the stormy night can be heard the incessant roar of cannon'. Be this as it may, one can agree with M. Breton's formulation of the basic conflict which is played out against this turbulent background, a background 'chosen', as he says, 'for the appearance of beings of pure temptation, combining in the highest degree the struggle between the instinct of death on the one hand . . . and, on the other, Eros who exacts after each human hecatomb, the glorious restoration of life.'

In the fragmentary 'Christabel' there is no 'glorious restoration of life' as, for example, in the business of the long-lost child of *Otranto* who is found at last and rules in the tyrant's stead. All the other elements of the tale of terror, however, are present—elements which Coleridge had admired in Mrs Radcliffe (see his review of *Udolpho* of 1794[2]) and was to guy later on when he sent to Wordsworth a satirical 'recipe'[3] on the subject of Scott's *Lady of the Lake*. His list of requirements (too lengthy for quotation here) is present, almost in its entirety, in 'Christabel'. The surprising thing is that 'Christabel', thought a minor work, is an entirely successful one within its particular limits.

We have in 'Christabel' perhaps the only tale of terror which expresses with any real subtlety the basic pattern of the genre, the struggle between the instinct of death and Eros. This struggle centres on the relationship of Geraldine, the 'fatal woman' (one of M. Breton's 'beings of pure temptation'), with Christabel herself, 'the maid devoid of guile and sin'. Geraldine does not appear among Dr Mario Praz's fatal women in his *The Romantic Agony* and one feels that she provides a far more compelling example than many of those we find there. She clearly belongs under Dr Praz's heading of 'La Belle Dame Sans Merci' (the genesis of Keats's poem of this title Dr Praz traces to Coleridge's ballad 'Love'), her characteristics being those of the fated and fatal men and women of Romantic literature, characteristics which are primarily the dramatization of an inner disturbance such as we find commented on by M. Breton. This condition, as Dr Praz shows, finds expression either in the inflicting of, or the passive submission to, pain. Both attitudes of mind are present in 'Christabel'.

2. THE TEXT

In 'Christabel' the struggle of evil and innocence is examined, although within the framework of the typical tale of terror, for the purposes of moral realization of the manner in which evil works upon and transforms innocence. Coleridge's success in achieving this realization by poetic means is due to a dramatic tension building up to a final, irrevocable climax and skilfully regulated by its background of symbols from the natural world.

As far as the poem goes (it is a 'fragment') it is complete.[4] The climax of,

> And turning from his own sweet maid
> The aged knight, Sir Leoline,
> Led forth the Lady Geraldine.

leaves Christabel in that condition of pathological isolation which
the Mariner also feels and which Coleridge must himself have
known. It follows upon the carefully ordered series of psychological shocks to which Christabel has been subjected and beneath
which her innocence is crushed. Mr Humphry House says of the
poem in his excellent book on Coleridge that it is 'fragmentary and
finally unsatisfying' and that its mystery remains both incomplete
and clueless. If one feels a certain incompleteness about the poem
it is because we are left with Christabel's pathological isolation
which is never, unlike that of the Ancient Mariner, to be resolved.
(Indeed, of the Mariner's, it would perhaps be more true to say
that it is only partially resolved.) The 'story', of course, was never
completed and the elements concerning the broken friendship between Sir Leoline and the father of Geraldine, relevant as they
are to the poem's theme of the division of the inmost being and of
the most intimate relationships, were never knit up into a more
organic significance. 'Christabel' offers, however, despite its abrupt conclusion in psychological stasis, a completeness concerning
what *does* happen, if only we pay attention to the premonitory
nature of the symbols at the opening and see the poetic interest
as centering on the uncertain balance which is represented here
between health and disease, good and evil, and the end as a
tragedy in which neurosis, not death, strikes the final blow. One
has in 'Christabel', in allegorical form, that same concern which
tormented the self-analyst of the notebooks and the reader of
John Webster's Folio on 'The Displaying of Supposed Witchcraft' : 'the mind's failure to guide the Will'. For Christabel,
bewitched, suffers simultaneously with the disintegration of personality the disintegration of the will.

Let us begin with the first important symbolical passage of
the poem :

> The thin gray cloud is spread on high,
> It covers but not hides the sky.
> The moon is behind and at the full
> And yet she looks both small and dull.

Everything hangs in this state of precarious uncertainty, of incipient disease. The cloud threatens the sky, but the sky still shows through, and to counterpoint this, the moon has achieved its most fruitful phase yet remains without the bright appearance of a full moon. Coleridge thus reinforces the idea of potentialities in Nature which are never finally to be realized in the story:

> 'Tis a month before the month of May,
> And the Spring comes slowly up this way.

The light of the moon is 'cold' and where it falls, it illumines a further symbol of decay, the toothless mastiff. In Christabel's room 'not a moonbeam enters here' and here she—ironically enough —feels safe.

Behind the moon in 'The Ancient Mariner' there is the association of the Queen of Heaven, 'the holy Mother' as Coleridge calls her. In 'Christabel' the diseased condition of the moon links suggestively with the inability of Christabel's dead mother, her guardian spirit, to operate in her defence. This symbolical use of the moon to reinforce the presentation of a psychological condition is characteristic of Coleridge's natural effects. 'In looking at objects of Nature', as he writes in *Anima Poetae* (Ed. E. H. Coleridge (1895) p. 136), 'I seem rather to be seeking, as it were, asking for, a symbolical language for something within me that already and forever exists, than observing anything new.' The sky – again, symbolically, a potential which remains frustrate – should offer Christabel the feeling of freedom and of free will:

> All they who live in the upper sky
> Do love you, holy Christabel

says Geraldine; and Christabel herself knows

> in joys and woes
> That saints will aid if men will call:
> For the blue sky bends over all.

But the sky is not blue during the time of the action of the poem: its sphere no longer operates upon that of the world below although, 'covered but not hidden', one can see it. Its presence adds to our appreciation of Christabel's growing feelings of helplessness and isolation. The diseased moon prepares us for her transition from a condition of organic innocence to one of complete division. What is the nature of this division and how is its appearance developed in the poem? The development, it should be noticed, takes place through instances of what happens *to* Christabel rather than what she does. Evil works upon her and by the time she feels *possessed* by it and, 'with forced unconscious sympathy' perhaps even becoming evil herself, she has lost her own free will.

It is worth while here to bear in mind Coleridge's interests in psychological phenomena, in Mesmerism, and also in witchcraft, where a powerful idea working upon the human psyche produces the feeling of guilt followed by mental deterioration. An interesting and relevant indication of Coleridge's interests as a psychologist occurs in the preface to his unsuccessful poem 'The Three Graves'. After the inevitable Coleridgean apologia for the subject, the metre and the fragmentary nature of the piece, he goes on to tell us that at the time of its composition he 'had been reading Bryan Edwards's account of the effect of the Oby witchcraft on the Negroes in the West Indies, and Hearne's deeply interesting anecdotes of similar workings on the imagination of the Copper Indians'. In settling on a story of psychological obsession brought about by a blasphemous curse (a story Coleridge says is 'positive fact, and of no very distant date') he had wanted to show 'the possible effect on the imagination from an Idea violently and suddeny impressed on it'. 'I conceived the design', he says, 'of showing that instances of this kind are not peculiar to savage or barbarous tribes, and of illustrating the mode in which the mind is affected in these cases, and the progress and symptoms of the morbid action on the fancy from the beginning'. All three protagonists in the poem are reduced to a condition of morbid introversion and their minds possessed by the image of the woman who has delivered the curse. Coleridge, despite a certain psychological acuteness, handles the affair somewhat clumsily as poetic material and we must return to Geraldine's onslaught upon Christabel to see what he is really capable of in dealing with this kind of subject.

To begin with, Christabel finds herself alone. Her lover is absent, her mother dead, her father sick :

Each matin bell, the Baron saith,
Knells us back to a world of death ...
These words Sir Leoline will say
Many a morn to his dying day.

Here is the position of the typical persecuted woman of the tale
of terror, defenceless and vulnerable, her isolation being intensi-
fied by its juxtaposition with the fine image of 'the one red leaf, the
last of its clan',

That dances as often as dance it can,
Hanging so light, and hanging so high,
On the topmost twig that looks up at the sky.

In this condition Christabel finds the Lady Geraldine who,
according to her own story, has been abducted, then abandoned,
and takes her into the castle. Coleridge conveys Geraldine's
character of fatal woman in a cumulative series of startling
touches. At the outset he gives no hint of the evil in her nature
and Christabel sees her as 'Beautiful exceedingly'. The first hint –
and it is scarcely even that until we re-read the poem – comes with
her unwillingness to join in Christabel's prayer:

Praise we the Virgin all divine
Who hath rescued thee from thy distress!
Alas, alas! said Geraldine,
I cannot speak for weariness.

Christabel's first disquiet occurs as they go into the castle and past
the sleeping mastiff:

The mastiff old did not awake
Yet she an angry moan did make ...

But even this disquiet seems connected rather with the circumstances of the night than with the actual character of Geraldine.
The third stroke is more direct. It takes up the motif of Geraldine's eye which is to be dramatically reintroduced at the climax
of the poem. As they are passing the almost extinguished hall
fire,

... when the lady passed, there came
A tongue of light, a fit of flame;
And Christabel saw the lady's eye,
And nothing else she saw thereby.

The fourth leaves us in no doubt. Geraldine, fearing the spirit
of Christabel's dead mother, the young girl's guardian spirit,
bursts out in a tirade against its presence. Coleridge gives the
situation an added uncertainty by withholding from us as yet
Geraldine's exact intentions. Indeed, whatever they may be, the
fatal woman, aware of her own fatality, seems half to regret what
she is about to do –

> Even I in my degree will try,
> Fair maiden, to requite you well. –

and as she undresses,

> Beneath the lamp the lady bowed
> And slowly rolled her eyes around . . .

As she lies down to sleep beside Christabel, she has put by all
her scruples :

> In the touch of this bosom there worketh a spell,
> Which is lord of thy utterance, Christabel.

They sleep and the suggestions crystallize into a final irony :

> , . . lo, the worker of these harms,
> That holds the maiden in her arms,
> Seems to slumber still and mild
> As a mother with her child.

– Christabel has lost her natural father and has found an unnatural mother : the guardian spirit has been worsted. The important final image of this passage of the sleeping mother
embracing her child comes to mind once more, as we shall see,
when we hear Bracy's dream of the same night.

In Part One the ground has been prepared : in Part Two the
evil of Geraldine begins to operate within Christabel herself.
Geraldine, 'nothing doubting of her spell/Awakens the lady
Christabel'. Christabel has, on the level of the conscious mind,
reassured herself and sees her tormentor as 'fairer yet! and yet
more fair!', but her unconscious fears become conscious once
more as her father embraces Geraldine and the latter prolongs
the embrace 'with joyous look' :

> Which when she viewed a vision fell
> Upon the soul of Christabel,
> The vision of fear, the touch and pain !
> She shrunk and shuddered, and saw again . . .
> Again she saw that bosom old,
> Again she saw that bosom cold
> And drew in her breath with a hissing sound.

It is the hissing of a horrified intake of breath, but its significance becomes deepened when Bracy the Bard tells his story and with what follows. During the night he has dreamed that he saw the tame dove which bears Christabel's name

> Fluttering, and uttering fearful moan . . .
> I stopped, methought the dove to take,
> When lo ! I saw a bright green snake
> Coiled around its wings and neck . . .
> And with the dove it heaves and stirs,
> Swelling its neck as she swells hers !

This moment is one of the most startling and suggestive touches in the poem. We are recalled by the image to that of the two sleeping together; we see in the movement of the snake an attempt to *imitate* that of the bird as well as to prevent its flight; we remember that the sound Christabel herself made resembled that of a snake. Just as the full moon that is dulled, holds in a frightful balance the image of health with the image of disease, the latter overpowering the former, so now there is a further frightful balance : we are on the brink of the suggestion that the identity of Christabel is coveted by Geraldine and that Christabel has unconsciously assumed something of the evil identity of the other. We come now to the most important dramatic climax of the whole, when Geraldine is kissed by Sir Leoline and the significance of Bracy's dream jestingly ignored by the Knight : *Geraldine looks askance at Christabel:*

> A snake's small eye blinks dull and shy,
> And the lady's eyes they shrunk in her head,
> Each shrunk up to a serpent's eye . . .
> One moment and the sight was fled !

Our worst suspicion is now confirmed by what follows :

> But Christabel in dizzy trance,
> Stumbling on the unsteady ground –
> Shuddered aloud, with a hissing sound.

She shudders with horror still, but she emits the sound a snake would make. Her imagination is so overpowered by 'those shrunken serpent eyes',

> That all her features were resigned
> To this sole image in her mind . . .

And not only does she see the image, she feels herself *becoming* the image :

> . . . And passively did *imitate*
> That look of dull and treacherous hate,
> And thus she stood, in dizzy trance ;
> Still picturing that look askance
> With *forced unconscious sympathy* . . .

The idea has rooted itself in her mind. Despite this fact, she still fights against Geraldine's spell by asking her father to send her tormenter away, instead of which he 'leads forth the Lady Geraldine', symbolically rejecting his own daughter. There is an extremely dramatic propriety about this incident as Sickness and Evil move off together. It completes the psychological fable with a succinctness in juxtaposition with which Coleridge's tacked-on conclusion to the second part sticks out uncomfortably from the rest.

One might note finally that Coleridge makes use of the old and familiar material of folk tale : the ageing ruler ignores his wise counsellor, rejects his 'natural' daughter and prefers his unnatural. None of the protagonists in Coleridge's narrative is in him- or herself complex : all are stock figures and therefore near to allegory and to what J. F. Danby, speaking of *King Lear* where Shakespeare uses the same fable, calls 'the unambiguous Morality statement' (*Shakespeare's Doctrine of Nature*). One is compelled to see the characters as symbols relating to Everyman's condition of inner psychological tension – the evil preying on the good, the sick undermining the healthy – which brings one back to M. Breton's statement of the symbolical conflict of the tale of terror, and to the fact that Coleridge's poem, limited though it is by its inability to resolve the conflict, presents an extremely individual variant on this basic return.

SOURCE: J. Wain (ed.), *Interpretations: Essays on Twelve English Poems* (London 1955) pp. 103–12.

NOTES

1. In *Surrealism* edited by Herbert Read (Faber and Faber).
2. In the Nonesuch *Coleridge*, p. 203.
3. In *Selected Letters*, edited by Kathleen Raine, p. 172.
4. On Coleridge's insistence that 'in my very first conception of the tale I had the whole present to my mind, with the wholeness, no less than the loveliness, of a vision', we have Wordsworth's comment : 'I am sure that he never formed a plan or knew what was to be the end of "Christabel" and that he merely deceived himself when he thought, as he says, that he had the idea quite clear in his mind'. (Recorded in Crabb Robinson's Diary, 1 Feb. 1836.)

SELECT BIBLIOGRAPHY

RECOMMENDED TEXTS

The Poetical Works of S. T. Coleridge, ed. E. H. Coleridge, 2 vols (O.U.P., 1912).
The Poems of S. T. Coleridge, ed. E. H. Coleridge (Oxford Standard Authors, O.U.P., 1912).

PRIMARY SOURCE MATERIALS

The Notebooks of Samuel Taylor Coleridge, ed. Kathleen Coburn, (in progress), (London :) Routledge & Kegan Paul; New York : Pantheon Books, 1957).
The Collected Letters of Samuel Taylor Coleridge, ed. E. L. Griggs, 6 vols (O.U.P., 1956–71).
Coleridge: The Critical Heritage, ed. J. R. de J. Jackson (London : Routledge & Kegan Paul, 1970).
The Journals of Dorothy Wordsworth, ed. E. de Selincourt, 1941; new edn. ed. Mary Moorman (O.U.P., paperback, 1971).
The Letters of William and Dorothy Wordsworth, ed. E. de Selincourt, (1935–9), vol. I, re-ed. C. L. Shaver (O.U.P., 1967).

BOOKS

M. H. Abrams, *The Milk of Paradise* (Cambridge, Mass. : Harvard U.P., 1934).
Patricia Adair, *The Waking Dream : A Study of Coleridge's Poetry* (London : Edward Arnold, 1967).
R. C. Bald, 'Coleridge and the Ancient Mariner', in *Nineteenth-Century Studies in Honor of C. S. Northup*, ed. H. Davis, W. C. De Vane and R. C. Bald (Ithaca, N.Y. : Cornell U.P., 1940).
J. B. Beer, *Coleridge the Visionary* (London : Chatto & Windus, 1959; New York, Collier Books, 1962).
M. Bodkin, *Archetypal Patterns in Poetry: Psychological Studies of Imagination* (O.U.P., 1934).
C. M. Bowra, *The Romantic Imagination* (O.U.P., 1950; Cambridge, Mass. : Harvard U.P., 1957).

R. L. Brett, *Reason and Imagination* (O.U.P., 1960).

R. L. Brett, ed., *S. T. Coleridge*, Writers and their Background (London : G. Bell & Sons, 1971).

Kenneth Burke, *The Philosophy of Literary Form*, 1941, 2nd edn (Baton Rouge, La, Louisiana State U.P., 1967).

R. H. Fogle, *The Idea of Coleridge's Criticism* (Berkeley : University of California Press, 1962) especially pp. 49–69.

D. W. Harding, 'The Theme of *The Ancient Mariner*', reprinted from *Scrutiny* IX (1941) in an expanded version in *Experience Into Words* (London : Chatto & Windus, 1963) pp. 53–71.

Alethea Hayter, *Opium and the Romantic Imagination* (Berkeley : University of California Press; London : Faber & Faber, 1968).

G. Wilson Knight, *The Starlit Dome* (O.U.P., 1941; 2nd edn London : Methuen & Co. Ltd; New York : Barnes & Noble, 1960).

J. L. Lowes, *The Road to Xanadu* (Boston, Mass. : Houghton Mifflin Co., 1927; rev. edn 1930).

A. H. Nethercott, *The Road to Tryermaine* (Chicago : University of Chicago Press, 1939).

Elder Olsen, 'A Symbolic Reading of the *Ancient Mariner*', reprinted from *Modern Philology* XLV (1948) in *Critics and Criticism*, ed. R. S. Crane (Chicago : University of Chicago Press, 1952) pp. 138–44.

Stephen Prickett, *Coleridge and Wordsworth: The Poetry of Growth* (C.U.P., 1970).

Elizabeth Schneider, *Coleridge, Opium and Kubla Khan* (Chicago : University of Chicago Press, 1953).

N. P. Stallknecht, 'The Moral of the *Ancient Mariner*', reprinted from *PMLA*, XLVII (1932), in *Strange Seas of Thought* (Durham, N.C. : Duke University Press, 1945, Bloomington, 1958).

Robert Penn Warren, 'A Poem of Pure Imagination' reprinted from *The Kenyon Review* VIII (1946) in *Selected Essays* (New York : Random House, 1958 : London : Eyre & Spotiswoode, 1964) pp. 222–61.

ARTICLES

E. E. Bostetter, '*Christabel*: The Vision of Fear', *Philological Quarterly*, XXXVI (1957) 183–94.

A. M. Buchan, 'The Sad Wisdom of the Mariner', *Studies in Philology*, LXI (1964) 669–88.

T. P. Coffin, 'Coleridge's Use of the Ballad Stanza in *The Ancient Mariner*', *Modern Language Quarterly*, XII (1951) 437–45.

O. B. Fulmer, 'The Ancient Mariner and the Wandering Jew', *Studies in Philology*, LXVI (1969) 797–815.

S. M. Parrish, 'The Wordsworth-Coleridge Controversy', *PMLA*, LXXIII (1958) 367–74.

C. J. Smith, 'Wordsworth and Coleridge: The Growth of a Theme', *Studies in Philology*, LIV (1957) 53–64.

E. E. Stoll, 'Symbolism in *Christabel*', *PMLA*, LXIII (1948) 214–33.

BIBLIOGRAPHICAL ADDENDUM, 1981

George Bellis, 'The Fixed Crime of *The Ancient Mariner*', *Essays in Criticism*, XXIV (1974), 243–60.

Norman Fruman, *Coleridge, the Damaged Archangel* (London: Allen & Unwin, 1972).

Allan Grant, *A Preface to Coleridge* (London: Longman, 1972).

Richard Haven, '*The Ancient Mariner* in the Nineteenth Century', *Studies in Romanticism*, XI (1972), 360–74.

Susan M. Luther, '*Christabel*' *as Dream-Reverie* (Salzburg: Romantic Reassessment 61, 1976).

Paul Magnuson, *Coleridge's Nightmare Poetry* (Charlottesville: University of Virginia Press, 1974).

Charles I. Patterson, 'The Daemonic in *Kubla Khan*: Towards Interpretation', *PMLA*, LXXXIX (1974), 1033–42.

Stephen Prickett, *Wordsworth and Coleridge: The Lyrical Ballads* (London: Arnold, 1975).

E. S. Shaffer, '*Kubla Khan*' *and the Fall of Jerusalem* (Cambridge: C.U.P., 1975).

Jonas Spatz, 'The Mystery of Eros: Sexual Initiation in Coleridge's *Christabel*', *PMLA*, XC (1975), 107–16.

George Whalley, 'Coleridge's Poetic Sensibility', in John Beer (ed.), *Coleridge's Variety: Bicentenary Studies* (London: Macmillan, 1974).

Carl Woodring, 'The Mariner's Return', *Studies in Romanticism*, XI (1972), 375–80.

NOTES ON CONTRIBUTORS

HAROLD BLOOM, Professor of Humanities at Yale University, is editor of works by Blake, the English Romantic Poets and Ruskin, and author of *Blake's Apocalypse* (1963), *Yeats* (1970), *The Anxiety of Influence* (1973), *Poetry and Repression* (1976) and *The Flight to Lucifer* (1978).

EDWARD E. BOSTETTER, author of *The Romantic Ventriloquists: Wordsworth, Coleridge, Keats, Shelley, Byron* (1963), was Professor of English in the University of Washington, Seattle.

A. M. BUCHAN, Professor of English, Washington University, St Louis, died in 1969. He wrote extensively on the Romantics, particularly on Coleridge.

HUMPHRY HOUSE was a Fellow of Wadham College, Oxford, until his death in 1955. He was author of *The Dickens World* (1941), *Coleridge* (1953) and *All in Due Time* (1955).

MARK REED, Professor of English, University of North Carolina and Associate Editor of the Cornell Wordsworth, has so far issued two volumes of a Chronology of the poet's life and works: *The Early Years* (1967) and *The Middle Years* (1975).

CHARLES TOMLINSON, poet, painter and critic, is Reader in English Poetry, University of Bristol; his *Selected Poems 1951–74*, appeared in 1978.

GEORGE WATSON, Fellow of St John's College, Cambridge, is editor of the *New Cambridge Bibliography of English Literature*, and also of critical essays by Coleridge and Dryden. His studies in criticism and literary history include *Politics and Literature in Modern Britain* (1977), *The Discipline of English* (1978) and *The Story of the Novel* (1979).

GEORGE WHALLEY, Professor of English at Queen's University, Kingston, Ontario, is the author of *Poetic Process* (1953) and *Coleridge and Sara Hutchinson and the Asra Poems* (1955).

INDEX

Figures in bold type indicate main entries